Interracialism and
Christian Community
in the Postwar South

THE STORY OF
KOINONIA FARM

Tracy Elaine K'Meyer

Interracialism and Christian Community in the Postwar South

THE STORY OF KOINONIA FARM

University Press of Virginia

Charlottesville and London

THE UNIVERSITY PRESS OF VIRGINIA

© 1997 by the Rector and Visitors of the
University of Virginia
All rights reserved
Printed in the United States of America

First published 1997

⊚ The paper used in this publication meets the minimum
requirements of the American National Standard for
Information Sciences—Permanence of Paper for Printed
Library Materials, ANSI Z39.48-1984.

Library of Congress Cataloging-in-Publication Data
K'Meyer, Tracy Elaine.
    Interracialism and Christian community in the postwar South : the
story of Koinonia Farm / Tracy Elaine K'Meyer.
        p.   cm.
    Includes bibliographical references and index.
    ISBN 0-8139-1712-3 (cloth : alk. paper)
    1. Koinonia Farm—History. 2. Christian communities—Georgia—
History—20th century. 3. Civil rights—Religious aspects—
Christianity—History—20th century. 4. Race relations—Religious
aspects—Christianity—History—20th century. 5. Georgia—Race
relations. 6. Georgia—Church history—20th century. I. Title.
BV4407.67.K54   1997
261.8'348'009758913—dc21   96-46374
                                                                CIP

To Jean and Jim K'Meyer,
my mother and father,
with love

Contents

Illustrations

Acknowledgments

In many ways this book is not only about a community, it is the product of a community effort, or at least an effort broadly supported in many ways. The research for this project could not have been completed without the contributions of past and present members of Koinonia. Former Koinonians welcomed me into their homes and shared their personal memories of the farm. Likewise, the Koinonia Partners opened up their community, allowing me to stay in the guesthouse and giving me insights into life at Koinonia. I should add that the research for this book would not have been as easy or as enjoyable without my good friend Tom Bickel, who let me stay at his house in Atlanta on my frequent trips to Georgia and who listened attentively as I talked about Koinonia for hours on end. Finally, two universities provided financial support for parts of the research. For their aid I am indebted to the University of North Carolina at Chapel Hill Mowry Fund and the New Mexico State University Faculty Minigrant Program.

In writing this manuscript, first as a dissertation and then as a book, I received more than the usual advice and support. I wish to express my sincere thanks to my faculty committee and to a number of my fellow students at the University of North Carolina for their input. In particular I am grateful to Peter Filene, who not only served as the best possible adviser any student could hope for but also went above and beyond the call of duty to continue reading the manuscript long after I graduated. In addition, three fellow students—Tom Baker, Kathryn Nasstrom, and Lisa Tolbert—helped me to focus my argument, led me to important new insights and, most important, gave me much needed moral support. Along the way from dissertation to book, a few colleagues perhaps unknowingly informed my method and argument. Rosalie Riegle shared her thoughts on oral history, religion, and activism, and Lee Formwalt discussed with me the civil rights movement in southwest Georgia. Others, especially Ken Hammond and Stephanie Cole, helped by just listening as I worked on ideas out loud. Lastly, the University of Louisville history department staff made sure I got the whole thing together and in the mail.

Finally, I would like to thank my family for their unconditional support first during my lengthy student years and then through the long wait for the book to be a reality. Their encouragement and frequent reassurances kept me going, and their pride in the book's completion makes all the effort worthwhile.

Interracialism and
Christian Community
in the Postwar South

THE STORY OF
KOINONIA FARM

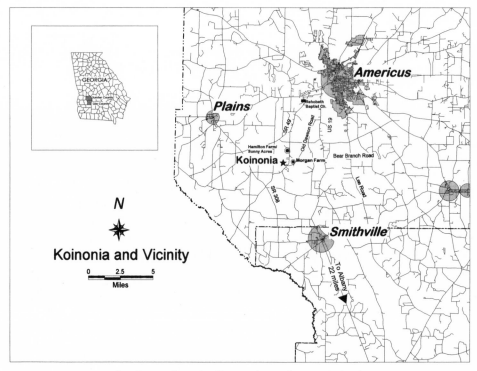

Southwest Georgia. (Drawn by Arthur W. Dakan)

Introduction

IN LATE APRIL 1992 I retraced a path traveled by thousands of people over the last fifty years, driving southwest from Atlanta toward Sumter County, Georgia. My destination was Koinonia Partners, an interracial Christian cooperative founded in 1942 under the name Koinonia Farm. The occasion was the community's fifty-year reunion and jubilee. I left behind the sprawling suburbs of Atlanta and drove over undulating roads, past new pine tree farms, and through shaded pecan orchards. The drive took me through small, hushed southern towns with names like Thomaston, Butler, and Ellaville. Though it was only April, the air was hot and dry. Every now and then the wind through the open window brought the scent of grass baking in the sun and the sweet odor of muscadine grapes. The fields by the road were a vivid green, though in a few months they would yellow with the summer heat. Along the edge of the highway a thin blood-red line hinted at the Georgia clay hiding just below the surface. Driving through the town of Americus, I passed large houses with well-manicured lawns and ramshackle homes in need of repair. Past the Rehobeth Baptist Church, a few small farms, then the winding road reached the white wooden gates of Koinonia.

For the jubilee Koinonia was dressed up like a festive oasis. A fresh roadside sign welcomed visitors, and in the center of the grounds stood a red-and-white canopy. How different the place looked from the pictures I had seen of the early years, when it was a dry open field with a few modest homes clustered in a near circle. Now the grass made a full green carpet, and flower gardens and chinaberry trees colored the landscape. An old barn was now a library, and a larger community building with rooms upstairs waited to house guests. A verdant wall of pecan trees blocked the horizon, which once had stretched across eroded Georgia farmland. When I arrived a few people milled about, but by the end of the weekend three hundred people gathered to remember Koinonia as it has been over the past fifty years.

The weekend celebration combined the spirit of a family reunion and a revival. Children who had been raised in the community greeted each other, and old friends got reacquainted. Chester Jackson, an African American who had grown up nearby, gave great bear hugs to anyone he recognized. Guests posed for photograph after photograph as they passed the time catching up on ten, twenty, and thirty years of separate lives. The different generations of Koinonians also came together as current residents and former members met to talk about their past. On Saturday guests used an open microphone to share reminiscences. G. McLeod Bryan told the story of how Clarence Jordan, the white Southern Baptist minister who was Koinonia's principal founder, had gotten the farm going with the help of his friends and supporters. Harry and Allene Atkinson, members from the earliest years, described building their first home by hand, with scarce material. And John Veldhuizen told harrowing tales of how Koinonians survived harassment and threats from the Ku Klux Klan and the White Citizens Council for their interracial activities in the 1950s and 1960s. The celebration ended Sunday morning with a service under the big top. During her sermon the Reverend Murphy Davis of the Open Door community in Atlanta evoked testimony and amens as she called on those assembled to stand on the shoulders of those who had gone before and look to the horizon for the future of the community's quest for peace and racial justice.

Behind the stories told at the Koinonia reunion lie fifty years of dramatic history, complete with religious idealism, interracial cooperation, boycotts, and bombings. I first encountered this story, almost by accident, years before. As a young graduate student, I had been in search of southern dissenters. Previously I had written about pacifists and had developed an interest in social action, particularly of a progressive or leftist nature, that was based on religious faith. Civil rights activism also had long interested me, especially that in the years before the "Movement"—the 1930s, 1940s, and 1950s. I wanted to know what white religious southerners did with regard to race relations during that time. Because of the nature of this subject material, I feel I should clarify my own position on region and religion. I am not a native southerner, though I attended both undergraduate and graduate school in the South. In addition, I am not a member of a church, though I was raised and confirmed as a Presbyterian. I do, however, have respect for religious faith and consider it an important social and historical phenomenon. This conviction informed my search for a story about southern religion and race relations.

I found such a story while flipping through old issues of the pacifist magazine *Liberation,* where I came across an article about a Ku Klux Klan attack on an interracial farm in Georgia. An interracial, cooperative, Christian community? In southwest Georgia? Despite the lack of scholarly attention to Koinonia, I quickly realized that not only would it be a story worth exploring in its own right, it would also lead to examining a range of historical questions.[1] What inspired these southerners to take this action, and what were they trying to accomplish? What effect did they have on the people around them and the broader civil rights movement? Did they succeed in creating an interracial community? And finally, of course, what could historians learn from them about southern religion and race relations?

The Koinonia Farm story cuts across three themes in southern history—religion, race relations, and community—and challenges the common understanding of each. For example, a mention of southern religion most often conjures up a Bible Belt dominated by a theologically, socially, and politically conservative white Protestantism. Most scholars have argued that southern white Christians, especially members of the Southern Baptist Convention, were concerned primarily with individual salvation and were uninterested in social ethics. According to this view the theological and social teachings of the Southern Baptist faith, in particular, emphasized conversion, personal right living, and evangelism. The mission of Southern Baptists was to do Christ's will, which was to convert the masses. Moreover, few people would find evidence of the Social Gospel or any progressivism in the denomination. This characterization of Baptist faith is given extra meaning because its size and institutional strength made the Southern Baptist Convention the cultural establishment of the South, and thus responsible for setting the "moral ethos" of the region.[2]

This picture of southern religion in general and Southern Baptism in particular does injustice to the diverse expressions of faith in the region. In the nineteenth century Baptist belief could be liberating for both women and slaves. Early in the next century, white and black women used southern churches as a launching pad for social action from which they attacked lynching and other evils.[3] Furthermore, there was a Social Gospel–inspired Progressive movement in the South, which addressed, among other issues, the problems of African Americans.[4] And in the 1930s and 1940s religious belief and membership in church institutions inspired white Christians to strive to improve race relations and to support the labor movement.[5] Biographies of people such as Will D. Campbell, Robert McNeil, and Jessie Daniel Ames help us to understand how these southerners broke with the dominant "moral ethos" of their time.[6] Studies of groups like the Young Women's Christian Association and Fellowship of Southern Churchmen illuminate the actions they took.[7] Taken together, these stories convey a new image of southern religion.

The story of Koinonia Farm can help us to understand the liberal Christianity of the South. By liberal Christianity I mean the belief in applying religious ideals to social issues in a way that calls for progressive change. The lives of Koinonians reveal the sources of this Christian liberalism in a generally conservative theological and social environment. Their actions and experience demonstrate how it can be put into practice and how it may be affected by changing circumstances. Over the years Koinonians created and maintained close ties with a wide network of like-minded southern Christians who supported them through their trials. Admittedly, Koinonians went further than most of their Southern Baptist or southern Protestant brethren. Nevertheless, understanding how Koinonians arrived at their beliefs can help explain how other southerners did so as well. The fact that they could win supporters and admirers sheds light on the pockets of Christian liberalism in the region. Finally, Koinonia's history reveals the diversity in southern religion and the range of possibilities for how religious belief could be put into day-to-day action in the social and political arenas.

Koinonia's history also adds to our knowledge of the civil rights movement at midcentury, especially white efforts to improve race relations. Over the years a narrative of that movement has been shaped by both academic and public presentations of history, most notably the popular *Eyes on the Prize* television series. The story begins with Martin Luther King Jr. in Montgomery, then runs through the sit-ins in Greensboro, the campaigns in Albany and Birmingham, and the marches on Washington and Selma. The Civil Rights and Voting Rights Acts are the climax. The epilogue describes the rise of black power and Malcolm X. Recently historians have paid more attention to "local people" and the role of women in the movement.[8] In addition, some scholars have explored the role of southern white liberals who worked for better race relations through regional organizations such as the Commission on Interracial Cooperation, Southern Conference for Human Welfare, and Southern Regional Council. The main concerns of these regional liberals ranged from decent treatment and improved conditions for African Americans to the end of the poll tax. More radical southerners such as those in the Southern Tenant Farmers' Union or at Highlander Folk School criticized both the southern racial and economic system, but these were always a tiny minority.[9] The scholarly consensus is that at least until the early 1950s, white liberals were interested in gradual change within the confines of segregation. Moreover, they sought to keep the pace of change in their own hands.[10]

Through Koinonia Farm we gain a different perspective on white support for, and participation in, the civil rights struggle. At the farm young white southerners took their religious beliefs and concern for African Americans further into social action than most southern white Christians or liberals would go. Koinonians developed their Christian beliefs into a unique alternate method for solving the race problem. They rejected the southern white liberals' reliance on gradual reform through legislative and court action. Instead, they pursued better relations through economic cooperation and building an interracial community where whites and blacks would live and work together. They believed tactics must match goals; political and legislative activities could not bring about economic equality or help create truly integrated and just social relationships. In the late 1950s Koinonia was supported in this effort by people across the country, including white Christians who rallied around them as a way to express sympathy for better race relations. In the early 1960s, furthermore, Koinonians cooperated to a great extent with the civil rights movement. Yet, while considered one of the hot spots of interracial activity in the late fifties, the farm is commonly overlooked today. In light of the continuing economic inequality and social distance between blacks and whites, we need to look at its history and evaluate its lessons.

Koinonia Farm was an attempt to build the beloved community. Koinonians shared that goal with the civil rights movement, as they also shared a religious basis and a belief in nonviolence. For Koinonians this meant tearing down the walls that separated people and making everyone a part of God's family. They sought to achieve that by bringing whites and blacks together in work, through cooperation and equalized economic conditions. Koinonians also sought to foster spiritual sharing through common worship and informal fellowship. Finally, at the farm whites and blacks would simply live together. Through these avenues Koinonians hoped to bring about racial reconciliation. Perhaps the most interesting distinction about Koinonia is that its members were interested in race relations more than just civil rights. Their approach brought a unique contribution to the early struggle for integration and to the movement in southwest Georgia. By considering the different meanings of beloved community, integration, and racial reconciliation, we can view the movement in new ways and perhaps also take a new look at current race issues.

Finally, the history of Koinonia Farm helps us to understand the diverse meanings of community. Usually when one thinks of communalism in the United States two subjects spring to mind: the utopian societies of the mid-nineteenth century and the hippie communes of the late 1960s. Yet in the postwar period of 1945–60, a time little associated with communalism, there were over 150 active cooperative societies in the United States.[11] Koinonia Farm is an example of this midcentury intentional community movement. More important, though, Koinonia was the intersection of several types of community. Its creators were attempting to build an interracial community. Koinonia was also a Christian cooperative, with economic sharing out of a common purse. Finally, the farm was part of a broader community of shared concern, that is, an interlocking network of Christian liberals, pacifists, and others who shared an interest in peace and justice. These three sorts of community were not always compatible, however. The farm's history allows us to unfold the layers of community and, most important, to explore the relationship between sharing—in cooperation or in a network based on shared concerns—and interracial fellowship.

In sum, Koinonia's history takes place at the intersection of race, religion, and community, rather than being about any one of them alone. This is not a story about civil rights as we usually understand it: the struggle of African Americans to achieve equality. Rather, it is about the efforts of white Christian liberals to participate in and support that struggle and the approach and ideas they brought to it. Furthermore, this story is not about intentional community. Although Koinonia is one of the longest-lived twentieth-century American communes, this narrative does not dwell on issues of intentional community development or persistence. Rather, it tells the story of Koinonia's effort to combine interracial fellowship, economic cooperation, and spiritual sharing in Christian community. Finally, this is not an investigation into the nature of southern religion or the southern church. It is, however, a story fundamentally about religion and the struggle to live according to one's beliefs while being engaged with the world and its problems. Specifically, Koinonia's history concerns Christian liberalism and race relations, and how some southerners drew upon their religious faith, especially their belief in sharing and brotherhood, and tried to build a "beloved community" where whites and blacks would live and work together.[12] Their lives illustrate the sources for such a liberal interpretation of religious faith and the myriad of ways it could be put into action. Throughout their history Koinonians were challenged by changing circumstances, attacks against them, and their desire to find a way to cooperate with the civil rights movement. These challenges led to hard times during which Koinonians redefined priorities, struggled to maintain their basic vision, and in the end found a way to restructure their community and reconcile their at times competing goals.

Both the academic and popular understandings of the civil rights movement have long established the importance in it of religious faith. Today we recognize the role of conservative Christianity in social and political life. The Koinonians' beliefs and actions demonstrate that religious faith can find expression across the spectrum of political and social ideology. In particular Koinonia Farm represents a liberal Christian approach to social issues, especially race relations. Koinonians brought to the problem a keen interest in interracial brotherhood and a unique approach for achieving it. They went further, sooner, than other white liberals of their generation toward cooperation and integration in its fullest meaning. Over the years they would gain success by a variety of measures. But they would also continually wrestle with the tensions within their beliefs—especially the relationships between communalism and interracialism—and between the desire to live as Christians while being effective against social problems. What the generations of Koinonians, gathered together at the reunion, shared above all was the struggle to reconcile their commitment to sharing in cooperative community and to brotherhood in interracial community. This struggle reveals the nature of a liberal Christian faith and the relationship between community, interracial brotherhood, and civil rights, while providing a potential model for us as we look for solutions to continuing problems of alienation and segregation.

Part I

*Beginnings,
1942–56*

I

Roots

KOINONIA GREW in southern soil. In order to understand the ideas and actions of the founders and the young people who joined them at the farm, it is important first to have a glimpse of the environment that produced the community. Koinonians were part of a particular southern religious culture. They held in common with other men and women of their generation a southern Protestant worldview, characterized by attention to individual conversion and evangelism. They grew up in churchgoing households, mostly Southern Baptist. Their mothers and fathers served as deacons and Sunday school teachers. As children they became members of the church early and participated in its boys' and girls' clubs. During college they joined campus groups and considered entering church professions. In short, they shared with Southern Baptists and members of other denominations across the region a set of socializing experiences. In the process of this socialization they learned about Christian beliefs, behavior, and social concerns.

A countervailing element to the traditional form of the education of these young white southerners was their exposure to Christian liberalism, which, although the minority view, was a constant element in regional church culture. Beginning with the Social Gospel and continuing in the interracial and student movements of the 1930s and 1940s, some southerners explored ways to apply their Christian beliefs to social issues, especially race relations. By the 1940s this viewpoint was often presented in various youth forums. A review of southern Protestant culture in general and the development of early twentieth-century Social Gospel and interracialism in particular reveals the nature of the liberal Christian tradition available to Koinonians and the ways in which they encountered it. Future Koinonians learned from both the traditional southern Protestant environment and the current of liberal thought in their churches and colleges. In the process they developed an understanding of Christianity and a plan for acting on it that challenged much of the culture around them. That they were able to do so demonstrates the potential for alternative religious faith and action in the region at the time.

Koinonians grew up in a culture informed by the southern Protestant church. As a result they shared with others of their age an ethos which was individualistic, Bible-centered, and mission-oriented. The main emphasis of southern theology was on individual conversion, personal morality, and strict adherence to the teachings of the Bible. Mainstream white southern Protestants believed that an individual conversion experience ushered one into a personal relationship with God. After accepting Jesus Christ as the savior, a Christian tried to live a moral life, guided by a careful and persistent reading of the Bible. In addition, southern white Protestants devoted much time and attention to evangelism. Again and again, they were called upon to support missions, in the hope that all nonbelievers could be converted, brought into the family of Christ, and taught to live a biblical way of life.[1]

Most of the first generation of Koinonians came from a particular part of the southern Protestant world, the Southern Baptist Convention (SBC). The SBC, along with the Methodist Episcopal Church, South, dominated the region's religious culture. By the turn of the century approximately 56 percent of southern white church members belonged to these denominations or the Presbyterian Church in the United States. Most of the others were in small local denominations or regionally defined churches that were similar in theology and practice.[2] The Southern Baptist Convention alone grew from 1.2 to 3.6 million members between 1876 and 1925. According to some scholars, these denominations expanded because they suited the experience and worldview of most southerners. Especially after the Civil War, Southernness was defined, in part, by the Lost Cause, poverty, and a rural lifestyle with its concomitant diffusion of population. These factors shaped a taste for an individualistic religion which promised the emotional satisfaction of conversion, the experience of being saved, and an ultimate reward. By holding forth this promise, Protestant revival religion won many converts. In addition, the Baptists built a strong institutional structure in the Southern Baptist Convention. Between 1917 and 1931 the SBC developed a central finance system, regionwide bureaucracy, and constitution. Central bodies produced and distributed literature, magazines, Bible lessons, and other materials aimed at giving Southern Baptists a common experience.[3] By midcentury "Baptists in the South were a cultural establishment enforcing moral conformity and sustained by an institutional structure that reached into all areas of church life."[4]

Southern Baptists, while sharing the basic elements of southern Protestant theology, held some additional tenets that were significant to the future development of Koinonia. Young Koinonians were exposed to a number of basic ideals. First, Southern Baptists believed that salvation, through the death and resurrection of Christ, is open to all. Because there is no intermediary except Christ between an individual and God's grace, all believers are equal and are priests to each other. Theoretically Southern Baptists held that "among Christians there are no superior or inferior classes." Moreover, Christians should live in communion with other believers, with the local congregation as a community. An important Southern Baptist article of faith is that each congregation represents the body of Christ and is autonomous. Finally, as in other southern denominations, the purpose of the Church is evangelism. In brief, the Southern Baptists have "no mission on earth save the carrying out of his [Christ's] will." That will is to evangelize the world.[5]

Southern Baptists devoted their time and energy to carrying out that will through missions. As children they gave pennies to, and learned about, missionaries in other countries. As young adults they attended Training Union programs where they were encouraged to go into service themselves. The Southern Baptist press constantly carried reports on mission activities and fund-raising campaigns as well as letters and articles from missionaries. Southern Baptist women organized in the Women's Missionary Union and, believing service and soul winning to be part of any Christian life, sponsored home mission activities including mothers' clubs, Sunday schools, hospital and prison visits, and nurseries. Since the turn of the century Southern Baptists had been expanding into new fields, including mountain missions, foreign language missions, and work in Cuba as well as among American blacks. Through the 1920s and 1930s financial hard times had forced some cutbacks, but Southern Baptists continued to proclaim the gospel to disadvantaged groups. After World War II the convention expanded, moving into rural church work and the West and increasing contacts in the mountains and cities.[6] Throughout the middle part of the century, Southern Baptists poured energy into evangelism in a massive effort to win souls for Christ.

The emphasis on evangelism reveals much about the social beliefs of most Southern Baptists. They believed in being "of the world" to save it. For them, saving society meant saving individuals within it and teaching them to live according to biblical prescriptions for right and wrong. The church did this through evangelism, education, and some charitable programs.[7] By and large, these were the acceptable outlets for social concern within the denomination. Southern Baptists made forays into social activism in the Prohibition and temperance movements, but even in these causes they aimed primarily at changing personal behavior.[8] The training of new ministers at the Southern Baptist Theological Seminary in Louisville, "the Granddaddy of Southern Baptist Seminaries," reflected this general theological and social conservatism.[9] Its curriculum was Bible-centered and focused on teaching the pupils to preach the gospel.[10] Future Koinonians, therefore, were socialized in a religious climate in which personal right living and the evangelization of others were the main concerns of a Christian.

The hesitancy of Southern Baptists to challenge existing social arrangements was most obvious in their failure to question the racial mores of the region. In the nineteenth century most Protestant churches had split over slavery, creating regional denominations such as the Southern Baptist Convention. After the Civil War the major denominations segregated into white and black congregations. While white Southern Baptists continued to evangelize blacks, particularly those in foreign lands, they showed no intention of inviting the newly won souls into their own congregations. Many white Protestants justified this rending of the Christian brotherhood with biblical passages. They said that blacks were the descendants of Ham, whom God had cursed to be forever the hewers of wood. They also maintained that God had created the color line and ordered men to stay within the "bounds of their habitations." Moreover, because most southern Protestants had little interest in saving or improving society, they were not particularly concerned with winning justice for the downtrodden, especially for blacks. Some Christians who worried that they might be neglecting Christ's message about universal love assuaged their doubts by being kind to blacks and showing a paternalistic concern for the salvation of "our Negroes." That concern only went so far. The vast majority of southern white Protestants were happy to maintain the racial status quo.[11]

A lifetime of socialization in church institutions impressed this worldview upon young people. Many of those who would later join Koinonia, for example, grew up attending church and Sunday school regularly and joining in young peoples' activities, such as choir practice and church socials. "It was my social life actually," remembered Willie Pugh, who participated in every denominational program for her age group, including the girls' auxiliary and the Baptist Young People's Union.[12] Young Baptists were encouraged to attend denominational colleges or join the campus Baptist Student Union (BSU). Because they spent so much time in church organizations, these young people had certain ideas, values, and experiences in common. The Southern Baptist Convention provided all the materials and directions for church activities, so that any member in the country went through the same rituals and lessons. From Sunday school books to church choir robes to the order of the service, there was a "Southern Baptist way to do everything."[13] For many young Southern Baptists, the church was a way of life; its work and lifestyle seemed natural.

The Southern Baptist church taught young people three basic lessons: to live a moral life, to do mission work, and to consider the church as a community. At a very young age boys and girls started learning about missionaries in India and Africa.[14] As members of the Sunbeams or Royal Ambassadors—girls' and boys' clubs—they donated money to help Christian missions among the poor of the world. The Training Union meetings on Sunday evenings prepared them to do church service, especially distributing charity for the poor and working for the salvation of souls. The adults around them and their Sunday school lessons provided the models for a pious Christian life. Personal morality meant adherence to the Ten Commandments and the Golden Rule, abstinence from alcohol and tobacco, and kindness to the less fortunate. Finally, young Southern Baptists were introduced to the concept of the congregation as a community. Their friends, relations, and most of their social contacts were in their congregation. Indeed, many found their future spouses there or at church camps and conventions.[15] This socialization process translated the basic tenets of southern Protestant and Southern Baptist faith into daily action and church culture.

Despite the generally conservative milieu, there was in the early twentieth-century South an alternate, liberal form of Christianity. This liberalism took many expressions, from Social Gospel reformism to interracialism to radical experiments in integrated unions or cooperatives. The early manifestation of this stream of Christian faith was the Social Gospel movement, which preached the application of Christ's teachings to the salvation of society as well as individuals. According to this theology the Kingdom of God was not heaven or an otherworldly hereafter but something which people could work to bring about immediately. Biblical descriptions of the Kingdom of God were a blueprint for the reconstruction of society. While the Social Gospel is most often associated with northern, urban churches, recent scholars have found evidence that it had followers in the South as well.[16] Southern ministers and lay men and women practiced applied Christianity and followed their beliefs into social activism. Much of this activity took place in other denominations but still influenced Southern Baptists, creating an ecumenical liberal culture which later had an impact on Koinonia. Regardless of denomination, these southerners were the spiritual and theological ancestors of later Christian liberals and reformers, including Koinonians.

In the early part of the century, the Social Gospel inspired its southern followers to engage in a wide range of reform activities, with a special focus on education. Women of the Methodist Episcopal Church, South, led the way, but Social Gospel ministers and lay leaders of other denominations participated as well.[17] Moral issues such as divorce, gambling, tobacco, and pornography attracted much of the attention. But Methodist women were also interested in conditions in the home. Believing that one must minister to the body as well as the spirit, they focused their attention on the physical conditions of the poor. As a result, they worked on public health and welfare issues, for temperance, and against child labor. In organizations like the Southern Sociological Congress, other adherents of the Social Gospel studied social problems in prisons and agriculture. The primary focus of the Social Gospel in the South, however, was on education, which ministers and laymen saw as the key to uplift for both poor whites and blacks. Ministers and churchwomen supported the movement to upgrade the schools and established home missions and settlement houses, such as the John Little Mission in Louisville and the Bethlehem Center in Nashville. These actions made the southern Social Gospel the backbone of the Progressive movement in the region. One scholar estimated that one-quarter of the members of the Southern Sociological Congress were ministers.[18] This alliance between Christian and secular reformers lasted through the interracial movements of the 1930s and 1940s and into the civil rights movement of later decades.

Any discussion of the roots of Christian liberalism or any reform in the South must address the issue of race. Scholars have recently argued that contrary to historical tradition, the Social Gospel was very involved with race issues, even in the South.[19] Southern Social Gospel leaders shared a concern for African-American conditions and education. They particularly supported the Tuskegee approach to education for blacks, while also advocating vocational education for poor whites. They established missions in urban areas to reach African Americans, who were moving there in larger numbers. This concern for black education did not mean that southern followers of the Social Gospel were not racist. Most believed firmly in the separation of the races and took white superiority for granted. They had a paternalistic concern for the conditions of African Americans and wanted to uplift the latter within the framework of segregation. Leaders such as Atticus G. Haygood and Edgar Gardner Murphy believed that separation was best for African Americans and looked forward to their improvement and development within their own sphere. Still, the simple fact that they showed concern for African-American lives and believed in development at a time of increased racial hostility and tension distinguished Social Gospel adherents from their fellow southerners. Moreover, this paternalistic concern often served as a starting point from which they traveled into the interracial movement and civil rights activism.[20]

The Social Gospel was the beginning of twentieth-century southern social Christianity and in many ways laid the basis for Koinonia's later work. It popularized, at least for an active minority of church people, the idea that

Christians could apply their beliefs to social conditions and relations. These individuals established institutions, such as missions and settlement houses, as well as organizations and alliances that nurtured progressive racial ideas and provided space for future generations to learn and practice them. Most important, perhaps, the Social Gospel led people into further action. Women who first worked in charity or missions moved into activism against child labor or for women's rights. Through their contact with black women, moreover, they involved themselves in the movement for African-American rights. Others who started out supporting education moved into broader action. Edgar Gardner Murphy, for example, eventually directed his energy to the study and amelioration of racial problems. For some white southerners, then, the Social Gospel was a bridge by which they moved into interracialism.[21]

In the two decades before the founding of Koinonia, the interracial movement provided a forum where members of the two races could meet and work together toward solutions to problems. Essentially, Christian interracialism was an effort to reach out to African Americans as brothers and sisters and work together in church activities or on particular problems. In the 1920s and 1930s interracialism—both within and outside the church—accepted the system of segregation and sought to work within it. Again, Methodist women were among the leaders. In their mission work they had met African-American churchwomen. Such encounters profoundly affected the white, middle-class women who participated, making them aware of black concerns and inspiring them to work with African Americans.[22] At first they concentrated on church-related activities. Methodist women sponsored summer Christian leadership schools with African-American church workers. They also held joint Bible schools, church visits, and youth programs. Outside of church work women fought lynching by sending interracial teams to visit jails and attend trials.[23] Throughout the early decades of the century, the dissident minority arranged interracial meetings and conferences to address racial problems. The most active organizations in this movement were the denominational social action bodies, the Young Women's Christian Association (YWCA), the Association of Southern Women for the Prevention of Lynching (ASWPL), and the Commission on Interracial Cooperation (CIC).

The CIC was perhaps the most organized expression of the interracial movement. Will Alexander and others founded the organization in the wake of post–World War I racial violence. To a large extent, though not completely, it was staffed by liberal Christians. The CIC created biracial partnerships by sending a team—one white person and one black person— into a southern community to bring people together to study and find solutions to problems. The Georgia Interracial Commission summed up the purpose of local committees: to provide an opportunity for people to get to know each other, a forum for settling conflicts, and a chance to improve conditions.[24] The work focused on concrete problems. For example, the CIC called for equal educational facilities for black children, job opportunity for black professionals, better housing, and more parks and recreational facilities for African Americans. By the late 1940s the Georgia state commission had succeeded in opening parks, setting up kindergartens, and preventing disturbances.[25] The CIC, by going against the grain of its time and focusing on concrete acts, served an important function. It gave whites an outlet for their ideas about improving race relations and an opportunity to work with African Americans. As a result they gained knowledge about problems in the black community. In addition, the CIC resolved conflicts and made contributions to better conditions in some places. Most important, membership in the organization led some individuals to support civil rights for blacks, particularly through the fight against the poll tax. The CIC was also a product of its time, however, and failed to challenge segregation or to call for social equality. The white members never went beyond a call for improved conditions for African Americans within a system of segregation.[26]

In the 1930s and 1940s there were some southerners, inspired by a radical interpretation of the gospel, who stood on the outer edge of white dissent to the racial status quo. A few, including Howard Kester, Alva Taylor, Claude Williams, Don West, and Myles Horton, questioned segregation itself. While churchwomen had led in the Social Gospel and interracial movement, these young ministers and seminarians led in combining interracialism with a critique of the southern economy.[27] The Fellowship of Southern Churchmen (FSC) was founded in 1936 by a loose-knit group of people interested in labor, race, and rural reconstruction. The organization fostered interracialism in southern communities by holding conferences, visiting campuses, supporting antilynching and anti–poll tax legislation, and serving as a clearinghouse for information and support. Because the members of the FSC believed segregation and discrimination were incompatible with the Bible, they broke with them in every way they could. Some members of the FSC helped to organize the Southern Tenant Farmers' Union (STFU), an interracial union of sharecroppers and tenants. The STFU challenged not only segregation, by including whites and blacks as equals, but also the southern agricultural system by organizing sharecroppers and calling a strike. The STFU argued that cooperative farms could be part of the solution to both agricultural and racial troubles and established Delta and Providence Farms in Mississippi to demonstrate cooperative farming and interracial solidarity. This small band of radical Christians went further in their interpretation and activities than even their contemporaries in the liberal minority of the white Protestant church. But they were never more than a tiny marginalized voice. The FSC never had over five hundred members.[28] Their contributions were their articulation of an interpretation of the Bible which criticized the race and economic system of the South and their effort to act on that interpretation by bringing whites and blacks together in cooperative work. Koinonians would learn from and join this circle of believers and activists.

Future Koinonians first encountered the dissident interpretation of Christianity as it filtered into Southern Baptist institutions, particularly youth organizations and college campuses. The men and women who were in college in the late thirties and early forties had grown up with war, depression, and now more war. They had seen the disillusionment after World War I and the economic devastation of the thirties. Some of them had been exposed to the Social Gospel of the interwar years. All these factors shaped the social consciences of some southern white Christians and made them ready to hear a progressive message.[29] At that time there were new voices to be heard. Student leaders for the churches on campuses often were out in front of their denominations on race issues. This was true in both the Baptist Student Union and the student YWCAs.[30] Organizations such as the CIC and FSC also made concerted efforts to generate interracialism among students. The FSC, for example, helped organize a gathering of collegiate interracial councils, at which students from Georgia Baptist College, Wesleyan, Georgia Southern College for Women, and Mercer discussed race issues and met black students from Paine College in Augusta.[31] The organization also spread its message through publications and campus speakers. These activities exposed a generation of southerners to ideas about improving race relations, as well as the opportunity to practice them. This stirring of interest in race relations greeted future Koinonians when they arrived on campus.

Despite the general conservativism of the denomination, the liberal Christian subculture reached Southern Baptist life. Particular beliefs of Southern Baptists, along with the influence of a few seminarians, made members of the denomination open to these new trends. The central tenets of Southern Baptist faith—the priesthood of all believers, the fellowship of the regenerate, and the freedom of conscience—allowed for a liberal interpretation. Some individuals argued that this creed implied that all Christians were equal brothers and sisters who should live together in fellowship. While most Southern Baptists interpreted this to mean that the church was a community and that all Southern Baptists anywhere were brethren, the minority went further and urged people to reach out to blacks and include them in that fellowship as equals. Meanwhile, some seminarians and ministers were urging Southern Baptists to apply the Bible's teachings to current social issues and to take responsibility in the region's problems. Professors Charles S. Gardner and J. B. Weatherspoon introduced their classes at the Southern Baptist Theological Seminary to the Social Gospel. By the mid-1940s the seminary had graduated several men who had written dissertations on social issues. These leaders, including Olin T. Binkley, Foy Valentine, and Clarence Jordan, influenced others through their ministry, participation in denominational bodies, and campus speaking tours.[32] Although most Southern Baptists continued to hold traditional interpretations, the support for the freedom of conscience allowed some acceptance of ideas about Christian social action, even in race relations.

In the pre–World War II era, the people in the Southern Baptist liberal minority mirrored the larger culture in their emphasis on converting African Americans and promoting education. This was manifested in a concern for blacks as a mission field and in support for ministerial training and vacation Bible school for blacks. Many local Southern Baptist groups were working with blacks in the 1920s, but most of their efforts were limited to donations of Sunday school materials or other church outreach. In the 1930s some people in the subculture started talking about the need to understand, appreciate, and respect African Americans. In 1936 Noble Y. Beall taught a course at a Mississippi college on "The Appreciation of the Negro" and concurrently hosted study groups, conferences, and public talks.[33] J. B. Weatherspoon called for an end to disenfranchisement, unequal education, discrimination, and prejudice. Another Southern Baptist Theological Seminary professor, Edward A. McDowell Jr., argued that segregation went against the idea of reconciliation in the Bible. All this activity was limited, however. Southern Baptists still lagged behind other denominations on interracialism. Although in the minority subculture individuals called for understanding, education, and even some rights, at this time they lacked a broader vision of social equality.[34]

During and after the war, a few Southern Baptists went further and began to seek fellowship with black Baptists. In 1946, in a publication of the Home Mission Board, Thomas Maston advocated that Southern Baptists cross the color line and cooperate with black churches and communities. Women's and student groups led the way in fostering interracial understanding. For instance, the Women's Missionary Union held interracial institutes around the South at which they studied and socialized with their African-American counterparts. In addition, in 1944 the women at an auxiliary meeting at the denomination's retreat in the North Carolina mountains, the Ridgecrest Assembly Ground, while trying to devise a list of ways to relieve racial tensions, pledged themselves to overcome stereotypes by getting to know black women personally. These actions resembled those of the interracial movement in other denominations. In student organizations young people gained experience working both for and with blacks in charitable efforts and churches, and along with it an interest in race issues. For example, in Georgia, white Baptist student groups passed a resolution enumerating a "Minimum Bill of Rights" for blacks. In addition, some student groups' conventions started to focus on the theme of the "Christian Approach on Races."[35]

Young Southern Baptists were most often first exposed to these new ideas about race relations in two main forums: youth conferences and the Baptist Student Union. At student meetings held annually at the Ridgecrest Assembly Ground and at other locations during the year, young people joined in campfire discussions and Bible study and heard speeches on biblical subjects and the application of Christian principles to social problems. Often, by week's end a young man or woman would dedicate himself or herself to a life of work for Christ.[36] On campus the students' life revolved around the BSU, just as it had around their congregation when they were children. The BSU helped individuals maintain their Baptist identity while away at school and served a social function for those who joined in recreation, meetings, and regional conferences.[37] It also introduced students to ideas and people who opened their eyes. One future Koinonian, Howard Johnson, remembered his debt to the campus minister at Auburn University and the older, more worldly students he encountered at the BSU there.[38] Because the student secretaries of the BSU were among the most forward-looking leaders in the denomination, they invited speakers and arranged programs that challenged the students' conceptions of what it meant to be a Christian.[39] In these forums young, idealistic white Christians took the idea of fellowship and extended it to include rights. Moreover, through these activities students built ties to a personal and organizational network, which would later pull them into action of various forms in the South's racial struggles.[40]

The men and women who founded and joined Koinonia took action on race relations, including trying to create an interracial fellowship, because of their understanding of Christianity. That interpretation grew from the interplay of several elements in the midcentury southern environment. Perhaps the overriding factor was the importance of the church in the lives of white southerners. It was the institution in which they grew up, made social contacts, and learned how to behave. From it they learned about the individual's relationship to God and the importance of missions. Most Koinonians were Southern Baptists and had absorbed the denomination's tenets of the fellowship of believers and the congregation as community, as well as its social teachings. A second informing factor in their upbringing was the tradition of southern Christian liberalism. The Social Gospel had made some impact in the region, fostering the idea that Christians could apply their principles to social problems. Those principles were behind the interracial movement of the thirties and forties. By the postwar era a minority voice of southern whites was calling for a Christian approach to race relations that included concern for African-American rights. This ecumenical movement of Christian liberalism made inroads into some Southern Baptist institutions and thus was accessible to the young men and women who would join Koinonia. By the forties Southern Baptist semi-narians, along with members of women's and student groups, talked about and acted on ideas regarding missions and education for blacks, coopera-tion, and even fellowship. The midcentury church culture socialized young white Christians to think of helping the less fortunate and to consider the church as a community of brothers and sisters. Contact with the liberal mi-nority through student and other groups gave them access to new ideas about race relations. The combination produced a fertile environment for Koinonia.

2

The Word

WHILE SOUTHERN BAPTIST religious culture provided the fertile environment for Koinonia Farm, the ideas of its founder Clarence Jordan were the seeds from which it grew. Jordan's experiences while growing up, studying in college and seminary, and working in Louisville, Kentucky, combined with his interpretation of the Greek New Testament to shape his beliefs about Christian life, race relations, and community. At college and seminary he encountered the liberal tradition of Christianity and absorbed from it an interest in reform, missions, and interracialism. He added to that an understanding of the economic roots of race problems, as well as ideas about community gleaned from his reading of the New Testament. Jordan translated those ideas into reality when he met Martin England, a Baptist missionary, in the early days of the Second World War. Together they worked out a blueprint by which they could put their ideas into practice in an agricultural demonstration plot, rural mission, and interracial community. While Koinonia's philosophy and action had many roots, the project began with Jordan. The story of his intellectual development and collaboration with England is the story of the shaping of an idea and its incarnation.

Clarence Leonard Jordan was a product of the Southern Baptist culture around him. He was born in July 1912, the seventh child in a large Baptist family in Talbotton, Talbot County, Georgia. A rural farming area between the state's piedmont and coastal plain, the county was "very sandy" with "poor soil, poor people."[1] The years of Jordan's maturation were hard ones economically for rural Georgia, mainly due to an attack of the boll weevil in the early 1920s.[2] But Clarence's father was not a down-and-out farmer. Rather he was a "puritanical businessman" who started the Bank of Talbotton and, with his sons' help, ran a general store. This provided his children with the opportunity to go to college. The Jordans were devout Southern Baptists who regularly attended services and Sunday school and read the Bible. At the age of ten Clarence was saved at a revival and joined the church.[3] Looking back through the lens of many years, Jordan's brothers and sister recalled that Talbotton was "typical" in race relations. "We were very close to all the blacks, had friends in the black community, had a black nurse and servants," said Jordan's brother Frank.[4] These recollections gloss over the fact that the 1920s were a time of increased racial tension and the rise of the Klan in Georgia. In doing so, the memory reveals that the Jordan family did not question the racial status quo. Clarence Jordan's roots were in this small-town, Southern Baptist environment where whites and blacks interacted, but their places were rigidly defined.

Jordan's temperament, a mixture of warm sociability and stubbornness, set him apart from his family at an early age. A tall youngster whose long, skinny legs later earned him the sobriquet "Tall-bottom," Jordan was good-natured and outgoing. He had a droll wit and a deep Georgia drawl. He was also unusually bright, even as a schoolboy.[5] Furthermore, according to his oldest brother, Frank, he "had an argumentative nature, always took the opposite side to be different. . . . He always was a little different, saw things differently than we did." Maybe it was being the middle son, maybe it was a childhood bout with scarlet fever, which had isolated him from the family with only his mother and a nurse to care for him.[6] Whatever the cause of Clarence's dissimilarity, instead of considering him a black sheep, his siblings were proud of him and urged him to "let your motto be to take the name of Jordan just a little bit higher than either one of us took it."[7]

Growing up in the segregated South accentuated Jordan's "different" temperament. His siblings recalled that because of the family's acquaintance with African Americans, Clarence had "learned to appreciate colored people." Unlike the rest of the family, little things began to bother him. The jingle they sang in Sunday school that said that Jesus loved all the children of the world—"red, yellow, black or white"—struck a nerve in him even as a child. Though the words said that God loved all children equally, Jordan saw adults around him treating dark children meanly. Once, when he was about nine or ten, he scolded his father for mistreating a black delivery boy who had come to the front door.[8]

In Jordan's memory his racial attitudes were most shaped by an experience involving the chain gang camp near his home. The prisoners, most of them African Americans incarcerated for "minor offenses like petty larceny or on trumped up charges," lived in cages. As a boy Jordan walked by the camp, visited with the prisoners, and made friends with the cook. One night after attending a revival, Clarence awoke to the sound of a man groaning. He knew it was a prisoner being tortured. He also knew the man responsible for it was the warden, who had been praising God at the service just a few hours earlier. Jordan recalled of that night: "This started a great conflict in me—almost against religion. I was bitter against God."[9]

When Jordan recalled and narrated this story, he packaged and explained his religious and racial awakening. His fury against God marked the beginning of his alienation from the mainstream religious culture around him, though not from religion itself. Indeed, here was the root of his radical Christianity. Jordan finished the story by saying that at first he considered being a lawyer but after mulling it over decided to become an agricultural scientist.[10] The narrative explained his awareness of the problems of both legal injustice and poverty and his conclusion that the latter was more important. Jordan used the story to try to pinpoint the roots of his approach to race reform, which emphasized economic over legal and political change. Chance are, Jordan was not really this self-aware as a teenager. The stories about Jordan's childhood are glimpses of his character seen in retrospect through the lens of his later work. When Jordan and his siblings tell these stories, they are looking for roots of difference and later racial attitudes. As a result, they recognize incidents like this one as turning points and infuse them with meaning as the trigger to a resolve to act.

Jordan's interest in alternative Christianity as well as his awareness of economic and racial problems grew while he was a student in agriculture at the University of Georgia at Athens. During these years his intelligence and personality served him well as he excelled in school and participated in a variety of campus activities. He joined a fraternity, the campus literary society, and the debate team. He also mastered his agricultural courses, published articles in the *Georgia Agriculturist,* and was elected president of the agricultural honor society.[11] At the same time he immersed himself in campus religious life. Like others of his generation he encountered, for the first time, the ideals of the liberal tradition in his denomination. In his first letter home, he wrote excitedly about the Baptist Young People's Union and the fine campus pastor. He also became close friends with the state and local Baptist Student Union director, D. B. Nicholson. Soon he was leading church groups and traveling to student conferences around the country. After one such meeting he found himself "resolving to live a better life for having been there." He and Nicholson also discussed racial issues and their spiritual implications.[12] Jordan's college years prepared him well for his career as a farmer and gave him the tools he would need to help African-American tenants. More important, the religious work in which he was engaged kept him in touch with transcendent issues, deepened his Christian devotion, and stirred his consciousness of social problems.

A turning point in Jordan's spiritual development came near the end of college. Jordan had signed up early in his college career for the ROTC program, and in 1932 a professor selected him for a special course which would lead to a commission as a second lieutenant.[13] While at boot camp in the summer of 1933, Jordan spent his free time reading the Bible, especially the Sermon on the Mount. One day during training exercises the words of Matthew went through his head: "Love your enemies, bless them that curse you, do good to them who hate you, and pray for them which despitefully use you and persecute you." On the spot Jordan decided that the ideas he had imbibed from the Bible conflicted with what he was learning in camp. To live according to the teachings he was beginning to cherish, he would have to give one up. That day he resigned his commission, and from then on he was a committed pacifist.[14]

Over the course of his college career, Jordan moved away from the material and economic concerns of agriculture and toward the spiritual ones of a religious vocation. By the end of his senior year, he was on the verge of a major life change. "Clarence struggled with a sense of call to the ministry, but he was very much dedicated at the same time to agriculture and working with farm people," recalled his good friend Claude Broach.[15] Jordan wanted to live the way of his Lord, but he hesitated to give up his dream of rehabilitating southern agriculture. He came to believe, however, that rural African Americans needed more than hybrid seeds and new fertilizers. They needed the Word of God. Finally, at a Baptist student retreat at Ridgecrest, Jordan determined that God's will was that he become a preacher. He described his call to the ministry as a yielding to a voice whispering in the back of his head: "If being called to the ministry means lending an attentive ear to a simple statement 'my child I want you to preach for me,' then most assuredly I have been called to the ministry. . . . You wish my answer? Here it is—'Yes Lord, whatever you say, just promise me that you'll go with me.'"[16] With quiet determination to learn the Word of God and prepare to preach it, Jordan set out for the Southern Baptist Theological Seminary in Louisville, Kentucky.

Jordan's years at the seminary and in Louisville not only taught him how to be a minister, they also exposed him to a new reading of the Bible and understanding of how to live according to it. He had chosen the Southern Baptist Theological Seminary because it was the most prestigious Southern Baptist academic institution. There, despite the generally conservative atmosphere, a few professors pushed him in a progressive direction. These instructors were part of the liberal minority leading their students and the denomination in general toward a Christian approach to race relations and other issues. From his New Testament professor, William Hershey Davis, Jordan learned to question standard interpretations of the Bible. The Christian ethics instructor, J. B. Weatherspoon, introduced him to social issues.[17] But the single most significant influence on Jordan in these years was Edward A. McDowell Jr., who inspired him to look more deeply into the Greek New Testament for the meaning of the Word. Equally important, he taught him "that the Word must come alive in currents of history and social change." McDowell, who believed that ministers had a special responsibility in conquering racial prejudice, also took his student to a meeting of the Southern Interracial Commission in the mid-1930s. "This too was a turning point in my life," Jordan later wrote, "for it seemed to bring into the open the deep feelings which had lain, like molten lava, within the inner recesses of my heart."[18]

After receiving his master's degree in 1936, Jordan decided to deepen his understanding of the Bible by studying for a doctorate in the Greek New Testament.[19] Later he explained that he knew his desire to help African

Americans would be controversial, and "I wanted to root myself firmly in the teachings of Jesus—in the Greek New Testament—to get it fresh from the stream."[20] While Southern Baptists generally emphasize Bible study and reading the Word, McDowell had taught Jordan to look for the essence of God's message in the meaning behind the words. The best way to do that, he believed, was to strip the text of the King James dialect and read it in the ancient tongues. Despite the controversy that would later surround him and leave him almost ostracized from Southern Baptist circles, Jordan shared with others of his denomination an essential Bible-centeredness. He saw it as the ultimate guide to life. His approach to reading the Bible was "radical," however, in that he was attempting to get at the root of Christianity. He was also becoming a radical in a more usual sense, because the ideas that he formulated while reading the Word led him to action that went against the grain of southern society.

One of those ideas was the meaning of community. Jordan first encountered the subject in the translation of the word *koinonia* in the Book of Acts. *Koinonia* is a Greek word which can be translated as church, fellowship, or community. In the New Testament it described the gathering of disciples in early Christianity. Reading further, Jordan came upon two passages in Acts that grabbed his attention: "The multitude of them that believed were of one heart and one soul" (Acts 4:32) and "And all that believed were together, and had all things in common; and sold their possessions and goods, and parted them to all men, as every man had need" (Acts 2:44–45). Baptists believed that the congregation is a community. Jordan's translations took him further. He decided that Christians should live in community, co-operating and sharing materially and spiritually, and that a Christian does not act as an individual but as part of the larger body of Christ.

In his reading of the New Testament, Jordan also discovered the centrality of the Christian message of the Kingdom of God. All Jesus' teachings, from his first words after his baptism to his parables, dealt with the Kingdom and how to get into it. Earlier Social Gospel ministers and activists had seen the Kingdom of God as a blueprint for reconstructing society. Again, Jordan went a little further. In a series of Sunday school lessons he argued that the Kingdom is the family of God. When a person accepts Jesus as the Christ, he or she becomes a member of this spiritual family, with God as the parent and fellow believers as brothers and sisters. He also believed that Jesus preached that this Kingdom was to begin now, not in some otherworldly hereafter or heaven. Most important, people became members of God's family and joined the Kingdom by reaching across barriers of race and class to their Christian brothers and sisters and sharing with them.[21] That required, above all, cooperation and fellowship between whites and blacks. Furthermore, Jordan argued that Christians should begin to live as if in the Kingdom of God and witness to it—or demonstrate that life—immediately. By doing so one became a true Christian disciple. These concepts, of communalism and the Kingdom of God as an interracial, cross-class family of God, distinguished Jordan from even his most liberal contemporaries.

Jordan experimented with putting his theories about community into practice a few years later while he was the director of a city mission in Louisville. He and his wife Florence, whom he had met while he was at seminary and married in 1936, gathered frequently with a group of students to discuss pacifism, racial equality, and the sharing described in the Bible.[22] When summer came, some of the student decided to stay at the mission. They called themselves "the koinonia" and emulated the early Christians by pooling their income and using a common bank account. The koinonia had meals together and decided by consensus how funds would be spent. According to member Bob Herndon, they also had a mission for blacks and hoped that their community "might work for the good of all." The experiment ultimately failed, however. All the members save the Jordans were students at the seminary at the time, which meant they had few resources and planned to move out of Louisville when they graduated. The Louisville koinonia lacked a core of people who were financially able or willing to see the experiment through over a long period of time.[23] Nevertheless, Jordan took from this experience lessons about the importance of a permanent membership base and economic self-sufficiency, and he remained determined to try community again in the future.

When he was not immersed in his Greek New Testament, Jordan worked with African Americans in activities that affected his attitude on race. While studying for his master's degree, he often went to preach in local churches, hospitals, and orphanages. These trips exposed him to shocking poverty in the worst sections of Louisville and the surrounding area. At one mission the "congregation was composed of a handful of ragged, dirty, hungry, and yes, starving humanity." Starving, in America, among Christians. How was it, he asked, "that such conditions exist alongside the mansions and places of luxury of another section of the city? No, America isn't Christian yet."[24] The disparity reminded him of the poverty in rural Talbot County. It also struck him as contrary to biblical teachings on the equality of believers and sharing among Christians. These experiences formed in him a strong opposition to materialism, which stayed with him all his life.

Later his graduate fellowship required him to teach part-time at Simmons University, a "small struggling black college" in Louisville which trained African-American preachers. In the course of his work there, Jordan became "deeply involved and sympathetic" with is students' lives. He discovered that they had to work as "waiters, cab drivers, delivery men, porters, or whatever," leaving them too tired to study. Like Christian liberals before him, Jordan became more and more concerned about the state of African-American education. Unlike his Social Gospel forebears, however, he also became convinced that something had to be done about the problem of racial separation.[25] He befriended some of his pupils and tried to involve them in the life of the larger and better-equipped Southern Seminary. On one occasion he proposed inviting some of his students for a prayer supper, but the seminary officials refused.[26] This experience at Simmons awakened his interest in race and gave it a focus. Jordan became determined to "do something" about African-American education, particularly that of black pastors.

After receiving his doctoral degree, Jordan pursued his interest in African-American education by becoming the director of the Baptist Fellowship Center (BFC), a mission in a slum neighborhood of Louisville. He did so because he believed, "These people [African Americans] are shamefully neglected," and it is "pathetic to see how hungry these people are for the Gospel, and yet how untrained and incapable their leadership is."[27] These words sum up the mission of the center at the time: to bring urban blacks into the Baptist church and to work with black pastors to improve their churches. Despite the condescending tone of Jordan's words and the center's mission, the work of the BFC was to some extent cooperative. The board had both black and white members, and Jordan worked with African-American pastors to organize training sessions, courses, and joint meetings.[28] The center accomplished its goals by holding programs for ministers, teaching summer school courses in the Old Testament, and establishing a training program for black Sunday school and young people's workers. In addition Jordan coordinated efforts to establish black churches in rural areas and sent young white students into the existing ones to help the ministers with administrative tasks. Finally, the BFC ran educational programs for African-American lay people, such as a vacation Bible school with an enrollment of twelve hundred and a religious camp for black girls.[29] The financial support for these activities came from the Long Run Association, which sponsored the BFC, as well as from small donations from Sunday school classes and branches of the Women's Missionary Union.

Jordan broadened the work of the center to the reflect his concern about poverty and to minister to the whole of the people's lives. The new program at the mission addressed material and social problems. Under his stewardship the BFC became as much a community and recreation center as a classroom. In this it reflected the example of Social Gospel era missions and settlement homes and joined the minority of Southern Baptist institutions that focused on "personal service missions." The term, originating with the Women's Missionary Union, referred to practical missions that reached out to the poor and outcast in the community and addressed their material as well as spiritual needs. In the 1930s an estimated one-quarter of Southern Baptist missions did personal service work.[30] As part of this trend, BFC workers organized mothers' clubs to help neighborhood women and hosted meetings for boys' and girls' clubs and for the whole community. Jordan and his coworkers also showed missionary films for the young people. For the littlest children the mission had a toy library and a playroom. Jordan experimented with his idea about Christian sharing by setting up a food pantry. Well-off people could contribute money or food, and those in need could draw from it. The idea was to provide "an outlet for those who have, to share with those who have not." Jordan believed that "people can't listen to a message when they are hungry."[31] The pantry and the BFC's work to ensure that people were well fed on both bread and the Word of God were based in part on Jordan's ideas about sharing and foreshadowed his career in providing material support for those in need.

Jordan sought not only to help the black population but to increase the understanding and fellowship between the races. He and his coworkers believed it was their Christian duty to practice "that great fact that in Jesus Christ the great 'middle wall of partition' was abolished." To do so, they sponsored activities in which whites and blacks worked together, such as bringing church leaders together for study, social times, and fellowship dinners.[32] The idea behind interracial meetings was not, as Jordan put it, "so whites can drop 'around to help you dear folks run things.'" On the contrary, he instructed whites to avoid "teaching" and "just go to worship, sit in on Deacons' meetings. . . . Avoid emphasizing differences by too much talk."[33] For example, when planning a night of music presented by local black churches, Jordan advertised it not as an interracial meeting but as a chance for white people to appreciate the music and learn that "the Negro has a great contribution to make to the religious life of the world and that he has an interpretation of Christ that the rest of the world needs."[34] In all such activities Jordan and others at the center emphasized that Christians should work together and appreciate each other instead of viewing cooperation as one group helping the other. This marked the beginning of a characteristic trait in Jordan's career. His approach to improving race relations was not for whites to uplift or give anything to blacks but for the two groups of people to come together in common work, worship, and recreation.

Jordan's work with African Americans while at the seminary and at the Baptist Fellowship Center angered many of his fellow white Baptists. Convention leaders tried to rein him in by drastically editing his articles on the white man's treatment of blacks.[35] Others objected to Jordan's "offensive and obnoxious" methods and complained that he tried to go too fast in the area of race relations. A few officials were incensed when Jordan suggested bringing African Americans to the student meeting at the Southern Baptist Assembly Ground in Ridgecrest.[36] The last straw was his practice of dining with African Americans. For many southerners eating together was a sign of social equality, and thus dining with African Americans was one thing they just could not abide. Mission workers tried to explain that eating together "grew out of the natural course of events," out of cooperative work.[37] This result was precisely what the opposition feared. The dispute over the center's sponsorship of integrated meals demonstrated the distance between Jordan and his coworkers, on the one hand, and the Southern Baptist Convention institutions on the other. These incidents foreshadowed the growing alienation of Jordan from the dominant southern social and religious culture.

At the same time, Jordan's developing reputation as a leader in interracial cooperation drew to him a host of admirers and supporters. As early as his seminary days he had befriended other students interested in social issues. When the school officials refused to allow Jordan's interracial prayer supper, his fellow students had threatened to leave, saying the school "was obviously not a Christian institution."[38] When he became director of the BFC, he received many donations from individuals and groups, such as the Kentucky Baptist Women's Missionary Union, who wanted to support his "work with Negroes."[39] Later his talent for preaching and his charisma made Jordan a well-respected speaker around Louisville, where church groups frequently asked him to talk about Christians and race relations. In addition, officials of various Southern Baptist bodies called on him to participate in programs at the Ridgecrest Assembly, on campuses, and at other young people's meetings. Jordan quickly became a student favorite and often left quite a ripple on the campuses. At Furman University, where he argued that the white church, and Christians generally, could do more for blacks, one young man felt inspired "to be a better servant of the master." Others began to work on the race question in Greenville, and the Sociological Club started working on projects for the education of African Americans.[40] Jordan's support in these groups reflected the stirring of progressive attitudes on race issues among some women's and students' groups at midcentury.

In the summer of 1941 Jordan was inspired to put his missionary urges, belief in community, and desire to address the problems of African Americans into action. Martin England, a missionary on furlough from Burma for the duration of the war, had written a letter to the editor of a newsletter about his communal philosophy. In the letter England argued that Christ wanted his followers to begin living according to the plan in the New Testament immediately. England proposed the creation of small communities, because "if the barriers that divide man, and cause wars, race conflict, economic competition, class struggle, labor disputes, are ever to be broken down, they must be broken down in small groups of people living side by side." When Jordan read the letter, he instantly felt a kinship with the writer's desire to experiment with community.[41]

England was a Northern Baptist minister, professor, and missionary who had long worked for education for the underprivileged. He had graduated with a B.A. from Furman University in 1924 and with a B.D. from Crozier Theological Seminary in 1933. After college he taught at the Yancey Institute in Burnsville, North Carolina, and Mars Hill College. As early as 1932 he had been interested in improving education with institutions modeled on the ungraded Danish Folk School system. England and his wife Mabel then went to Burma, where they were missionaries until 1939. The family was home on furlough when war broke out in Asia, preventing them from returning to their post. For a while England traveled around looking for work that would enable him to do some good in the United States. He ended up in Wakefield, Kentucky, attracted there by an experimental farmers' cooperative.[42]

Jordan met England through their participation in a pacifist organization, the Fellowship of Reconciliation. At that time Jordan, who had been getting restless in Louisville, was predisposed to consider combining their ideas and putting them to work. He believed that the overcrowded and poor conditions of blacks stemmed to a large extent from the rural poverty that had pushed them off the land and into the city. This conclusion reawakened his desire to go into a rural area to improve the lives of poor African Americans.[43] Moreover, despite the way in which the Louisville koinonia had dissolved, Jordan was ready to experiment with community again. After their first meeting Jordan and England quickly became friends. In talking to England about Christian stewardship, the community of believers, and the sharing among the disciples in the early church, Jordan became convinced that community, combined with a mission, could address social problems. The two men spent long nights talking about how to act on their beliefs, until one day Jordan simply said, "Well, what are we waiting for?"[44]

Full of excitement, Jordan and England considered a myriad of potential functions for their project. England wrote to a friend that the two men wanted "to go into backward southern community, set up as farmers . . . and try to bring to bear, in the spirit of Christ, all the resources within and without the community to minister to the individuals and to the groups we can reach."[45] Drawing upon their training and the example of Baptist missions, they thought they would hold vacation Bible schools and regular Sunday schools and establish a school to train black pastors. To minister to the material side of life they would run recreation and health programs, organize cooperative farming and marketing operations, and perhaps hire a doctor or nurse for their staff.[46] Letting their imaginations go, they envisioned a rural community center where white and black could come together to rebuild southern society.

The Koinonia experiment combined Jordan's concern for improved race relations, determination to live a Christian life based on the New Testament, and commitment to community. The material aspects grew out of Jordan's lifelong intention to return to the rural South and help impoverished black farmers. Like others interested in rural reform at the time, Jordan had concluded that the root problem of African Americans in the South was the tenant system, which depleted and exhausted both the land and the people on it. With his agricultural knowledge, he hoped to train share-croppers to use the land more productively and thus lift themselves out of their virtual servitude. To accomplish this he would run agricultural extension programs including demonstrations and classes in scientific techniques at Koinonia, and set up cooperatives.[47] Jordan hoped that by cooperating with African-American farmers, he also would get to know them on a personal level. He believed that such face-to-face relationships and work provided the foundation for better race relations.

Jordan and England also intended Koinonia to be a place where men and women could put their Christian beliefs to action. Because of their training in Baptist institutions, they expressed their religious concerns through missions. As Jordan put it, "We want to be humble, rural missionaries." So, besides conducting agricultural education, Koinonians would hold a training school for black ministers and send missionaries into the surrounding rural community.[48] In addition to conducting vacation Bible school and Sunday school, they would visit their neighbors' homes and sponsor recreational activities. Finally, they would work with local African-American ministers and congregations to improve their church buildings and program. To a large extent, then, the founders organized Koinonia like a Southern Baptist personal service mission. Jordan and England went further, however. They believed that Christian faith was the potential source of better race relations and that introducing people into God's family made them all brothers and sisters. Through evangelization and common worship they hoped to bring whites and blacks together. In this, Koinonians would use common Baptist forms to take the interracialism of the denominational liberals further than most of their contemporaries had yet intended.

Finally, acting on their interpretation of the Word, Jordan and England intended to live in community. Martin England explained that "we call it Koinonia Farm because we want to discover the community of spirit and life of the early Christians."[49] They drew the idea for a Christian commune from Acts 2 and 4 and understood it essentially as the sharing of both fellowship and resources. More than just a way of being faithful to the life of Christ's first followers, to Jordan and England community served a social purpose as well. For one thing, community was the key to breaking "down barriers between people of different race, class, and economic opportunity." In addition, the Koinonia community could serve as a witness for different peoples living together.[50] Koinonians hoped that by living as an example they could banish the fears, primarily held by whites, of a desegregated society. Taken as a whole, through its educational programs and experiment in cooperative living, Koinonia hoped to provide an economic basis for equality, bring whites and blacks together in Christian fellowship, and prove to the world that the two races could live and work side by side.

With this program Koinonia would establish an approach to addressing the problems in race relations, which, although it grew out of liberal Christianity, went further than most of the farm's contemporaries. Instead of emphasizing only missions or aid for black churches, as did their fellow churchmen, Koinonians used these efforts to promote understanding and a fellowship of equals. While they would often work alongside secular white liberals, there were significant differences between them. Most liberals tended to be paternalistic, desirous of keeping the leadership and pace of change in their own control, and interested in uplift before equality. Many shunned the idea of social equality and until the 1950s even hesitated to advocate integration. They gathered in organizations such as the Southern Conference on Human Welfare and the Southern Regional Council, focused on organizing and acting in urban areas, and worked on legal or political issues such as the poll tax and the desegregation of higher education. Koinonia's program shunned gradualism and reform in favor of immediate acts such as eating and sharing together. Its members focused on economics, personal relationships, and bearing witness to the way whites and blacks could live together, rather than on political or legal change.[51]

Koinonia's work for better human relations was more influenced by groups and individuals involved in rural reform in the 1930s and 1940s. During that time private and governmental reform efforts aimed at changing the basis of southern agriculture and making it more equitable and stable, by putting it on a more cooperative basis. Radical Christians addressed rural problems and sought to improve farm life by creating cooperatives like those at Delta and Providence Farms, cosponsored by members of the Fellowship of Southern Churchmen, the Southern Tenant Farmers' Union, and others. The federal government had also become involved in rural rehabilitation through the Resettlement Administration and its successor, the Farm Security Administration. Together, these agencies established thirteen communities across the country for black agricultural workers.[52] Through the early 1940s farm communities, including Macedonia in North Georgia and Little River Farm in South Carolina, tried to create a better and more economically stable way of life in rural areas. Jordan sought advice from these cooperatives and other groups and individuals involved in rural reform while he was planning Koinonia. Although some were inspired by social or political philosophy and others by religion, nearly all agreed that cooperative farming was the way to free poor farmers from debt and dependency. Some also went further than contemporary white liberals and shared Koinonia's commitment to using economic change as a basis for racial change. The founders of Delta Farm, for example, foreshadowed Koinonia's approach when they declared that "biracial organization through cooperatives of every kind . . . is the best immediate approach to the race situation in the deep South."[53] This rural reform tradition, and especially those within it who criticized both the racial and economic system, provided the closest model for Jordan and England's plan for Koinonia.

Once England and Jordan had the plan for Koinonia clearly formulated, they set out to locate and finance it. First they needed to find a farm. They wanted to be in the Black Belt region, preferably in Alabama. When looking at land they considered factors such as the white-black ratio, average income, soil type, amount of tenancy, climate, and the spiritual needs of the people, meaning primarily the number and condition of African-American churches. After much consideration they chose Chambers and Barbour Counties in Alabama. In August they traveled south to look at the available land. Jordan's brother Frank was a farm appraiser and helped them weigh the value of various properties. Then in the early fall he told them to wait until they had a chance to look at a piece of land in Sumter County, Georgia. When Jordan and England visited the 440-acre plot near the town of Americus, Clarence pronounced, "This is it."[54]

Georgia as a whole suffered from many of the problems in which Jordan and England were interested. A few years earlier, in 1937–38, Paul W. Chapman of the University of Georgia School of Agriculture had surveyed farm and religious life and found disturbing facts about the level of indebtedness and tenancy. Of farmworkers in Georgia, 65 percent were tenants of some sort. Farm conditions were also poor. The state ranked thirty-ninth in farm income, with yields per acre among the lowest in the agricultural states and more eroded acres than any other state east of the Mississippi. These numbers had a human effect. The average tenant home was a small, dilapidated, two- or three-room structure. Most lacked electricity, running water, a bath, or phone. In the area of religious life, by contrast, the picture seemed more hopeful. The vast majority of Georgians were church members, with 85 percent of whites and 95 percent of blacks identifying themselves as Baptists or Methodists. Still, the rural churches were in trouble. White churches were losing membership and lacked the publications and women's and student groups that were shaping new attitudes on race in the urban areas. The black church, struggling to survive financially, emphasized individual salvation. Neither was in the position to sponsor outreach programs or foster better racial and economic conditions.[55]

Sumter County suited Jordan and England's purposes on several grounds. Excluding the county seat of Americus, the black-to-white ratio was more than 2:1. The vast majority of African Americans were agricultural workers. Although some blacks owned land, most worked as sharecroppers their entire lives. The land they farmed was badly depleted from overuse, poor techniques, and failure to rotate crops or diversify from cotton, corn, and peanuts, which comprised 80 percent of the county's agricultural product.[56] The agricultural needs of the community obviously attracted Jordan and England. As for spiritual needs, Jordan found a fertile field there as well. Ludrell Pope characterized the churchgoing habits of local African Americans simply as "some do and some don't." The black churches were small, often just one-room country buildings scattered along the county's back roads. Two of them had small schoolrooms out back. These, along with the Seay Industrial School, served the educational needs of the county's blacks. Local people remember Sumter as a poor place, whose African-American population was willing to accept help, especially from fellow Christians.[57]

Jordan and England's final task before buying the land in Sumter County and beginning to make their dream of Koinonia Farm a reality was to find

financial support. Local church groups, Sunday schools, and charitable individuals had always supported Jordan's work at the Baptist Fellowship
Center.[58] But their offerings of dimes, nickels, and dollars would never
make up the sum needed for the down payment on the Sumter County
land. With help from Marjorie Moore of the *Baptist Student,* Koinonia's
founders put together a brochure about the farm and sent it out, hoping to
get support from friends and interested parties.[59] About the same time Jordan met Arthur Steilberg, a wealthy businessman and member of the board
of the Union Gospel Mission in Louisville. Steilberg was instantly affected
by Jordan's "utter sincerity and by his idealism" and pledged his support to
the Koinonia project. When Jordan desperately needed money—the down
payment on the land was due in a matter of days—Steilberg handed him an
envelope containing a check for the exact amount required.[60] With the
down payment in hand, Jordan and England bought the property in
Sumter County and formally incorporated Koinonia Farm.

3

Incarnation

J ORDAN'S IDEAS about race relations, a Christian life, and community were incarnated in Koinonia Farm. Immediately upon their arrival in Sumter County, Jordan and England began conducting their agricultural and mission outreach and building their community. Over the next few years young men and women from around the South came to join them. Between 1942 and 1950 the activities of the group at the farm, while embodying all of Jordan's principles, centered on addressing the race problems of the South. Jordan, England, and the young men and women who soon joined them embarked upon that task by working for economic independence for, and developing personal relationships with, the county's poorer African Americans. During this period Koinonians took the ideas of the liberal minority in their churches and put them to practice through missions and outreach. By emphasizing fellowship and complete sharing, they went further than most of their contemporaries. But because they drew on existing models and presented the actions as the work of concerned Christians, they were accepted by the white community. Over time tensions did increase, however, demonstrating the limits to that acceptance. In their first decade, then, Koinonians experimented with putting their liberal Christian beliefs about race relations to work and tested the limits to which interracialism could go within the church and other southern institutions.

When Jordan and England arrived in Sumter County in November 1942, they had to start from scratch to build both their community and their farm. The soil on their land was eroded and rutted, with bright red Georgia clay peeking out from just below the surface. Some gashes were so deep it seemed unlikely they could pull a plow over them. The dry rolling terrain stretched off into the distance, with few trees breaking up the dusty horizon. Farm buildings and equipment had fallen into disrepair from misuse and age and slumped in decay. The main building on the property was an old four-room farmhouse with a big front porch and wide hall. It was so bug-ridden that Jordan and England affectionately nicknamed it the "rabbit hutch" and eventually converted it into a chicken brooder.[1] Across the road were three rundown tenant shacks. In one lived the Johnsons, a black family who stayed on the property to work for the new owners. Jordan and England had their work cut out for them.

The first task was to build residences and set up a system of sharing, so that they might call themselves a community. The housing situation was complicated not only by the particularly ramshackle state of the existing buildings but by the fact that the previous owner's white tenant refused to leave until the next crop came in. Florence Jordan, Mabel England, and their children stayed in Wakefield, Kentucky, while the husbands moved into one room in the farmhouse. Once the surly tenant moved on, Clarence and Martin fixed it up, even though the war made it hard to get materials and building permits. In January, Jordan received a permit to build a shop and designed a two-story structure, with a shop on the ground and a four-room apartment upstairs. In April the apartment was finished, and the two families settled into their new homes. Martin England suggested they live together with an allowance system and separate finances. Clarence Jordan, however, insisted on "total community" of goods. So they put all the resources in a pot, and as a group decided how all the funds would be spent.[2] With this decision, the community was founded.

The Koinonia community grew as Jordan visited southern campuses and Baptist student meetings and lectured about the farm and his beliefs about Christian race relations. When Jordan spoke, the effect was electric. His dynamism, sincerity, and ability to tell a story attracted students to him and inspired them to look at their lives and discover ways to be better Christians. As one young woman, Willie Pugh, put it, "We thought he was so sincere and was doing something really worthwhile to get at the root of the problem of racism in the South."[3] Most important, he motivated some listeners to follow him. After hearing Jordan at Ridgecrest, a young man named Howard Johnson pledged to change his life and to do something to address the "great material and spiritual needs of the people of our Southland, the White and Negro too."[4] Almost immediately people started visiting Koinonia. In February 1943 Henry Dunn and Howard Johnson came over from Auburn University. Later that summer Stetson University student Harry Atkinson visited while he was preparing to go to seminary. Koinonia's first female guest was Willie Pugh, the Baptist Student Union president at Blue Mountain College in Mississippi whom Jordan had so impressed.[5] These young people brought with them a lifetime of experience in the Southern Baptist church culture. Those experiences helped to shape the ways in which Jordan's ideas would be put to action.

The life stories of the first Koinonians illustrate both their roots in southern culture and the sources of their commitment to better race relations. Howard Johnson recalled those roots: "I was born in a log cabin in a cotton patch near Reeltown, Alabama." His family owned a small farm, which they worked with the help of black sharecroppers and convicts whom they bailed out of jail. As a young boy Howard joined the 4-H Club and aspired to teach farm boys and girls when he grew up. As for his religious training, he said "I'm from a long line of Southern Baptists." His difference from his peers on race issues began early. "The first time I remember that it [segregation] disturbed me was when I was ten years old," recalled Johnson. In the early 1930s sharecroppers had organized a union in Tallapoosa County, Alabama, his birthplace. When the sheriff tried to seize a member's property for debt payment, the blacks armed themselves. As Johnson remembers it, law enforcement officers and white farmers riddled the sharecroppers' homes with bullets. It was, in his words, "a massacre." "The incident started me thinking about why some people are at the bottom of the ladder, so to speak. It was a long time before I could see the answer to that."[6]

The seed of doubt planted in Howard Johnson by the massacre in Tallapoosa County was nurtured by his connection with the Southern Baptist network. At Auburn University, Johnson joined a very active Baptist Student Union and went with other members to visit black churches for worship, Bible study, and training courses. In the summer of 1942, he attended a student conference at the Ridgecrest Assembly Grounds and heard Jordan speak on the Sermon on the Mount. Inspired in part by the talk, Johnson and other students tried unsuccessfully to get African Americans invited to the next conference. After that meeting Johnson visited the farm with his friend Henry Dunn, who lived at Koinonia in 1946 and 1947, and afterwards corresponded with residents there regularly. Eventually, Johnson concluded that he would not live according to the dictates of the southern racial caste system. He joined Koinonia, he later explained, because "there was no [other] place in the South where I could get a job which wouldn't require a compromise with segregation."[7]

Willie Pugh learned religion and concern for blacks from her family. Pugh, who "had been steeped since tiny childhood" in the Southern Baptist tradition, remembers her family as "more decent than most" when it came to the treatment of African Americans. Both her mother and father had been Sunday school teachers, and her father was a lawyer who occasionally helped black clients. Her father taught her in quiet ways to help and be kind to African Americans. For example, when she was ten years old, she was walking home on a blustery day, and when she turned to walk backwards to keep the wind off her face, she knocked down an elderly black man. "I was horrified. I helped him up, told him how sorry I was." She looked across the road to her father's office, and "I saw him beckoning to me from his office door. He just wanted to tell me how proud he was at what I did, helping the old black man back onto his feet." Watching her father's actions and this incident in particular impressed upon her the importance of kindness toward African Americans and the responsibility she had to help them.[8]

Harry Atkinson's acquaintance with African Americans made him question the southern caste system. Before he went to college, Atkinson built houses in Florida with his father. Like the Johnsons on their farm, the Atkinsons hired African-American laborers, including convicts. It was Harry's responsibility to go the jails and bail them out. As he remembered, "I knew what their financial situation was. I met their wives and children. I tried to help them, to get Dad to give them raises." While at Stetson, Atkinson continued to work with African Americans, this time in the dining room on campus. When his coworkers could not take time off for church on Sundays, he organized a small prayer meeting. At the Southwest Baptist Theological Seminary in Fort Worth, Texas, he tried to minister to the local underprivileged blacks and Hispanics.[9] Over the years these experiences convinced Atkinson that whites and blacks should worship together and share Christian fellowship. Atkinson, like Pugh and Johnson, had personal experiences that had awakened a concern about African Americans which was then reinforced by lessons about the Christian responsibility in race relations learned at college or seminary. These and other young men and women came to Koinonia with a desire to act on those lessons by living a Christian life and doing something about the race problem of their region.

Jordan and England's three main goals—to teach better agricultural techniques to African-American farmers, to minister to the spiritual needs of their black neighbors, and to live in community—manifested themselves in three faces of Koinonia. During the 1940s Koinonians focused on outreach in agriculture, missions, and relationships. Their first task was to improve their land. They believed in the "enrichment and preservation of the soil—for the sake of the soil itself" and immediately initiated conservation efforts by cutting terraces into the land.[10] At first they planted cotton, but they gave it up because it depleted the soil. Instead, they planted field crops, including their main cash crop, peanuts, garden vegetables, and grasses "with names people couldn't pronounce."[11] They were also among the first in southwest Georgia to use ground-up peanut vines as fertilizer for the next year's crop. As Howard Johnson remembered, "We tried to find out as much as we could from whatever source," so that Koinonia could improve the land and demonstrate the techniques to others.[12]

The Koinonians' next task was to minister to the material needs of rural southerners by demonstrating their techniques to, and cooperating in farm enterprises with, their neighbors. They strove especially to teach African-American tenants, renters, and sharecroppers how to make their land more productive, so that they could be more economically secure. To do so, Jordan, Howard Johnson, and others drew on agricultural extension models they had learned at southern universities. Jordan kicked off the demonstration part of Koinonia's mission as soon as he arrived in Sumter County by leading occasional gardening or machinery classes in town. The men at Koinonia also visited individual farmers on the neighboring land to counsel them. Carranza Morgan, one of the few African-American landowners in the area, met Jordan when he went down the road to Koinonia to borrow some equipment. After that, Jordan and Morgan visited, discussed farm life, and helped each other bring in their crops.[13]

Once Koinonians were more established, they began trying to bring white and black farmers together. Henry Dunn and Harry Atkinson organized a group of black farmers into a seed cooperative. They gathered at a school nearby to plan their strategy, compare prices, and figure out a distribution system. The co-op did not attract much attention or opposition because they met "as just farmers, black and white, and no one cared much about farmers getting together."[14] In addition, on Monday evenings Koinonia held classes at which Jordan and others talked about fertilizers, chicken brooders, or the proper use of a peanut combine. The men stayed for questions, conversation, and occasionally refreshments. At first both whites and blacks came, and as Con Browne remembered, they "would have marvelous times at [the] classes until it came time for the refreshments." Then the "white guys would drift out, or the blacks would drift out." Eventually there were about ten African-American farmers who came, with an occasional white straggler peeking in.[15] Through these classes and meetings Koinonia introduced the farmers to new machinery, conservation techniques, and the use of fertilizers and hybrid seeds.[16] They also got to know African Americans in programs that because of their educational nature, local whites, while not always joining, did not try to stop.

Koinonians also started cooperative relationships with neighboring whites. They built friendships with Rob Hamilton and Kenneth Short by helping them with their income tax forms, having dinner, and lending a hand on the farm. The families worked together, sharing gasoline, plowing, and bringing in crops.[17] Most important, they collaborated in an egg and poultry business. Jordan built a brooder and laying house at Koinonia, and a friend in Virginia, Jacob A. Shank, donated 500 young hens. Jordan then helped his neighbors build brooders on their farms. Koinonia used its wheat and corn for feed, and the cooperative bought more. Con Browne, who was later in charge of the enterprise, arranged a joint marketing scheme. He collected the eggs from all the partners, cleaned and put them in cartons, and sold them to area hotels, stores, and restaurants. The project proved to be a boon to the local economy.[18] Moreover, the egg business gave Koinonians and their white neighbors a mutual interest and fostered a sense of cooperation and community.

In their farm work Koinonians tried to give African Americans economic support. To some extent this took the form of charity. Whenever Koinonia had extra vegetables from their garden or meat from a slaughtered cow or pig, they took it to neighboring families. Inspired by an idea from the Church of the Brethren's post–World War I Heifer Project, they devised a "cow library." When a family lacked sufficient milk, they could borrow a cow from Koinonia, use it till it went dry, then return the animal and get another one.[19] These efforts, although not fostering economic independence, did help Koinonia build relationships with local African Americans. Koinonia also hired African Americans as field hands and day laborers and paid their workers twice the going wage. They reasoned that if parents made more money, then they could keep the children out of the fields and in the schools. Also, such a simple thing as paying a few extra dollars challenged the southern labor system because it forced other landowners to do the same.[20] With its employment and charity Koinonia made its first small steps toward changing the area's economic and social status quo.

The Koinonians' attention to agriculture and economic improvement made them part of a movement of religious people concerned about the problems of rural areas. This movement paralleled the rural rehabilitation work of some New Deal programs and groups such as Delta and Providence Farms but added an interest in the spiritual side of life.[21] Participants believed that poor economic conditions for farmworkers were causing a crisis in rural communities and churches. To address this crisis several groups sponsored programs in agricultural and rural church development. The Christian Service Foundation of Florida engaged in agricultural extension and demonstration work similar to Koinonia. The Fellowship of Southern Churchmen took an interest in religious life in the country and hosted programs to train church workers in the concerns of rural people. Their Brush Arbor Institutes, for example, included courses on cooperatives, credit unions, and rural labor issues. The organization also coordinated other groups working on similar problems, including the Christian Rural Fellowship, American Country Life Association, and the Rural Life section of the Fellowship of Reconciliation.[22] One of the FSC's most noted projects in its early years was Eugene Smathers's church in Big Lick, Tennessee. Smathers had gone to this small Cumberland community and developed a program for the whole life of the people, including recreation, religious education, and even health care.[23] The FSC characterized Koinonia Farm in its publications as another example of work, like Smathers's, in rural community development.

Like Jordan, many people involved in the rural reform movement were concerned about the relationship between agricultural conditions and race. The Commission for Interracial Cooperation, then mainly interested in the conditions of returning black soldiers, was organizing in small country towns such as Americus and nearby Cordele. Early in the decade president Howard Odum urged the group to pay attention to agricultural development and economics as race relations issues. In the late 1940s and early 1950s the Southern Regional Council organized conferences and institutes on rural life. During the same period the FSC, which had long been concerned with rural and labor issues, increased their attention to interracialism. The organization's Rural Reconstruction Commission began to sponsor biracial workshops on rural community development in 1945.[24] To take interracialism into the countryside, the FSC organized a series of work camps at sites around the South, at which white and black students would work and live together. These activities demonstrated the recognition on the part of some southerners that economic conditions in rural areas were linked to problems in race relations. Jordan had long understood this link and immersed himself and the farm in this interracial activity for rural reform. In addition to the farm's work in agricultural training and cooperation, Jordan belonged to the FSC and went on speaking tours on its behalf to college campuses.[25] Koinonia also served several times as a site for an interracial student work camp. After the *Brown* decision, when integration became the main focus of the civil rights struggle, activity in rural reform diminished. But just as its agricultural development effort made Koinonia part of a broader movement in the 1940s, its continued work in the area of economics would make it a leader when the issues resurfaced in the late 1960s.

As devoted as he was to teaching better farm techniques and raising the economic level of rural African Americans, Jordan also had gone into the southern countryside to spread the Word of God. Because of their training in Southern Baptist institutions, much of the Koinonians' energy went into mission efforts. Like the Baptist Fellowship Center, they strove to help African-American churches by teaching a study course for ministers and running a training union program for other church workers.[26] The training of black pastors never reached the scale Jordan and England envisioned, however. Koinonians devoted much more effort to bringing white and black Christians together for study or fellowship. They started with an interracial Sunday school and sing-along on the farm. Then Howard Johnson, Willie Pugh, and Gil Butler, a friend of Johnson's from Auburn, started a Friday night fellowship hour for young people, where they would play games and sing songs.[27] Koinonians also went into the community and led informal meetings at the homes of local black families. Then they visited African-American churches and Sunday schools. Chester Jackson, an African-American teenager who lived nearby, remembered Koinonians visiting the Sunday school that his church set up in a local schoolhouse.[28]

The Koinonians' best-received mission effort was its vacation Bible school. Willie Pugh and Norman Long, a minister who had worked with student evangelicals in Europe, organized the farm's program.[29] As Pugh later explained, vacation Bible school (VBS) was "an old Baptist habit. Most of us had grown up in the Baptist Church, so it was a natural thing to happen." They held the sessions during the laying-by time of the summer, after they had put up the crops and there was a break in farmwork. Early in the morning Pugh and Long drove a truck around to the farms within a five- to six-mile radius and picked up as many as seventy children. Usually the session lasted eight days. During this time Pugh and Long held Bible classes, showed educational films, and taught crafts such as woodworking and sewing. On the last day the parents of the pupils came along for an afternoon of socializing.[30]

Local whites helped in Koinonia's early mission activities, displaying their acceptance of interracial work within traditional southern forms. Because of their shared Southern Baptist backgrounds, religion and religious programs were a common ground between Koinonians and their white neighbors. This enabled the latter to understand and to some extent condone the farm's work. The children of the Short family came to the Friday night fellowship hour. In addition, some young people from the Rehobeth Church, a white Southern Baptist church down the road, helped at the early VBS sessions.[31] In these cases Koinonia's interracialism was acceptable because it was pursued through traditional southern Protestant practices. White involvement, however, eventually decreased. When the Koinonians visited the Jacksons' Sunday school, the county superintendent of schools asked the church to end the classes.[32] This order, the only action taken against one of their interracial mission endeavors, showed that the white community was most offended when Koinonia's work either went further than religious instruction or took place in a public arena. Even so, during this period, after they ceased participating, whites were willing to allow Koinonians to worship and have fellowship with African Americans on the farm or in their own homes.

The Koinonians' understanding of the Christian message led them to go beyond traditional Sunday school activities and address the neighbors' educational and social needs. In keeping with Jordan's long-held interest in African-American education, they worked to improve the services available to local blacks. Jordan held literacy classes for African Americans at the farm and, since there was no bus to the Seay School, drove black students to class. Koinonia also raised money for a bus and some new books. But the school board would not accept their donation.[33] More than just for charitable uplift, Koinonians made these efforts because they considered education along with economic independence the road to equality. In addition, like the Baptist Fellowship Center in Louisville, Koinonia served as a community center where people could come together for work, worship, and fellowship. The farm sponsored recreational activities including volleyball, basketball, square dances, and community parties. The members believed that bringing whites and blacks together in wholesome activities would allow them a chance to get to know each other in an informal situation where fellowship could come naturally.[34] This forwarded their goal of serving their neighbors and breaking down social barriers between people.

Koinonia's work was an extension of contemporary trends in Southern Baptist evangelism and missions. In the recent memory of Koinonians, just before World War II, the Southern Baptist Home Mission Board had set up city missions to reach the urban poor and minorities. Personal service and practical missions were also spreading in Southern Baptist institutions. In these missions church workers helped the disadvantaged with material needs by organizing clubs and hosting programs for children. In addition, by the early 1940s Southern Baptist missions had begun to address the needs of African Americans in cities by running Sunday school programs and training institutes for black ministers. Most Southern Baptists rarely saw activities such as vacation Bible school, missions, or aid to the less fortunate as agents of social change. There was, however, a minority of men and women who were using these traditional forms to foster brotherhood, fellowship, and a sense of Christian responsibility in race relations. By the end of the decade some Southern Baptist missions included efforts to bring whites and blacks together as equals.[35] Koinonia Farm's work took the example of the urban mission efforts of the progressive minority and moved them to a rural setting. Its members also took the format further and sought to create from these mission efforts an interracial family of God.

Koinonia's work in agricultural training and missions took place in the context of living in community. To the members Christian living required complete sharing and equality. Their communalism distinguished them from other Christian liberals of the time, who focused mainly on missions, education, and uplift. During this time, however, exactly what living in community meant was an open question. They used a common bank account, distributed resources as equally as possible, and shared a fellowship that bound them in all aspects of life. They arranged their daily schedule in order to spend time together and foster a sense of group living on the farm. Their focus in the first decade, however, was on the outer society and its problems, rather than on their internal fellowship. Koinonians lived together in order to accomplish their other goals. As Marion Johnson recalled, "Clarence's thrust was the witness to racial brotherhood and attempt to help the local black or white people in agricultural ways." They did not think of themselves as a Christian church community yet.[36] In the 1940s when Koinonians talked about community, they meant sharing, cooperating, and having good relationships with the people around them, both black and white.

At this time Koinonians had a very broad definition of who was in their community. The core of Koinonia was made up of southern white Christians who came to settle on the farm: the Atkinsons, Johnsons, Pugh, and others. These individuals came to Koinonia determined to make a long-term commitment, and they set the tone for life in the community. In addition, the fellowship encompassed people who came to the farm for shorter periods of time. The founders had hoped that students would come to Koinonia to help with the work, and from the start the farm attracted scores, even hundreds, of visitors and volunteers. Students, seminarians, ministers, and lay people came to Koinonia to work in the fields, enjoy the fellowship, and then depart. While at Koinonia the volunteers lived in the farm's housing, shared meals, and were provided for out of the community's resources. Anyone who stopped by or stayed was considered a part of the community.

The tenants and day laborers from the surrounding area who came to work at Koinonia also became part of the community. Young black men took these jobs to supplement their family income. Brothers Chester and Alma Jackson, their nephew Henry Jackson, and Bobby Engram were regulars. At times the men lived at Koinonia during the week and went to their parents' homes on the weekends.[37] The Koinonians' philosophy dictated that they treat laborers as equals. They did so by sharing meals and including them in social functions. African-American workers participated as they felt comfortable. In this period some took a wage and others lived off the resources of the farm like the white residents. Bo Johnson chose to remain a sharecropper, while Denice Alman, a man who came to Koinonia in 1944 when Martin England and his family returned to Burma, gave up his salary and lived out of the common purse.[38] In any case, the white Koinonians made the effort to include the African Americans in the communion as much as they could.

Koinonians ordered the relations between all those participating in the community by parity and sharing. First, they tried to maintain the equality of all believers. They made no official distinctions between "member," "volunteer," "guest," or "hired hand" and strove mightily to keep the farm as democratic as possible. To make decisions they met, sometimes for hours, to discuss all the aspects of the issue that occurred to them and to try to reach a consensus. They did not want to have a leader because they did not want any one person to have authority over others.[39] In practice this produced a very loose authority and administrative structure. Before 1950 people took responsibility for various jobs, but until the end of the 1940s there were no officers. For most of the early years the core group was small, and face-to-face meetings and decision making were easy. This enabled Koinonians to have little authority structure and to be officially, and in spirit, equals.

The Koinonians' effort to preserve equality did not always live up to the ideal. In the first decade the community resembled a traditional family, in which certain figures hold more power and authority than others. Because of his role as founder Jordan was looked to both within and outside the group as the leader. He tried to dispel that image, but with little success. Local people still considered it "Mr. Jordan's farm," and in differences over policy he usually had his way. There were personality clashes and occasional struggles of will. Usually, if someone really disagreed with a decision, he or she left.[40] Moreover, "complete equality" only extended to visitors and laborers in some aspects of life. Everyone did share meals and resources equally. But the permanent residents directed the farmwork, keeping the traditional employer-employee relationship intact.

Besides equality, Koinonians tried to base their life on sharing. The essence of the disciples' *koinonia,* after all, had been living out of a common purse and distributing according to need. The first experience Koinonians had when they arrived was shared housing. In the early years Koinonians lived in a small circle, with the Jordans in a house that had an apartment for visitors or single members in the basement, Willie Pugh in a modest house, and the single men in a building across the road.[41] As new families arrived, they played musical houses, moving from one to another to make the best use of space. Koinonians believed that like the land, these homes were not their own but were held in trust. Besides housing, anyone who came to Koinonia shared in the resources of the farm. As Willie Pugh remembered, "You gave what you had and got what you needed." The group did not have much money, so decisions concerned the use of scarce funds. Florence Jordan took responsibility for doling out money for groceries and individual needs.[42] Because the core group was small and homogeneous, there was no need for more elaborate financial arrangements.

Koinonians arranged their daily lives in order to maximize the time they shared. They rose early in the morning. Just after dawn they made their way to the community building where they would have meditation and devotional. In the earliest years they ate together because there was only one kitchen. Later, the single people continued to eat together in a community room. After the men met to decide what extra work needed to be done, everyone went off to take care of their responsibilities. At noon, no matter what they were doing, they interrupted their tasks to gather for lunch. This was the high point of the day. Hired field hands, friends, visitors, and members sat down to break bread together. Along with the meal they prayed, read from the Bible, or shared a silent moment. Then in the afternoons Koinonians finished their chores, played with their children, and ran the youth programs for the neighborhood boys and girls. Or they might visit a neighbor, read a book in the library, or chat with a guest. After a family dinner in their homes, they met again on the porch of the main house to sing songs or share their thoughts and feelings.[43]

Anyone associated with the farm could partake of as much of the sharing as he or she cared to. All residents, visitors, or laborers who stayed on the farm shared the housing. The morning devotional and evening visits were open to anyone. It was during these sunset talks that resident Koinonians got to know their guests. The most important communion was the noon meal. Dining together has important symbolism in southern culture broadly and southern religion particularly. When there is a unity of feeling in the group, Southern Baptists share bread and wine as a sign of communion. While eating together is a sign of Christian fellowship, it also denotes social equality. Although southerners gathered weekly on church lawns to share a meal, the dining table was, along with the church, one of the most strictly segregated spaces in the region. With its noon meal Koinonia kept the Christian tradition of breaking bread but violated southern custom by sharing it with African Americans.

In these early years Koinonians spent a great deal of energy fostering good relations with the people around them. Jordan and England believed it was important to become part of the community before they started introducing the innovations they had planned. They immediately joined the Rehobeth Baptist Church and involved themselves in the life of the congregation by teaching Sunday school and leading revivals.[44] In doing so, they made the church an arena in which they worked out a relationship with local whites based on a common religious culture. Jordan and England also reached out to their neighbors, black and white, with material help and friendly gestures to let them know that they wanted to work together and help each other out. For the most part their neighbors, black and white, welcomed these overtures. Jordan wrote to a friend that "instead of bitter antagonism, which so many of our friends prophesied, there has been the utmost friendliness and cooperation."[45]

In its first decade Koinonia was accepted into the white community. The members became friends with the Hamiltons, Shorts, and other families on the farms nearby. They also got to know people through canning and other chores of agricultural life. Koinonians won admirers with "their generous and humane actions" and because of the economic benefits of their poultry business.[46] Essentially Koinonians and the local whites had a lot in common, sharing an agrarian lifestyle and a Protestant worldview and upbringing. They got to know each other in church activities because the former had been very active members, preaching, leading the music, and teaching Sunday school. The ladies of the Rehobeth Church liked Harry Atkinson and Henry Dunn so much that when the men first moved into the area, the women tried to introduce them to their single daughters. Later, when Harry married Allene Griffin at the church, the ladies of the congregation gave them what Harry described as paintings of traditional southern belles, a common gift in the local area.[47] In Baptist faith the congregation is considered a community. By welcoming Koinonians into the pews, the local whites signaled their acceptance of them into the community.

The Koinonians' acceptance by white Sumter Countians was mirrored by the support for them in broader southern white Christian networks. Jordan continued to be a popular speaker for church and student groups around the South. In fact, he estimated that he spent as much as one-third of his time spreading the Word to these groups through various speaking engagements around the region.[48] In addition to preaching at Rehobeth, Jordan and others traveled around the area leading revivals. As his reputation spread, he was invited to participate in Religious Emphasis Weeks in North Carolina, Mississippi, and other places around the South.[49] More often than not, on these occasions Jordan spoke about the Koinonia Farm experiment, community, and Christian race relations. He started putting his interpretation of the New Testament onto paper when an official of the American Baptist Publication Society asked him to write lessons on the life of Christ. He also wrote Sunday school lessons and topics for young people's discussions.[50] Jordan's popularity on the lecture circuit and in Baptist publications showed that he was touching a nerve in southern white Christians and giving a message many of them not only accepted but wanted to hear.

Although the white community accepted Koinonia in the early years, there were isolated incidents of opposition. The first objections came when some white neighbors dropped in and saw Jordan and England having lunch with their black tenants. Soon after that, some men claiming to represent the Ku Klux Klan visited and declared, "We don't allow the sun to set on anybody who eats with niggers." Jordan thrust out his hand and said he was glad to meet men who could stop the sun.[51] Neither the Klan nor other whites made any other effort to stop the Koinonians from dining with African Americans on the farm. The Koinonians' effort to drive black children to school also eventually aroused the ire of local landowners. As one school official put it, "Niggers do our work for us around here and if we educated them they will all move away, so I don't intend seeing them educated."[52] Local whites were more angry about Koinonia's busing black children than about the members eating with their African-American help because the former threatened the whites' livelihood by potentially removing their low-wage workforce. When Koinonia's practices infringed on white prerogative, the opposition was more severe. Still, in the early years none of this opposition amounted to a direct attack. The incidents did, however, highlight the fact that the Koinonians' racial practices occasionally pricked the benevolent attitude of the outside community toward the farm when they stepped out of the boundaries of tradition in church or agricultural extension models.

Meanwhile, Koinonians also developed relationships with African Americans in the surrounding area, as the experience of the Jackson brothers illustrates. The Jackson family worked on a farm adjoining Koinonia. They heard a little about the community but at first did not have much to do with it. Then, around 1948 Chester Jackson ventured over to pick up some extra money doing field work. He started attending classes and stayed over night occasionally. Then he traveled with Jordan, Pugh, and Butler to a national meeting of the Fellowship of Reconciliation. This, and his own reading of the Bible, convinced him to become a conscientious objector. Meanwhile, his younger brother Alma started going to the farm for Bible lessons and recreation. Later, he worked there as a hired hand, living with Koinonia during the week and going home on weekends. After he got married, Alma and his wife lived at Koinonia full-time.[53]

Koinonians had mixed success, however, in fostering a sense of fellowship and community with African Americans. On the one hand, many of their black friends responded gratefully to the farm's efforts to improve the lives of the local people. Carranza Morgan characterized Jordan's work succinctly: "He was trying to help less fortunate people, I'll put it that way."[54] Moreover, Koinonia's friends welcomed the treatment they got from members of the farm and the relationships they had there. On the other hand, some African Americans hesitated to work with Koinonia or Jordan. Alma Jackson remembered that his father "wouldn't have too many dealings with him, I guess cause they were white." He characterized the reaction of many older people the same way: a little frightened and unwilling to have much to do with the farm.[55] In particular, blacks feared what would happen if they were caught eating at Koinonia. Con Browne remembered that the older people used to sit separately at lunch, out under a tree, instead of at the table.[56] In addition, many whites, including the sheriff, and even some older blacks steered people away from Koinonia.

Even the African Americans who were close friends with Koinonians and active participants in the programs did not often become permanent residents or give up their salaries to be full-sharing members of the community. Quite the contrary, they often consciously remained separate. Chester Jackson considered settling on the farm, but his mother's concerns about what might happen to him or the family stopped him. Besides, he felt that becoming a resident, giving up his salary, and sharing out of the common pot was just too big a step all at once.[57] Alma Jackson did live on the farm for a while. Later, when hostility against it increased in the mid-1950s, the pressure was too much, and he eventually moved off the farm. He also frankly admitted that besides being concerned about danger, he did not like the discipline of living communally. "There were things I wanted to do and I wanted [that] they didn't approve of," he remembered. He wanted to go into town occasionally, and Koinonians wanted him to devote his free time to the community. He concluded, "I wasn't used to that, I wasn't ready for it."[58] Over time, Koinonians came to realize that the African Americans who lived on the farm did not join because they would not accept voluntary poverty. Blacks in Sumter County had never had much, so it was hard for them willingly to give up what they had. It was easier for them to work on the farm for a wage.[59] While the Jacksons enjoyed their relationship with Koinonia, they and other African Americans at the farm did not share the communal philosophy. As Koinonians became more interested in community per se, a gap opened between them and their African-American friends.

Although Koinonians did not accomplish all that they dreamed of in their relationship with African Americans, they did have more social relations with blacks than most people at the time dreamed of or wanted. Even though they still held paternalistic beliefs common in their day about uplifting and helping African Americans, they tried to get beyond them by stressing social equality and fellowship. And while they mistakenly assumed blacks in Sumter County would want to join them in a koinonia defined by white values, in the 1940s they combated that by focusing on developing a fellowship that did not depend on complete economic sharing. Despite these weaknesses, in their first decade Koinonians were pioneers in the area of race relations. They broke southern tradition daily by eating and socializing with blacks, having them in their homes—welcoming them through the front door—and treating them as much as brothers as they knew how. They also laid the groundwork for change in Sumter County by assisting black education, giving blacks extra work when they needed money, paying high wages, and being an example of people of different races living together. Their actions, based on their understanding of community, the Kingdom of God, and brotherhood, benefited local African-American families while earning the farm respect and friendship that would long be remembered.

It was this closeness to their African-American friends that eventually drove a wedge between Koinonians and the local white community. Ironically, the local Baptist church, formerly the place where Koinonians and local whites came together, was the scene of the rupture between them. Around 1948 the rapport between Koinonia and the Rehobeth congregation became strained. Bad feeling was brought to a breaking point when Harry Atkinson invited the black chauffeur of one of the members of the church to join his Sunday school class at Rehobeth. With this gesture he extended the Baptist concept of fellowship to an African American. He did so not in his own home or at the farm but on church grounds. The Rehobeth congregation saw this as a violation of their ideal of their congregational community, which was inclusive only of whites. They were so angered that they pressured Koinonians to withdraw from the church. The Atkinsons did quit over the issue. But most Koinonians refused. Consequently, the church denied them the right to hold any office or responsibility. The Koinonians continued to attend the church, even though other parishioners made it quite clear that they were not welcome.[60]

In 1950 the growing animosity against the farm within the church disrupted the fellowship with local whites. Koinonians unwittingly triggered the event when they brought a visitor, a dark-skinned man from India, to

Sunday services. The Rehobeth congregation mistook him for an African American and charged Koinonia with trying to integrate the church. A crisis followed. The minister notified Koinonians that "because of our differences in opinion on the race question . . . and the proper relationship to the church, it seems to be the consensus of opinion that members of the 'Koinia' Farms cannot be retained in the fellowship of Rehobeth Church."[61] Florence Jordan, Gilbert Butler, and some of the children attended services on the day they were to be stricken from the roles. The resolution excommunicating them from the congregation accused them of visiting black churches, holding interracial services, and publicly disagreeing with "some doctrine and practices of the church."[62] The motion effectively banished Koinonians from the white Baptist fellowship in Sumter County. While their common southern Protestant theology and practices had bound them together, their difference over the inclusion of African Americans in public worship had torn them apart. The Koinonians' work had crossed a boundary, making them no longer acceptable members of the white community.

This incident, and the resulting break with the local church community, demonstrated the limits to liberal Christian interracialism at the time. So long as Koinonians carried out their work through forms that were recognizable to southern whites—agricultural extension and missions—and were confined to their own property or the homes of African Americans, it was acceptable to local whites. That is, when they met as "just farmers" to discuss agricultural methods or in that old "Baptist habit" vacation Bible school to read the Bible, they caused little stir. Although whites at times objected, as in the first Klan visit, or ceased to participate, as in the farm classes and Bible school, they did not prohibit the programs from taking place. But when the Koinonians' work spilled out into the public sphere, it inspired a more hostile reaction. When they visited the Jackson family's Bible study in the school, the superintendent asked the class to move. When Norman Long went to a movie with Alma Jackson and sat in the colored section, authorities removed him.[63] The incidents that angered the Rehobeth congregation similarly involved Koinonians' relationships with African Americans in public or in the church. Koinonians also raised hackles when their educational and agricultural work indirectly intruded upon the landowners' prerogative to have cheap labor. Thus, the space in which Koinonians worked was circumscribed. They were free to develop relationships with

African Americans and help them economically as long as it was done through traditional forms and in private space.

During the 1940s Koinonians began to put their liberal Christian ideals into practice through agricultural education, missions, and fellowship. At this time their primary goal was to improve African-American lives and in so doing take the first step toward addressing southern race problems. The young men and women who had come to the farm during this time did so because of the racial witness and outreach. The idea of community was not particularly well developed or important. Koinonians lived together cooperatively in order to accomplish other goals, and when they did think about community, it was as a way to bring whites and blacks together. Koinonia's program combined contemporary Christian interracialism with attention to economic problems. To some extent, models in southern institutions such as agricultural extension and missions and the work of contemporary activists and progressive Christians provided a precedent for the Koinonians' work. But they distinguished themselves from both secular and religious liberals by bringing whites and blacks together in day-to-day life, work, and worship as equals. Although they had success in the first decade in fostering interracial relationships and helping local blacks, however, there were limits to how far Koinonia's program could go. Koinonians underestimated the amount of hostility to real challenges to the status quo. They also showed naïveté by believing that the solution to race problems was as simple as bringing whites and blacks together in community. Finally, they underestimated the very real cultural, social, and economic differences between them and their sharecropper neighbors. While Koinonians spent the next several years looking inward and developing their inner relationship, outer events would heighten the importance of these factors for their interracial work.

Bo Johnson (at wheel) and Shaq and Doll Paschal (*foreground*) with Howard Johnson and Jim Jordan, 1948, in what was possibly the first mobile peanut harvester in Georgia, converted from a stationary peanut picker by Clarence Jordan. (Courtesy of T. Howard Johnson)

The Koinonia community at work in the fields, ca. 1948–56.
(Courtesy of Leonard Jordan)

Children at vacation Bible school at Koinonia, 1948.
(Courtesy of T. Howard Johnson)

Children learn Indian lore at Koinonia's interracial summer camp, ca. 1954–55.
(Courtesy of Leonard Jordan)

Clarence Jordan meets with the first college work camp at Koinonia, 1951.
(Courtesy of T. Howard Johnson)

4

Christian Community

BEGINNING IN 1949 and for the next six years, Koinonia turned its energy toward learning how to live in community. In their first decade Koinonians had lived together in order to accomplish certain goals in race relations and rural reform, and communalism had been a relatively low priority. By the end of the decade, however, population growth, the interests of newer members, internal strife, and contact with other Christian colonies led them to devote more time to ordering their communal life. That meant defining membership and leadership as well as the extent of their commitment. During this process conflict and compromise among the people at Koinonia produced changes in both the way they lived together and the way they reached out to African Americans. This change raised to the surface inherent tensions in their philosophy and forced them not only to decide just what sort of community they wanted to be but also to struggle thereafter with balancing their two goals of communalism and interracialism.

Koinonians were not trying to create a Christian community in a vacuum. Other groups had pursued many of the goals and principles set out by Jordan for Koinonia.[1] At the turn of the century there had been a burst of communitarianism based on cooperative ideals. In the 1890s the opposition to private monopoly on resources or land and a belief in the single-tax system had inspired Fairhope in Alabama. During the same period two groups of Social Gospel idealists merged to form the Christian Commonwealth, a colony based on "unselfish" or "Christian" socialism located just east of Columbus, Georgia.[2] Just as these colonies had been reactions to a troubled economy, during the Great Depression of the 1930s reformers turned to cooperation for solutions. During the fifteen-year period of the thirties and early forties, over fifty efforts were made at rural rehabilitation through community. In particular the Delta, Rochedale, Providence, and Little River Farms set a precedent for Koinonia by using cooperative economic arrangements to address the problems of rural southerners.[3] In each of these cases participants sought to use Christian-based cooperation to relieve the damage caused by capitalist competition.

The Second World War inspired a new wave of communities devoted not only to cooperation but also to pacifism and a return to Christian roots. After the war pacifists converted Macedonia, a rural reconstruction community founded in 1937 in northern Georgia, into a demonstration of a nonviolent way of life. A postwar mood among American religious people of experimentation and a desire to get back to basics produced a growth in evangelical communities in which people tried to live like the early disciples.[4] The postwar movement included cooperatives, anarcho-pacifist communities, and loosely bound groups of people seeking a new life. In 1953 communitarians formed the Fellowship of Intentional Communities to serve as a clearinghouse for information and a forum for sharing experiences. Koinonians attended meetings of the organization and even served as officers. In doing so they joined a network of cooperatives, pacifists, communitarians, and Christian socialists.

Because of their participation in Christian and progressive circles, the early Koinonians had some prior knowledge of the communitarian movement. When they were planning Koinonia, Clarence and Florence Jordan had familiarized themselves with existing models by investigating other communal experiments.[5] Other early members of Koinonia had likewise studied the subject. Howard Johnson, for example, learned about Macedonia from a brochure. Con and Ora Browne, who joined the farm in 1949, studied the history of community and were familiar with groups in New Jersey and Illinois. Moreover, Con had been involved with pacifist groups at the Civilian Public Service (CPS) camps, which were often communal in spirit. Finally, Harry Atkinson had grown up in the Moravian Church, which, although he did not recognize it until years later, was communal in nature. Therefore, individual Koinonians had some acquaintance with communalism and arrived at the farm with an understanding of community drawn from their own experiences and Christian ideals.[6]

In the early years, however, Koinonians had not elaborated on the meaning of community beyond the basic ideals of living together, sharing economically and spiritually, and working toward a common goal. During these years a core group of residents, visitors and guests, and workers stayed at the farm. The meaning of "belonging to Koinonia" was rather loose. As Con Browne remembered years later, "You just came to live," and "anyone who came was a member."[7] In the period 1942–48 the main group included at various times the Jordans, Englands, Harry Atkinson, Howard Johnson, and Willie Pugh.[8] In 1948 Gilbert Butler, Millard Hunt, and Jack and Gene Singletary joined them. Two African Americans, Bo Johnson and Jessie (Bobby) Engram, also moved onto the farm. When people arrived, as a matter of course they joined the common purse established by the Jordans and Englands.[9] Most of them had been students and did not have many possessions anyway. The African-American workers shared as much as they felt comfortable with, some earning a salary, some sharecropping, and some living out of the common fund. The consensus among the early participants was that they lived together to accomplish the outreach, which was to minister to African Americans in a variety of ways, work and worship together, and thereby improve race relations. Because the number of people at the farm was small, there was no need to define community or structure themselves any further.

Beginning in 1949, several factors, including population growth, disagreements on day-to-day issues, and the influence of other communitarians, turned the Koinonians' attention to the meaning of community. In 1949 and 1950 the population expanded with the arrival of Con and Ora Browne, Allene Atkinson, Marion Johnson, and Norman Long, pressuring the group to define exactly who was a part of Koinonia. At the same time the farm started attracting more visitors and short-term residents. Problems of order and accountability began to arise as more and more people started coming. As Ora Browne explained: "You'd have a meeting and discuss some big issue like economics. Then these transients would spend all the time airing their opinions, then they'd be gone."[10] The long-term group wanted to make sure the only people helping to make policy were the ones who were going to stick around for a while, work, and be accountable for their actions. Another difficulty was that the newer people were treated the same as those who had been living there long enough to get used to community. Con Browne thought that new people often left quickly because "we put so much on them," meaning responsibility and pressure to yield to the will of the group, by treating them as members from the minute they arrived.[11]

Additional people at the farm meant a greater variety of opinions on day-to-day operational issues. The first big disagreement concerned financial matters. Some people arrived at the farm with personal health or life insurance, and others did not. A few Koinonians strongly believed that holding insurance was inconsistent with a dependence on God. With the common purse and pledge to take care of each other, they argued, "we have something bigger and better than insurance." Others thought insurance might be a worthwhile investment or at least should be left up to the discretion of the individual.[12] With more people coming and going, Koinonians also began to face the question of how to provide for those who might leave, either temporarily or permanently.[13] They also debated the role of the children and how they might be educated in community values. "Some thought the education of children, the responsibility for the children was all with the family," Marion Johnson recalled, "and . . . some felt it should be a community thing, so mothers would be free to participate [in group activity]."[14] Disputes such as these made Koinonians realize that while they agreed on the basic philosophy of living according to Christ's teachings, they disagreed sharply on how to translate that into practice on mundane issues. Eventually, they began to feel uncomfortable with this lack of unanimity and started talking about how to resolve their differences.

Besides population growth and its attendant tensions, Koinonians were influenced by their new friendship with the Brüderhof, or Society of Brothers. The Brüderhof, founded by Eberhard Arnold in Germany in the 1920s, was a Christian community modeled on earlier European examples and populated by people from the Christian youth movement.[15] The group had been forced to migrate out of Germany because of its pacifism, staying briefly in England and then moving on to Paraguay. In 1949 Koinonians read about the Brüderhof in *Fellowship* magazine. They immediately wrote to them. The Brothers replied that they were planning a trip to the United

States and would like to visit Koinonia. In April 1949 Herman Arnold and Alan Stevenson of the Primavera *hof* in Paraguay arranged to meet members of Koinonia at Macedonia. After that initial meeting, whenever someone from the Brüderhof traveled to the United States, they stayed at the farm.[16] Koinonians saw the Brüderhof as a close-knit community with a strong sense of harmony and purpose. The comparison made their own fellowship seem weak.

A final factor in pushing Koinonia's attention toward community was a change in the priorities of the people gathered there. The growth of 1949–50 included people to whom living in Christian community meant as much as or more than working for better race relations. When Con and Ora Browne arrived, for example, they brought with them a keen interest in community. Con Browne had experienced community in the Civilian Public Service camps in World War II, to which he had been assigned as a conscientious objector. After having heard Jordan lecture in Green Lake, Wisconsin, he devoted his studies in seminary to community. "I have been grappling with communal ideas for six years at least," he wrote Jordan in 1949; "I feel we [he and his wife Ora] must seek a spiritual family like Koinonia."[17] Some people already at the farm began to regard developing more of a communal life as vitally important. Jordan summed up the feelings of himself, the Johnsons, and perhaps others. Their conflicts arose from too much concentration on particular ideas and goals rather than on the community itself, he said. "I think my biggest problem has been that I've been thinking in terms of committing myself to principles, when it seems to me that I must commit myself to the people of Koinonia who are making the same struggle as I am."[18] The new members and new concerns of some older residents began to tip the scales and shift Koinonia's concern away from outreach and missions and toward developing their internal relationship and deciding what it means to live in community.

At the start of the new decade, Koinonians took a series of steps to formalize their relationship and provide more structure to their community. In 1950 and 1951 Koinonians devised a membership process. Whereas earlier one became a member by walking in the door, now there was a three-step procedure. First a newcomer declared his or her interest in becoming a part of the community and entered novice status. After a few months, if the person was still interested, he or she became a provisional member. This step lasted usually six months and ended with a vote by the full members about whether this new person was ready for commitment. The last stage was full membership, when the individual surrendered fully to the will of the group. The whole process usually took a minimum of a year, during which time the newcomers weighed whether they could be fully committed to community. The process gave people time to get used to community life, committing a little more as they were ready. In addition, it set up guidelines for how much responsibility an individual had at any given step in the process.

Koinonia arranged the economic commitment to match the membership process. At first the novice put his or her possessions in trust outside the community or gave it to Koinonia to hold pending further decisions. At the provisional level assets were given to Koinonia to use but were retrievable if the person decided to leave. Finally, upon becoming a full member, the new Koinonian shared his or her belongings with the group, with the understanding that ownership was relinquished and they would never be returned.[19] Income from the farm provided food and shelter for all residents, of whatever membership level. Full members also received medical care and money for individual needs such as shoes, books, or whatever the treasurer deemed a necessity. With this financial arrangement there was less pressure on people who were exploring the idea of community because they could hold on to their possessions until they were ready for full commitment. In addition, the process ensured that the people making important decisions were the ones with the greatest stake in the community. With this change, membership became a formally defined status linked to a willingness to give up personal property, share completely, and abide by the will of the group.

At the same time Koinonians established a system of authority for the farm. Until then, there had been a very loose sense of who was in charge. Jordan had even made a special effort, by declining any elected office, not to be the leader of the group.[20] In 1950, in order to maintain efficiency as the population grew, Koinonians organized an administrative structure. The executive committee, which consisted of president, secretary, and treasurer elected for one year, held the overall authority. Below that there was a financial coordinator for the household and farm and a work coordinator who assigned jobs. Each of the farm enterprises had someone in charge. For example, Howard Johnson supervised the field work and was responsible for caring for the crops.[21] This system dispersed authority but ensured that major tasks got done. The positions also rotated so that no one could build up any excessive power, and men and women shared the jobs equally. Only full members held the top positions, however.

As Koinonians took these steps in reorganization, they debated the nature of, and their commitment to, community. For a year they had been discussing ways to clarify their legal status and had considered requiring each person to carry with them a notarized statement of membership. Some, like Howard Johnson, sought ways to combat problems of instability caused by the turnover in population and ambiguity in relationships. Finally, Jordan, Browne, Johnson, and some others were influenced by their friendship with the Brüderhof. Visitors from the Brüderhof, especially Will Marchant and Heini Heinrich, had convinced them of the importance of unity, meaning uniformity and agreement on all issues. Furthermore, the Brothers argued that the individual should accept the decisions of the group, because the community is the highest expression of the will of God.[22] Under this influence, and seeking clarity and stability, Koinonians debated their commitment.

"Surrender to God is the basic thing," Con Browne said, opening the discussions on commitment in November 1950. It was a statement with which most Koinonians could agree. But how was that surrender expressed? Gil Butler, Clarence Jordan, and Con Browne argued that it was expressed through commitment to a group which represents the will of God. Jordan called that the body of Christ, which is a group of believers trying to live in a certain relationship to Christ. He added that "I think our duty is to make Koinonia as nearly the body of Christ as we are able—that is our task."[23] To do this they needed to be committed to each other, not to particular work or principles. Over the next several months other Koinonians agreed with this characterization of their priorities. One member argued that "the idea of community is so vital and important that we have to struggle to make it what Jesus had in mind." By March the secretary noted, "The idea of being committed to God was indicated as our supreme desire."[24] While they agreed they wanted to avoid dogmatism, they advocated signing a written pledge to clarify and declare their commitment.

Other Koinonians opposed both this theological shift and its practical consequences. Willie Pugh and her new husband, C. Z. Ballard, in particular, could not accept the group as "the highest expression of the will of

God." Even before this debate Pugh had had disagreements with the group over money and her freedom to go visit her mother. "I began to wonder if a group could be as selfish as an individual and if it was really possible if a group will could be the highest expression rather than something an individual feels within him or herself." Moreover, she feared that such an inward focus on community would mean an abandonment of their race relations work. "To C. Z. and me the important thing was the outreach and the ministry to the outer community. We lived together simply to make that outreach," she later remembered. To her, the debate over a commitment boiled down to the "age-old question" of outreach versus community.[25] Others also had misgivings. The Atkinsons and Singletarys had displayed their own uneasiness with the community earlier by moving to Smithville to farm independently, though Harry and Allene Atkinson had come back to Koinonia just before this debate. Cliff and Ann Sanford had become disillusioned with Koinonia because they wanted to give more to their neighbors.[26] As a whole, this group resisted adopting a pledge which would commit them to the community per se rather than to the work it did.

In April 1951 those who wanted to anchor Koinonia in a commitment to community, following the example of the Brüderhof, accomplished their goal. Although the number of people on each side was approximately even, the outcome was influenced both by the weight of Jordan on one side and by the inclination of C. Z. Ballard and Jack Singletary to leave regardless of the outcome. The resulting pledge read: "We desire to make known our total, unconditional commitment to seek, express, and expand the Kingdom of God as revealed in Jesus the Christ. Being convinced that the community of believers who make a like commitment is the continuing body of Christ on earth, I joyfully enter into a love union with the Koinonia and gladly submit myself to it, looking to it to guide me in the knowledge of God's will and to strengthen me in the pursuit of it."[27] On April 4, 1951, the Jordans, Johnsons, Brownes, Norman Long, and Gilbert Butler signed the statement, thus making them officially members of Koinonia.[28] From here on, full membership, and the responsibilities and benefits that came with it, required signing this pledge. With this commitment Koinonians signaled that their primary goal was to live together as a community.

This turn away from outreach and toward inner relationships had both immediate and long-term consequences for the farm. While it satisfied some Koinonians' desire for more definition, the drawing up of the commitment led to the departure of the longtime residents who had fought the move, including the Singletarys, Sanfords, and Willie and C. Z. Ballard, as well as the Atkinsons, who would eventually return to Koinonia for a few more years. These families feared that the change meant giving up the outreach to blacks, which they considered the most important thing about Koinonia. Instead of staying with Koinonia and its new preoccupation, they found other ways to continue their race relations work. Cliff and Ann Sanford left the area and went to work at a Baptist children's home. The Atkinsons, Ballards, and Singletarys bought a farm in nearby Plains where they established a Sunday school for black children and tried to "relate on a one-to-one basis" with African-American families.[29] Their departure helped to seal a shift in the community's priorities by removing the voices arguing for a concentration on outreach.

Koinonians did not completely stop working with African Americans, as some of these members feared, however. Instead, they began a process that would characterize Koinonia for years to come: the attempt to balance outreach work and attention to community. This meant trying to incorporate the new understanding of a unified community, and its priority, into the race relations work. Over the next several years the mission work did continue in some form. Norman Long and newcomer John Eustice sponsored a boys' club. There were also neighborhood fellowship nights, a craft program, and the usual vacation Bible school. Koinonians also maintained a relationship with African Americans, both near and far. Norman Long led a group to visit Vernon John's church in Montgomery. Local blacks, including Bobby Engram and Alma Jackson, continued to live at Koinonia and work closely with the members. Over time, however, the emphasis was placed on finding ways to make this work support the goal of living in community. They strove to include neighbors and laborers in the "whole of life" and taught about the community movement during the work camps. Koinonians also laid the groundwork for making their new children's day camp relate to the ideals of community. In general there was a shift from making contacts to trying to convince African Americans to become members. This change in emphasis was reflected on their promotional literature, where the slogan "An Agricultural Missionary Enterprise" was replaced with "A Venture in Christian Community."[30]

Koinonia's summer camp illustrates its effort to integrate the two goals of reaching out to African Americans and creating a community. The idea for a weeklong sleep-over camp was raised in December 1954. Con Browne and Claud Nelson took responsibility for it and in the spring of 1955 started recruiting participants. The brochure called the Koinonia camp "An Adventure in Community Living and Sharing." It went on to describe the experience: "At Koinonia your child will live with people whose vocation and concern is sharing and the development of mature persons."[31] After emphasizing the importance of community in the advertising material, Koinonians then highlighted the race relations aspects. In personal letters Koinonians affirmed that the experience would be interracial and cosmopolitan. The list of campers included African-American children from the local area, Atlanta, and Nashville, as well as other children from Indiana, Louisiana, and even the United States Embassy in India. Over the summer the children worked on the farm, made crafts, went swimming in nearby creeks and ponds, learned Indian lore, visited neighbors, and went on educational trips. Koinonians were seeking to give the children a taste of life in community. In the process the camp turned out to be one of Koinonia's most successful interracial ventures.[32]

While the camp showed that Koinonians could integrate their two goals in their work, they had less success combining concern for race relations and community in their relationships. Koinonians debated how to maintain relationships with African Americans in their new life as a community. Con Browne summed up the problem: "Are we trying to bring people into Koinonia and our patterns rather than reach them through their own experience?"[33] In response Jordan indicated his priorities: "We shouldn't be encouraging people to think we can help them with living arrangements if they aren't going to come into the Koinonia relationship."[34] Not many of their black friends were interested in that kind of commitment, however. Individual Koinonians like Norman Long put a lot of effort into recruiting black members. For several years Koinonians tried to work out arrangements with Bobby Engram and the Jacksons, encouraging them to become more a part of the group. In the end, while some blacks continued to work at or associate with the farm, none of them signed the commitment to community.[35] Bo Johnson almost immediately signed up as a novice, but changed his mind and moved to Florida. When he returned to Sumter

County, he remained for years only an employee and friend. One couple, Rufus and Sue Angry, did begin the membership process. They had first become acquainted with Koinonia when John Eustice came to pick up their children and take them to the farm for recreation. In 1954 the couple decided to move to Koinonia.[36] The Angrys' stay at Koinonia was soon cut short by outside pressure, however, and the community was unable to gain or keep any other African-American members. In effect, the Koinonians' effort to strengthen their inner community led them to define membership in a way that alienated African Americans, setting up a barrier between whites and blacks and creating separate categories for them at the farm. While local blacks continued to come to the farm to work, visit, and even live for varying periods, they did so as friends, not as full-sharing members of Koinonia.

Despite their agreement on their commitment, Koinonians discovered they still suffered from personality differences and problems with communication. They wanted to live the life of Christians in community, which Jordan said was the body of Christ. But what did that mean in day-to-day practice? In particular, to what extent did they need consensus and internal harmony? Koinonians spent much of their energy through early 1956 debating the extent of unity they desired and the nature of their community. A particular thorn was the role of the Jordans in the community. Koinonians tried to avoid relying too much on a charismatic leader. Although Clarence Jordan steadfastly refused to hold office, people outside the group insisted on regarding him as the leader. This caused resentment within Koinonia. At one point Claud Nelson accused him of putting himself above others as the "judge of Koinonia." Jordan admitted his weakness and with the group sought ways in which he could minimize his own role further. He even suggested that he take a leave of absence from the farm, to devote time to translating the New Testament and to give the group a break from the tension. The matter was left open for the time being, and events soon made Jordan drop the idea. At the same time some members faulted Florence Jordan for not attending meetings and for trying to keep her children separate from the others. By late 1956 Norman Long also was not participating to the same extent as others.[37] These tensions raised the issues of how much an individual should yield his or her own time and desires and how much commitment and involvement in community activity was expected. Some

Koinonians believed that if the group wanted to be, as in Acts, "of one heart and one soul," then they had to let go of their individual selves and accept the will of the collective. Technically they had agreed to this principle when they signed the commitment. But when they spoke of unity, it was not clear whether they meant absolute agreement on all issues and uniformity or consensus on basic principles with an acceptance of differences on day-to-day issues.

In their effort to determine how to live in community, Koinonians looked to two models, the Brüderhof and the Hutterites, whom they first encountered in the early 1950s. The Hutterites, "the oldest continuing intentional community in the world," had originated with Jakob Hutter in sixteenth-century Europe. Centuries of persecution, due mostly to their pacifism but also to their communal lifestyle, led them to the northwestern United States, specifically the Dakotas, and to Canada.[38] The Hutterian Brethren seemed to have the closeness in spirit and harmony that Koinonians were seeking. Jordan, the Johnsons, and others saw these older groups as models and tried to solve their internal troubles by borrowing some of their mechanisms for improving relationships. First, they adopted the Brüderhof's idea of loving admonishment, which meant that if one member was hurt or offended by the action of another, he or she approached the perpetrator directly and spoke honestly of it. Con Browne remembered that Koinonia for a while tried to make the principle of "frank and earnest speech" a foundation stone of its community. The members also used the Brothers' concept of a "Servant of the Word," an officer who was selected to be a mediator in interpersonal problems. Claud and Billie Nelson believed that part of Koinonia's problem was that no one had time off from farm duties to think or do anything about these sorts of tensions. Koinonia rectified the problem by making the vice president responsible for resolving personal differences.[39] With these changes Koinonians set up a structure by which they could strive to foster a closer fellowship.

For the next few years Koinonians grew very close to these other communities and even debated joining the Brüderhof. The Brothers had suggested that if someone from Koinonia joined them, it would bring the communities closer and benefit the farm, because the Brothers could give it the spiritual direction it lacked. Claud and Billie Nelson were selected to visit a hof and were greatly impressed by the life there. Indeed, they urged

Koinonia to become a hof, promising that the Brothers could bring a "re-newal of life" to Koinonia. Howard and Marion Johnson also visited the Brüderhof and wanted to explore a relationship with them further.[40] On the other side, Norman Long argued that Koinonia needed to work things out on its own "rather than taking on the form and practices of the Brüderhof or any other group." Florence Jordan also pointed out that "they are much more regimented than us. We've always been smaller and that let us be freer."[41] Finally, for a few Koinonians, "part of the feeling was if we became Hutterites or Brüderhof we wouldn't be in Georgia anymore" and thus would have to leave behind the potential for fellowship with African Americans.[42] The Brüderhof and Hutterite model did not explicitly include the interracial character of community as Koinonia understood it. These members were unwilling to give up their opportunity for fellowship with blacks in order to join these other groups.

As important as these particular critiques was a doctrinal difference over the ability to know God's will. The Brüderhof seemed to the Koinonians to "believe it has, and it is possible to have, a full knowledge of God's will."[43] Koinonia rejected that certainty. Instead, its members believed one could never completely understand God. It followed that different people would have different interpretations of God's will and would act accordingly. Con Browne argued that "Koinonia should be open regardless of stated belief or theology" and that its members should allow differences in theology to co-exist without considering one to be more or less Christian.[44] In the end Koinonians decided to define unity as a consensus on the commitment to living a Christian life, according to the New Testament description of the Kingdom of God as they interpreted it. But they would allow disagreements and lack of complete uniformity in belief or on the day-to-day aspects of how to accomplish that. This result left Koinonia with the flexibility to adapt to changing circumstances and the open-mindedness to consider alternate ideas and arrangements in the future. As for the relationship with the Brothers, the majority of Koinonians chose to remain independent for both personal and philosophical reasons. According to Clarence Jordan, co-operation and sharing between groups were enough because "God is big enough to love us all even though we do have differences."[45]

By 1956 Koinonia had established a rough framework for its internal community. At the turn of the decade its members had devised the administrative structure and membership process to define who had a voice in decisions and how the authority was distributed. At the same time they defined the economic commitment that went along with membership. In addition, they arranged day-to-day living in community by setting up communal meals, job rotations, child care options, a weekly worship service, and a holy communion service for new members. They also made efforts to improve the relationships within the group by practicing admonishment and having the vice president be responsible for working with aggrieved members. Above all, and most significant for their future development, they agreed to be open and accepting of disagreement. This is not to say that all was settled. Building a community is a never-ending process. Throughout its history Koinonia would be forced to reevaluate the nature of its community. Most significantly, when attacks against them threatened their existence, the members would be forced to decide between the witness for racial equality and the strength of their inner fellowship.

These changes did more than give Koinonia an authority structure; they shaped the character of the community. Koinonia went from being an amorphous gathering of rural missionaries to an organized community dedicated to embodying God's Kingdom on earth. Accordingly, the membership process by which someone became a Koinonian changed. Twice the farm lost residents because of decisions made during the discussions about the meaning of community. First the Ballards, Singletarys, and others departed rather than give up missions for the sake of internal unity and commitment. Then, when Koinonia decided to remain independent, the Nelsons and Johnsons cut their ties to the farm in order to join the Brüderhof. With the membership procedures, newcomers became part of Koinonia when members voted them in and they signed the pledge. This process meant that new people were accepted on the existing group's terms. This fact had two consequences. First, few blacks were willing or able to join on Koinonia's terms. Second, the process, combined with voluntary departures, ensured relative homogeneity and agreement on basic principles. At the time of the debate over joining the Brüderhof, Koinonia had decided to reject regimentation and to be a flexible, democratic community. Koinonians could accept disagreement on day-to-day issues because of their self-selected homogeneity; all potential disputes would be within the parameters defined by agreement on basic principles, and all changes in policy would be decided by consensus among the people assembled at any given time. While they defined their community by a commitment to living according to their interpretation of the New Testament, they were willing and able to be flexible and to adapt their philosophy to different problems and a changing environment.

The changes of this period significantly altered Koinonia's ability to address race relations. In their early years Koinonians had focused on segregation and "doing something about the race problems of the South." Their original approach had been to use economic development and relationships in worship and work to heal racial division. But in their effort to clarify their internal relationship, they inadvertently had raised a conflict between their attempt to build a Christian community of total sharing and commitment and their vision of a "beloved community" of whites and blacks working and living together as equals. The changes they made set up a barrier as the membership rules excluded African Americans. Moreover, because their communitarianism made it difficult to work with others, the Koinonians' new emphasis eventually created a gap between them and other liberals who were working for racial equality.

Community can be a withdrawal from society, or it can be an agent for social change. The communitarians of the thirties and forties had wanted to change society through cooperatives and providing an example of a new way of life. Martin England saw community as a strategy for altering society by breaking down the barriers between races and classes. When the Koinonians turned inward and defined membership as total sharing and commitment, they made it harder for that strategy to work. From this point on in their history, they continually suffered from the tension between their goals of working to improve race relations and to live a Christian life in a sharing community. Ironically, because of events in society around them, it was at this point that Koinonia was attacked for its interracialism, an assault so vigorous it forced Koinonians into the civil rights arena and disrupted their community at all levels.

Part 2

The Crisis,
1956–58

5

The Crucible

I N T H E L A T E 1950s Koinonians became the target of violence, legal harassment, intimidation, and economic boycott. As civil rights became more of a national issue, Koinonia's interracial activity drew attention and anger. The resulting pressure damaged its farming and reputation, disrupted the internal fellowship, hurt the relations with the local community, and even threatened its existence. Under these adverse conditions Koinonians had to find a way to hold on to their basic beliefs while adapting their communal structure and program in order to survive. Furthermore, the attacks heightened the importance of some of their work and ideals. The violence shone a spotlight on their interracialism and, because it was integral to their response, their belief in nonviolence. During this period, which lasted until the eve of the civil rights movement in southwest Georgia, Koinonians confronted the fact that in the heightened racial atmosphere, the different elements of their program might not all survive. The attacks challenged Koinonia to maintain their religious faith literally under fire. Moreover, the pressure forced them to reevaluate their priorities, as well as the relationship between their interracialism and their life as a community.

In the mid-1950s Koinonia lived a quiet life in an uneasy but peaceful co-existence with the local people. By that time the number of people living or working at the farm had grown to approximately sixty, about one-quarter of whom were African American. During the six years after Koinonia's expulsion from the Rehobeth Church, its interracial programs had aroused little overt hostility. Although the members had not abandoned their opposition to segregation and discrimination, they rarely made a demonstration of their beliefs in Americus, confining much of their activity to the farm. Their lack of public demonstration in part stemmed from their turn inward and focus on their own fellowship. As important, however, Koinonians did not believe in making a scene, using the courts, or agitating for legal measures that would advance racial equality. Instead, they preached that having fellowship and cooperating in work would lead to changes in the laws, economic circumstances, and prejudices that kept people separate.[1] This approach to improved race relations distinguished Koinonians from others who were advocating civil rights for African Americans by working through the courts and legislation. The distinction later would be greatly misunderstood.

While Koinonia was looking inward and sorting out its communal life, however, race relations rose to prominence as a national issue. During World War II the federal government made a series of moves in the area of civil rights. Throughout the 1940s and early 1950s the Supreme Court chipped away at segregation in higher education. President Truman desegregated the armed forces and appointed a presidential commission to study the problem of race relations and make recommendations. National and international events produced this interest in civil rights. For many people the war against Nazism had delegitimized racism. Meanwhile, the movement of blacks to areas where they could vote made civil rights a political issue. Then, as the postwar boom made economic issues and poverty less pressing, the attention of liberal activists was freed for other things. Finally, in the postwar international climate, America's race problems became a liability, prompting cold war liberals to advocate removing this blemish from the national record.[2] Over this period the nature of the race issue also changed. In the 1930s liberals had seen racial inequality as part of a larger problem of economic injustice and exploitation. In the forties attention focused on civil rights in campaigns against the poll tax and white primary. By the 1950s race had become a moral problem with desegregation as the primary solution. Instrumental in this change was the publication of Gunnar Myrdal's *An American Dilemma*, which portrayed the race problem as a result of the contradiction between American ideals and reality. What was needed was laws that would bring the races together so that whites could overcome the moral sickness of racism and treat all people equally.[3]

The rise of race as an issue affected white southerners, galvanizing opinion on all sides. In the 1930s and early 1940s southern liberals had supported the New Deal and worked for progress on economic and class issues. They had sought to build a coalition which would address economic and labor problems. To accomplish that, they worked to enfranchise blacks and poor whites through repealing the poll tax. During and after the war southern liberals became more interested in race per se. Some groups were particularly interested in conditions for black veterans. Other liberals joined in coalitions of church and labor organizations. In the late 1940s the Southern Conference for Human Welfare (SCHW) and the Southern Regional Council (SRC) debated and finally endorsed integration over the separate but equal policy. From that point through the mid-1950s, the SRC and the Fellowship of Southern Churchmen concentrated on preparing communities for the expected school desegregation decisions.[4]

Through the same period, however, anti–New Deal sentiment and racist politics combined to close down the window of opportunity for a change in race relations. Resistance to the federal trend on race issues rose slowly. Between 1950 and 1954 the fight over the renewal of the Fair Employment Practices Commission, McCarthyism, and Supreme Court decisions on segregation energized conservatives. Meanwhile, anticommunist attacks silenced the SCHW and others who tied civil rights to economics. Individual who, in the words of the FSC, held "racial views which are too Christian or democratic" were victims of the association of anything liberal with subversion.[5] The *Brown v. Board of Education of Topeka, Kansas* school desegregation decision split and isolated liberals and gave their opponents a rallying point. Anger against the Supreme Court and black militancy intensified. Avenues for liberal action shut down. A "wave of reaction" rolled across the South, hitting one of its first targets at Koinonia Farm.[6]

Before *Brown* the white people of Sumter County were unaroused by or uninterested in race relations or civil rights. Indeed, there had been little open questioning of the status quo. As far as Koinonians could tell, whites and blacks had contact at work but were socially separate—a separation marked by little overt hostility. When in January 1954 Tuskegee Institute released a report documenting a decline in lynching, the local paper wel-

comed the news and hoped it would silence "the rabble rousers and communists who try to stir up anti-American sentiment."[7] Before this time
African Americans had launched few civil rights protests in the area. There
had been a chapter of the NAACP in Americus in the 1920s, but by the mid-
1950s it was inactive and on the brink of disbanding.[8] The expectation and
announcement of the *Brown* decision disturbed this calm. The official public reaction of the white community was at first measured. The *Americus
Times-Recorder* called for reason and predicted that nothing would change
because the decision was unenforceable.[9] The local white residents, however, became steadily more agitated as the paper carried daily headlines
about the governor's race, which the school issue dominated, and of desegregation crises such as the Montgomery bus boycott. In June 1955 the paper
reported on a tristate rally of the White Citizens Council at which there was
a promise of "a social boycott of the 'scalawags and carpetbaggers of the
modern era' who fail or refuse to join in the fight to preserve segregation."
Six months later local citizens organized their own effort to protect "consti-
tutional government" and school segregation.[10]

Clarence Jordan added a spark to a tinderbox of racial feeling in the
spring of 1956 when he decided to help two black students apply to the University of Georgia system's business school, an all-white institution. Sam
Williams, a longtime African-American friend in Atlanta, had called Jordan
and asked him to help the students because the university system required
the signatures of two alumni for an application. Jordan hesitated to help the
students if they were only interested in causing a legal battle over desegregation. He did not believe in starting a demonstration for its own sake. But he
did support any civil rights action which came up naturally as people tried
to live fairly, or as African Americans tried to improve their lives.[11] When he
was assured that the students sincerely hoped to further their education by
taking business classes unavailable at the "Negro" schools, he arranged to
meet them. The applicants were Thelma B. Boone, a graduate of Tennessee
State College and secretary to the president of Clark College, and Edward J.
Clemons, an insurance executive at North Carolina Mutual Life. Jordan and
Harry Atkinson met with them, Williams, Grace Hamilton of the Atlanta
Urban League, and Jim Weldon, pastor of the Oak Grove Methodist
Church in Atlanta. Seeking to avoid publicity, Jordan took the students to
see George Sparks, president of the business school. The group spent the day

being shunted from one official to the next. In the end Jordan could not sign the applications because of a technicality. Frustrated by this turn of events, Jordan and Atkinson decided to return to Americus. In the meantime, word had spread about what they were attempting to do, and as they left the university offices, reporters surrounded them. By the time they got back to Americus, the governor had called the local sheriff to find out who "this Jordan fellow" was, and the *Americus Times-Recorder* had printed an inflammatory account of the whole incident.[12] Jordan's attempt to help these students, combined with the agitation of the people of Sumter County over the race issue, suddenly transformed Koinonia from a community of Christians trying to live together into a threat against segregation.

The local people almost immediately resorted to violence, legal intimidation, and economic boycott to remove the threat. The violence began with vandalism and random gunfire. The farm's roadside market, on a highway four miles from the main part of the property, became the first target. Unknown vandals repeatedly tore the sign down. On other nights bullets fired from passing cars riddled the storefront. Soon shots also struck the community buildings, and the Jordans began receiving threatening phone calls. Concurrent with the physical threat was a legal and economic assault. Soon after Jordan and Atkinson's attempt to help the black students, merchants stopped handling the Koinonians' eggs, and one of their insurance companies canceled the policy on the farm property and equipment. A long period of siege and struggle for survival had begun.

The violence escalated that summer. The roadside market was severely damaged when a car pulled into the driveway of the store and a passenger threw ten to fifteen sticks of dynamite toward the door. The explosion blasted a hole in the ground and damaged the front and roof of the building. Fortunately no one was inside at the time, but the damage cost Koinonia $3,000. When Koinonians rebuilt the market, it was repeatedly fired upon. On one occasion a Georgia Bureau of Investigation agent found fifty-five slugs of a .22 rifle in the walls. Dynamite blasts destroyed the refrigerated meat case, ruining one of the farm's profitable enterprises. The final blow to the market business came shortly after midnight on January 14, 1957. Sheriff Fred Chappell called Jordan to inform him there had been another explosion. When he and Atkinson arrived on the scene, they found the structure blown to bits and fire burning what little remained. This time

Koinonia decided to give up on the market and, instead of rebuilding it, left the rubble as a monument to violence.[13]

The attacks on the residential part of the farm also intensified. In late December shots were fired into the gas pump near some of the homes. Throughout the winter and into the spring, shotgun fire threatened the lives of the people at Koinonia. One night seven shots were fired into a room where people were sleeping. On another, ten or twelve shotgun blasts struck the buildings. While Harry Atkinson sat watch in a car by the road, someone drove by and shot into it. Atkinson was leaning over at the time, and the bullet went through the seat next to him. In April, as the Jordans' oldest child, Eleanor, dressed for bed and turned out her light, four or five shots were fired into her room. The bullets passed through her wall, into her father's chair, and on into the next room where they finally stopped in a child's toy closet. Clarence Jordan, just moments before, had gotten up from the chair to go to bed. Another time, a passerby fired into a volleyball game in the yard of the community, sprinkling the children with buckshot.[14] These attacks were part of a larger, regionwide pattern of violence which greeted anyone who pushed for integration. In effect, they pulled Koinonia into the movement for civil rights by making it, along with Montgomery, an early flash point in the battle for racial equality.

Neighbors who befriended Koinonia also came under attack. Gene and Jack Singletary still lived on their farm in Smithville and maintained a close relationship with the community. One night in mid-January, after receiving a warning call, Jordan and the Butlers drove out to the Singletarys' and found a small fire set by three kerosene flares that had been thrown under their barn. Another white friend, J. D. Clements, incurred $30,000 in damage when his barn was burned down. Koinonia's black friends were even more vulnerable to the campaign of terror. Mr. and Mrs. Top Wilson were African Americans who lived on the farm and sometimes did a little work for the community. One night John Eustice saw an unfamiliar Plymouth headed for their house. The passengers of the car shot into the building as they drove by. No one was hurt, but shortly after that a cross was burned on the Wilsons' lawn, and they decided to move out of the area. In early February three more crosses were burned on the property of sympathetic neighbors, including at the home of Alma Jackson's parents. Koinonians tried to get some kind of protection for their African-American neighbors, but

Sheriff Chappell simply urged black families to get away from the farm and warned that anyone who kept up an association "would get hurt."[15] To a great extent the threat worked, but some of Koinonia's friends refused to be scared off. As Billy Monts, a hired hand, explained to a reporter, "I'd rather die like a man than live like a coward."[16]

People also tried to intimidate Koinonians themselves. The crosses burned on their neighbors' properties were meant for Koinonia's notice; especially the one near the Wilsons' home, which could be clearly seen from the residences on the farm. In addition, one night in late February, Klansmen visited Koinonia. They had held a rally nearby at which speakers whipped up the crowd, declaring that segregation was God's law. Then they led a group of seventy to eighty cars to Koinonia. When Margaret Wittkamper greeted them at the gate, they demanded, "Take us to your leader." Wittkamper tried to explain that they had no leader, they were all equal. The frustrated visitors insisted she knew what they meant. Just then Norman Long, John Eustice, and Chris Drescher came out. The spokesman for the Klan said they came to offer to buy Koinonia out, guaranteeing them full value for their property. After a brief discussion Koinonians refused the offer.[17]

Throughout this time Koinonia protested against the violence and tried to get police protection. The police did little to help, however, and turned the blame on Koinonia instead. When Jordan and Atkinson had arrived on the scene of the dynamited market, they found Chappell there but making no effort to put out the blaze or investigate the blast. The sheriff refused to let Koinonia put lights on the road and turned down its request to have a patrolman stationed nearby. He also scolded Jordan for placing watchmen on the road and bothering drivers by shining flashlights on their license plates. He and others charged Koinonia with being in complicity with those doing the violence, suggesting that to elicit sympathy and cash donations, the members had faked attacks on themselves. At the same time the sheriff accused the community of not cooperating with his investigations and of calling the media before his office when there was violence.[18]

Realizing they were not going to get protection from the local authorities, Koinonians went over their heads and contacted the Georgia and Federal Bureaus of Investigation. They knew they had a case when, in mid-January, machine-gun fire strafed their houses. Con Browne's brother-in-law, who was a military man, said that the weapon must have been government issue. Jordan believed that if United States weapons were being used against citizens in peacetime, then it was a violation of federal law and the FBI could get involved. Shortly thereafter, Koinonia's lawyer, Osgood Williams, heard that the FBI had established a tie between the weapons and the National Guard.[19] Koinonia had long suspected this because most of the shootings were on Monday night, after National Guard meetings. The investigation never went any further, however.

Lacking official protection, Koinonians acted to defend themselves. For the most part their response to direct violence consisted of displaying their vulnerability and trusting in their attackers' unwillingness to hurt unarmed people. Soon after the shooting started, Koinonia put guards on the road. At first only the men took turns until Ora Browne suggested that it might be more effective, and would be more equitable, to have the women join them. Then they strung lights on the road and had the men and women stand beneath them. Although cars and equipment continued to be fired upon, no one shot directly at the defenseless people sitting under the bright lights.[20] Sometimes people on watch would try to get license plate numbers in order to report them to law officers. John Gabor frightened cars off just by flashing a light on them or pretending to call for help. Others would follow cars until they left the vicinity. No one from the farm ever carried a weapon for defense even while on watch, however, or challenged an attacker face-to-face.

Whatever Koinonians did in defense had to be carried out within the bounds of their understanding of nonviolence. To them, that meant not responding to violence in kind and not showing aggression or hatred for the "enemy." Nonviolence had always been part of Koinonia's philosophy. In fact, the issue had been the center of some controversy in the forties when the FBI investigated the group for their pacifism and when two members had been prosecuted for resisting the draft.[21] Besides those incidents, however, to this point it had been less a part of daily life and less well articulated than belief in community or racial brotherhood. The circumstances in the mid-1950s, however, forced Koinonians to give nonviolence more priority and decide what it meant in practice. Some actions, such as posting unarmed guards, seemed clearly nonviolent. But was chasing a car or flashing lights on it confrontational or aggressive? Eventually, Koinonians would consider whether using the courts to defend themselves or confronting businessmen was within the confines of nonviolence. Over time, their understanding of this part of their philosophy evolved, becoming better defined and more important as a guide to confronting problems.

While Koinonia's nonviolent defense seemed to diminish the level of physical attacks, it could not protect the farm from legal harassment. The primary target for local officials was the interracial summer camp. Before the 1956 summer season could start, the county got an injunction against the camp based on questions about the sanitary conditions at the site. Con Browne filed for a health inspection on June 8, and on the twenty-fifth the public health engineer carried it out. The official found no conditions warranting the closing of the camp. He testified later that Koinonia had complied with all of his suggestions, including making all campers bring health certificates from their physicians, moving the site two thousand feet from any paved road, and installing fire extinguishers.[22] Soon after that four local white farmers brought a companion suit, charging that Koinonia violated laws against operating a business which lodged and fed travelers or guests. They further alleged that the operation of the camp would be detrimental to the morals of the children because they would witness the birth of animals and would live in coed facilities. They asked the court to prevent Koinonia from holding the camp.[23]

The battle over this injunction raged on throughout the summer, forcing Koinonians to expend time, energy, and financial resources to defend themselves. At the first hearing, in early July, the government attorney asked for and received a postponement of the trial to better prepare his case. The judge ordered the parties to submit evidence by affidavit in two weeks, at which time they would have a week to give a rebuttal. These measures meant that time was running out for Koinonia to be able to hold the camp. When the judge further postponed the trial until September 20, it looked as if Koinonia would have to cancel the camp. In the meantime the nine-year-old son of Myles Horton, the leader of Highlander Folk School, had heard about the farm's predicament. With his father's permission he invited the Koinonians to hold the camp in Monteagle, Tennessee. Koinonia accepted and managed to have a successful season despite the injunction. In September, Judge Cleveland Rees ruled the issue moot.[24]

The camp injunction demonstrated the new restrictions on Koinonia's interracial activity and forced it to be flexible in order to maintain some of

its programs. In the court case it became abundantly clear that what farmers really objected to was black children being brought in to mix with white
children. Koinonians had sponsored the interracial camp successfully and
without incident the year before. The farm also had a long history of vacation Bible school and other youth programs that included both black and
white children. Although other whites had not participated, they had not
tried to stop these programs before. Now, however, local people saw the
camp as a prime example of Koinonia's trying to force integration. In the
newly charged racial atmosphere the space for Koinonia's work was limited.
Local whites successfully removed this threat to segregation from their
neighborhood. Koinonia, however, found a way to continue the program
by moving the camp. Although in a slightly altered and smaller form, it
maintained an integrated program and expressed its interracial beliefs.
Koinonians continued to host the camp at Highlander, with the help of former members Willie and C. Z. Ballard, for several years.[25]

Local officials next began to investigate activities of Koinonia that they
deemed potentially subversive. There had been suspicions about Koinonia
before, when the FBI investigated its pacifism. The government took another look at it in February 1957. Around the same time Long notified
friends that the GBI was investigating the farm's "connections."[26] The next
month the government subpoenaed members of the community to appear
before the grand jury in the case of *The State of Georgia v. C. Conrad Browne.*
The order asked Clarence Jordan, John Eustice, Jack Singletary, and Alma
Jackson to present themselves. The court also required Jordan to bring with
him their mailing lists, records of all donations since 1942, names of all their
contributors, and all other financial records for 1955 through March 1957.
Although Koinonia did not know exactly what the charges were against
Browne, the members quickly realized that the case was meant to prove the
theory that they were perpetuating the violence themselves and to be a "general fishing expedition" into supposed subversive activities.[27]

The hearing illustrated the overlap of anticommunism and anti–civil
rights sentiment in the South at this time. Around the region investigative
boards called liberals to testify. Anne and Carl Braden, who had helped a
black family acquire a home in a formerly all-white neighborhood, were investigated by the House Un-American Activities Committee and a local
grand jury. Virginia Durr, who had worked on the poll tax issue, had to an-

swer to Senator James O. Eastland's Internal Security Subcommittee. The two forces, anticommunism and resistance to racial change, reinforced each other and were used to silence reformers.[28] In Koinonia's case the prosecutor probed the supposed communistic and race-mixing practices of the community. To begin with, Jordan had to answer questions about his connections with Aubrey Williams, Myles Horton, and the Southern Conference Education Fund. Then Alma Jackson was pressed to provide damaging information about his treatment on the farm. The prosecuting attorney wanted to know why he referred to Florence Jordan by her given name, why he did not say "Yes ma'am" and "No ma'am," and the extent of his social relationships at the community.[29]

The grand jury did not gather enough evidence to bring formal charges against Koinonia. Nevertheless, it released a series of presentments that had the desired effect of "proving," in the minds of many local people, that Koinonia was a subversive organization. The jury reported that it believed the farm was a communist front because of the members' friendship with several known radicals. It further found that the community was committing acts of violence against itself and receiving large cash gifts as a result. The jury went on to accuse the farm of keeping blacks in a state of "brainwashed peonage."[30] In short, this was not a harmless Christian group but a subversive organization presenting a clear danger to the traditions and racial mores of the white community.

These charges threatened to be the final cut severing Koinonia from the local white community. Koinonians tried to diminish the impact of the grand jury presentments by releasing a rebuttal that explained their position regarding communism and violence. "No person at Koinonia has now or has ever had any affiliation with the Communist Party. Marxist communism is diametrically opposed to all we stand for," the statement read. "We would do violence to no man, even in our thoughts."[31] The local paper would not print the community's more detailed answer to the informal charges, citing the danger of libel suits from members of the jury and the solicitor general.[32] Koinonians printed their response and mailed a copy of it to every person in the Americus phone book. They hoped this would impress their innocence upon the local people and forestall further attacks.

Their effort failed. People in Sumter County and around Georgia not only accepted the evidence presented by the grand jury, they built on it with further investigations. The state of Georgia sent photographer Ed Friend to the Highlander Folk School's twenty-fifth anniversary seminar partly to spy on Koinonia. This was the same mission which produced photographs and billboards linking Martin Luther King Jr. to communists. At the seminar Friend attended a session at which Con Browne told the story of Koinonia Farm. The spy testified that the prayer service led by Browne was "subversive, sir, to the way that I have been taught to live in America." He added that "it is the primary motive of this group [Koinonia] to tear down the forces that were trying to keep the races separate in the South" and thus bring chaos and communist aggression.[33] This was all the "proof" the state of Georgia needed that Koinonia was subversive and un-American. Most white Sumter County residents, angered by Koinonia's racial practices and confirmed in their suspicions about its subversion, pulled away from the community completely.

The violence and harassment that Koinonians suffered sapped the energy of the community, as it worked to defend itself, fight off legal attacks, and rescue its reputation and relationship with the local people. Yet, with only these troubles Koinonia might have continued to be a successful farm and mission enterprise. Concurrent with all this, however, the white community unleashed its most devastating attack, a near-complete economic boycott of the farm. It began when local merchants stopped buying the farm's eggs. Before the trouble Con Browne, who was in charge of the eggs, had been handling 125 cases a week. Then a young man whose taxi fare was paid by the White Citizens Council started following him around and scaring off his customers. For a while Browne sold eggs in the black community in Albany with the help of Slater King.[34] When that business failed to yield enough money, Koinonians were forced to liquidate their flock.

After that, the boycott quickly began to devastate the farm. Local merchants would not sell it supplies such as fertilizer, gasoline, lime, and seed, which were vital to farming. Insurance companies canceled the members' policies, leaving them unprotected against the damage to equipment caused by the violence. Finally, banks notified them that they could no longer accept their business. Slowly a noose was drawn around the community. A farm needs the cooperation of local businesses to survive. Koinonia's earlier success showed its good relations with farmers, merchants, and businessmen. Now its isolation from the local community robbed it of its economic lifeblood.

Koinonia tried to rescue its fellowship with the local people by talking to some of the merchants. Typically the businessman would express sympathy with the farm and admit that his actions were un-Christian, but he would not change his position. Harold Still of the Still Gas Company, for example, told Koinonia that he would lose business if he continued to deal with it, although no customers had complained yet. He admitted the policy was wrong but was determined to stick by it. Koinonia asked if he was a Christian, and if he was, did he not think he was behaving a little unbrotherly, perhaps even like a Judas? He confessed he was, and claimed to feel just awful about it, but would not reconsider his decision.[35] At other times Koinonians encountered great hostility from local merchants. When Jordan went to talk to Willis Shiver of the lumber company, he was met with a venomous barrage against the NAACP, ministers who would let blacks into the church, and Koinonia. Jordan tried to explain that the farm was a religious, law-abiding organization and that the members' beliefs should not be taken into consideration in business deals. In response Shiver denounced Koinonia for trying to "ram things down our throat."[36] Koinonia seemed less saddened by men like Shiver than by the people who, like Still, claimed to agree with them but could not stand up to the pressure.

When Koinonians failed to break the boycott, they developed several strategies for surviving the economic devastation it was causing. They maintained the basic practice of economic sharing among themselves but adopted new moneymaking ventures and financial arrangements to fit the circumstances. Because the egg business had been destroyed, along with most of its other profitable agricultural ventures, Koinonia turned to other products and creative marketing techniques. In order to maintain their cash income, Koinonians went into the pecan-processing business. Because it marketed the nuts through mail order, Koinonia could sell them to its supporters and bypass the local boycott.[37] This enabled Koinonians to reach beyond the local people to a wider community. Moreover, they could hire African Americans to work in the plant and keep providing employment at high wages, despite the decline of their agricultural program. Although Koinonians were forced to make changes in their financial basis, they continued to share economically and to provide material assistance to African Americans through jobs.

Late in the spring the boycott took a violent turn. Herbert Birdsey, owner of a feedstore in town, decided that his local store and another he owned in Albany would serve Koinonia. Soon thereafter, on May 19, 1957, someone drove by his Americus establishment and threw several sticks of dynamite onto the sidewalk at the doorway. The blast damaged other buildings, including the Citizen's Bank and the Sumter County Courthouse, but no one was hurt. The local people reacted with shock and dismay at the violence. Birdsey said he would try to keep his store open, although he now knew how "voluntary" the boycott was.[38]

This incident created a crisis atmosphere in town and led to an official request for Koinonia to leave the area. Several leading citizens, fearing the violence would spread, decided to ask Koinonia for a meeting. A delegation from Americus, which included Frank Myers of the Chamber of Commerce, Charles Crisp of the Bank of Commerce, Mayor Fred Bowen, J. R. Blair, publisher of the *Americus Times-Recorder,* and several others, visited with the members of Koinonia. Crisp, speaking for the group, stated that their main concern was for the safety of the 25,000 people of Sumter County. It was not only the leaders, he said, but most people in Sumter County who wanted Koinonia to leave. Another spokesman warned, "When the masses of people in the United States want something, they get it, if they have to resort to armed force to do it." They charged Koinonia with causing the unrest in the county and asserted that 99 percent of the people in the area would be glad to see the members move on.[39]

The people of Koinonia refused to believe there was no other solution. Clarence Jordan, speaking for the community, pointed out that they were not the ones doing the violence. He suggested that all those in the room could make common cause to stop it, especially if the civic leaders would put pressure on law enforcement officers. Other Koinonians added that Sumter County was 65 percent African American and doubted that all of them wanted the farm to close. The larger issue, according to the community, was whether the members should be run out because of their beliefs. Koinonians suggested that the two sides compromise and set up an impartial panel to hear the facts in the case. The panel could be staffed by three men selected by the civic leaders, three by Koinonia, and three by some outside group. This committee could hear the grievances and decide whether Koinonia should leave.[40] This proposal was rejected, ending any dialogue between Koinonians and the leaders of Sumter County.

In late 1959 Koinonians reevaluated their attitude toward the boycott.

Until this time they had used the methods of nonresistance. They confronted individual merchants once, then left them alone in order not to create hostility or put undue pressure on individuals. When there was an emergency, they sent visitors to buy supplies for them secretly. In 1957 they expressed uneasiness with their practices, declaring that "we feel the initiative for reconciliation lies with us and we wish we could find more ways to contact the 'enemy' with good will."[41] They felt that they were both cooperating with evil and being dishonest and wanted to change their approach. This represented an evolution in their nonviolence away from just not responding to violence to actively seeking reconciliation through goodwill or love for the "enemy." They started shopping in the local stores for the items they needed, forcing the merchants to make a daily decision on where they stood on the boycott. Koinonians announced this change in letters to area businessmen because they wanted to be more open about their attitude toward the boycott and to witness "against the application of such tactics in society."[42] Unfortunately, the reevaluation did not have much effect. Many merchants did not start doing business with them until the mid-1960s. However, it left Koinonia more assured that they were handling the problem in a manner consistent with more active nonviolence.

The crisis created tension, both within Koinonia and between members and the local people. The violence and the economic damage caused by the boycott took a heavy toll on the emotional life of the residents of the farm. First, the strain of overwork and loss of sleep wore people out. They grew physically exhausted from standing watch at night and working on the farm during the day. Even when not on watch, they were awakened almost every night by gunfire. On top of the weariness, Koinonians were justifiably frightened. They agonized over whether to send their children away from the danger. Ora Browne had been reading about the psychosis suffered by the British children evacuated during the Battle of Britain. When a little neighbor girl died instantly after her dress caught fire from a stove, they realized how precious their children were to them; they decided to keep them at the farm but to teach them to lie low. Mrs. Browne also remembers the anger she felt. "I was angry a lot of the time because I couldn't logically see why white southerners were behaving like they were, when they said they were all such great Christians. It was just so inconsistent with the Christian message."[43] Tiredness and frustration led to squabbles over little issues that were not important. The tension also created internal debates over how to respond. This dissension, according to Harry Atkinson, hurt the community as much as the violence.[44]

Besides causing internal tension, the crisis also wrecked the fellowship that had existed between Koinonia and some of the people of Sumter County. Mrs. Frank Sheffield told a friend of the community, "We've known some of the Koinonia people for a long time and feel much more kindly toward them than most other people, but we do wish they would move out and let things alone." Another person called Con Browne a "fine Christian gentleman." But the local people also believed the grand jury. If Koinonia Farm was communist, and if the members were breaking racial taboos as well, then they should get out.[45] Local whites had considered Koinonians "nice" as long as they had quietly gone about their ways. But now they were flouting local custom by helping blacks get into white schools. "There was no boycott so long as they stayed in their own backyard. We didn't like it, but we put up with it."[46] Now that they had tried to force their ideas on people, it was time for them to leave. The friendly relations Koinonia had enjoyed with its white neighbors were terminated.

The crisis led to mixed results in Koinonia's relationship with African Americans in Sumter County. The violence and turmoil over Koinonia's attempt to have fellowship with African Americans, ironically, made many blacks back away from the farm. Some blacks claimed that the "Negroes in the community don't talk about the Farm, and they don't think about it." Sam Weston, a former member of the NAACP, tried to distance his organization from Koinonia by telling reporters that it "wouldn't lower its dignity to bother with" the farm.[47] A black repairman told a friend of Koinonia's that while he thought highly of the community, it would hurt Koinonia, and local blacks, if he spent a lot of time there.[48] Thus, the attention on the race issue was a double-edged sword, cutting Koinonia off from both the white and the black community.

Some blacks, however, found ways to visit and help the farm. Carranza Morgan brought supplies to the farm under the cover of darkness, and Doc Champion did some of the members' shopping for them.[49] Koinonians were gratified at signs that the black community appreciated what they were trying to do. One day during a Klan rally some local blacks stood by watching, seemingly unafraid. When asked about it, a leader in the community said, "You should know, Koinonia has taught us not to be afraid."[50] Most of the blacks who actually lived on or worked at the farm left, but a few stayed. Alma Jackson told the grand jury prosecutor that he was not afraid and he would stay because "I wanted to be there. I liked it there. It was a nice place to live—the right way of living." Alma and his wife Mary, as well as another black couple, Eddie and Mildred Johnson, continued to live at Koinonia for a while and to attend novice meetings.[51] Koinonians tried to find ways for these African Americans to stay but understood why some would want to leave. Moreover, they felt that these departures were not a true breaking of fellowship but rather a separation imposed on them from the outside.

Although it seemed Koinonia's relationships with those around them were crumbling, the members were heartened by signs of support from friends both near and far. In addition to their African-American friends, in the local area a few whites stuck by them. Their friend Dan Rhyne and his brother continued to visit. The Episcopal minister, the Reverend Paul Ritch, accepted the Brownes briefly into his church and commended Koinonia's witness from his pulpit. Other upstanding citizens tried to talk to the townspeople about Koinonia. Dr. Lloyd Moll, president of Georgia Southwestern College, worked with friends of Koinonia to hold a meeting at his home to talk about the situation. Although he was not very successful, for years he stood by Koinonia and the local black people in their struggles.[52] Liberals around the region and country also responded to the attacks and race-baiting and helped them. Anne Braden corresponded with Koinonia regularly and warned the members when the farm's charter was being investigated in Louisville.[53] Although Koinonians were losing the friendship of most local whites, they were discovering it in other places.

Koinonia Farm survived the hostility, violence, and economic boycott, but it emerged from the crisis as a different entity. In 1956 the community had about sixty residents, a quarter of whom were African American. By 1959 the numbers had dropped dramatically to three families and a handful of long-term guests and newcomers. Many of the original families, including some of the signers of the first Koinonia Commitment, and most of the blacks had moved away. New families came, wanting to help Koinonia survive and to make a witness for better race relations, but they tended to stay for shorter periods of time. As circumstances around them changed, Koinonians struggled to maintain as much of their program as possible and to remain true to their ideals. The agricultural program was completely altered as the pecan mail-order business replaced the egg business and cash crop farming. The crisis had also damaged Koinonia's educational and mission program. The vacation Bible school ended with the summer camp. Koinonia kept up contact with the local black people, however, and continued to do service work such as counseling alcoholics and juvenile delinquents. The members also continued to work with African Americans and hosted integrated programs as much as possible without sacrificing the safety of their friends. They also remained steadfastly nonviolent in the face of physical and economic threats, refining their understanding of nonviolence over the period. And, despite financial hardship, they continued to share economically among themselves.

Their ability to adapt, however, could not mask the fact that the attacks fundamentally tested their commitment to, and their ability to maintain, an interracial fellowship. The violence and legal investigations had brought attention to their racial practices. This occurred at a time when race had become the preeminent domestic social and political issue. In confluence with anticommunism, heightened racial feeling limited the extent to which Koinonia, or others, could work for better race relations. Moreover, the attacks made the farm one of the foci of civil rights activity in the mid-1950s. This forced members to reconsider their priorities, the place of their racial beliefs in their overall philosophy, and the direction they would proceed as the civil rights movement developed. Their interracial fellowship had been damaged because so many of their African-American friends had had to distance themselves from the farm. There were always a few blacks who continued to associate with Koinonia and more in the community who respected their position. But as African-American participation diminished due to the violence, Koinonia was left standing up for the right to have interracial fellowship and for the chance to have relationships in the future, rather than for the current existence of such a community. By the late 1950s Koinonians spoke of their witness, their refusal to give up the principle of interracialism, which at the time seemed all they had left of their race relations work. But was that worth the threat to their lives? During the next few years Koinonians debated how to work with others, and how much they were willing to sacrifice, in order to keep that witness to racial brotherhood alive.

6

A Fellowship of
Believers

KOINONIA FARM survived the attacks against it to a large extent
because of the help it received from friends across the country. While the crisis damaged Koinonia's internal fellowship and its relationship with neighbors in Sumter County, at the same time the members formed a bond with
a new sort of community. Koinonians had long understood *community* to
mean a group connected by economic cooperation, common work and worship, and sharing in all aspects of life. But in modern society mobility, the
specialization of labor, and other forces prevent people from sharing their
whole lives with those around them. As a result, people look for kinship elsewhere and find it in relationships based on shared beliefs.[1] Koinonia's cause
attracted people who believed integration was the road to equality for
African Americans; the relationship between them and members of the farm
was based on their perceived common interest in better race relations. The
resulting sense of community was a source of moral support where people
got reinforcement for their beliefs. Koinonia's crisis gave these individuals a
rallying point and something to do to support better race relations. Meanwhile, the external community helped Koinonia survive. Although the relationship had mutual benefits, it was also fraught with potential tension. The
external community lacked a total understanding of Koinonia's Christian

liberalism and mission. As a result, the relationship between the farm and its friends raised the issue of the difference between civil rights per se and the Koinonians' belief in interracialism through community.

The network that supported Koinonia included white liberals around the country who, after the war, became involved in efforts to improve race relations or to encourage the nonviolent resolution of conflicts. For the most part these individuals had been inspired by the idealism of the New Deal or their contact with the student Christian movements of the 1930s. In addition, the experience of fighting a war against fascism abroad led them to want to fight for social justice at home. These postwar activists included pacifists, men from the Civilian Public Service camps, New Dealers, southern liberals, clergymen, and members of groups such as the Baptist Peace Fellowship, the Fellowship of the Concerned, or the Women's International League for Peace and Freedom.[2] In the postwar years these people pursued different paths toward the goal of better and more peaceful human relations. Pacifists joined Peacemaker cells and investigated ways in which to live nonviolently, founding communities such as Glen Gardner in New Jersey and Macedonia in Georgia. In the upper Midwest the Congress of Racial Equality used Gandhian tactics against segregation and sponsored interracial workshops on nonviolence. In the South individual clergymen risked alienating their flock and losing their churches by speaking out against racial hatred.

By the mid-fifties these people were finding themselves more and more isolated. Their initial activity in the field of race relations and nonviolence had taken place during a postwar burst of idealism. The atmosphere of liberal excitement had quickly given way to a backlash of conservative sentiment. In the South whites were retrenching against further advances and, in the wake of the *Brown* decision, rallying to defend the status quo. Meanwhile, across the nation anticommunist hysteria targeted anyone calling for change, especially in foreign policy or race relations. In this unfavorable climate activists had to bide their time, pursuing their goals quietly. In such an atmosphere they became isolated and had to gain solace from the knowledge that there were a few others of like mind out there, in what the Fellowship of Southern Churchmen called "a community of kindred spirits." Koinonia's crisis came just when isolated individuals needed a way to get and keep in touch with one another.[3]

In 1956 and 1957 Koinonia Farm's story began to appear in various national magazines. Almost immediately after the first attacks, the *Christian Century* reported the story, exposing the farm's dilemma to its national, liberal, and Christian audience. From the beginning Koinonia was portrayed as a race relations story. The editors of the magazine set the tone for the early coverage by saying that Koinonia was under attack because it was trying "to demonstrate a Christian way of life in which members of both races can share." Shortly after that, *Time* echoed the *Christian Century* and called Koinonia "a Christian experiment in racial equality." The media also linked Koinonia to other racial hot spots around the South. The *Nation* listed the three forces in the South—"partisans of the past, silent onlookers, and the brave who are trying to change things"—and named Koinonia along with the black children involved in school desegregation as examples of the latter. A few months later *Newsweek* called Koinonia "a case study of the social upheaval that has rocked the South since the Supreme Court [*Brown*] decision."[4] Over the next year the print media, in particular the *Christian Century,* updated its readers on the violence at the farm. Smaller organizational journals, including the *Catholic Worker* and the *CORE-lator,* reported on the situation. In this way Koinonia became familiar to people involved in peace or civil rights activism. Although accounts usually mentioned other aspects of Koinonia's philosophy, the image in the media that attracted attention to the farm was of a besieged integration effort.

From its beginning Koinonia had attracted supporters. Now, as the violence against the farm and its cause became known, Koinonia's circle of friends grew to encompass students, members of church organizations, communitarians, and secular liberals who were part of the postwar community of people interested in change. Those whom Koinonians befriended included a minister in Etowah, Tennessee, who lost his church for preaching on the race issue, a student who wanted to crusade against hate in South Carolina, victims of the House Un-American Activities Committee, and rising civil rights leaders. These people could look at Koinonia's nonviolence, communal lifestyle, and interracial fellowship and say, "I believe in that, too; we are brethren." At a time when the national and regional mood was against them, they could turn to Koinonia and to each other for moral support and fellowship.

The Koinonians' interracialism attracted the attention of most of their new friends, overshadowing other parts of their philosophy. Throughout Jordan's career and Koinonia's history, the mission to African Americans had been a focal point. Jordan had developed a reputation in Louisville and in Southern Baptist circles for the work he had done with blacks at the Baptist Fellowship Center. He advertised his intention to continue that work at Koinonia, proclaiming in preliminary literature on the farm that its purpose would be to help black sharecroppers and to train black preachers. Then from its beginning Koinonia had intrigued people who were concerned about prejudice and who were interested in the farm's "project with Negroes."[5] The Koinonians had lived and worked side-by-side with African Americans, and while in recent years they had turned inward and focused less on their race relations work, they had not completely abandoned it. They still courted African-American members and hosted an interracial summer camp. When local and national attention turned to race issues, these activities drew notice.

Once Koinonia came under attack, activists who considered themselves campaigners for racial justice and believers in "the Christian principle represented by integration" saw the farm as an example of that principle and rallied around it. Letters poured in praising the Koinonians' stand against segregation and applauding their approach to integration. Said one observer, "I believe in what I call 'opportunity of association,' i.e., get the races together in a day-to-day setting and race prejudice will drop away. I believe you are doing it." Another praised Koinonia for "seeking integration in the best sense of the word."[6] Ironically, Koinonia would not have considered what it was doing to be integration. The members associated that word with a coercive political and legal process and did not believe in pursuing change through these channels. Instead, they believed they were fostering interracial relationships within a community based on spiritual and material sharing. That interracial fellowship was part of a total reorientation of life. Despite frequent admonishments by Koinonians to their supporters to consider the total vision, however, the pacifist and communitarian aspects of their philosophy went unnoticed. Supporters misunderstood the nature and extent of Koinonia's interracialism and superimposed a contemporary vision of integration on the community's work.

This misunderstanding went unrecognized at first, as white liberals around the country responded to the crisis and came to the farm's aid in ways ranging from voicing moral support to arranging secret deliveries of supplies. Koinonia received letters nearly every day from men and women around the country who expressed their solidarity with the farm's witness: "Our school has been integrated for three years with no problem." "My family refrains from doing business with Jim Crow merchants." "I have preached plainly on the race question several times and a movement has started to get rid of me."[7] The writers did not explicitly ask for anything from the farm. These letters were brief statements, usually a few handwritten lines, expressing the writer's beliefs and sometimes accompanying a small donation. At times the authors might ask for more information or for advice on how to pursue their goals in their own life. Mostly, however, these people were looking for a chance to say, "We are fighting the same battle." This built bridges between them and Koinonia and gave them a sense of fighting together. This kinship helped each to carry on.

In addition to individuals, state and regional organizations voiced moral support for Koinonia. Church bodies and interdenominational groups of ministers passed resolutions condemning the violence and calling for an independent investigation.[8] The ecumenical nature of these groups revealed that religious people of various faiths supported Koinonia, not just those within its own denomination. In fact, at the height of the crisis, while most Southern Baptists—with the exception of a few liberals in particular convention bodies—ostracized Koinonians, other denominations and faiths embraced them. In the wake of the grand jury presentments against Koinonia, for example, clergy from several denominations joined forces to rescue the farm's reputation by issuing a statement denying the investigations' findings and asserting that Koinonia was a Christian community with no connection to the Communist Party. Even the Americus and Sumter County Ministerial Association adopted a resolution in support of the Koinonians' right to hold their opinions. Although the declaration did not exactly sanction Koinonia's beliefs, members of the farm appreciated the effort because it showed them that "all was not darkness."[9]

Besides writing letters or passing resolutions, many friends came to Koinonia in person to show their concern and help on the farm. Because of the crisis, Koinonia Farm had lost its labor pool of local blacks and needed people to work in the fields. To satisfy Koinonia's labor needs when individuals were not enough, organizations assembled groups of volunteers to participate in work camps at Koinonia. These groups usually numbered around fifteen. The workers came from as far away as Denver and the University of Hawaii. Sometimes they came as organized groups, and sometimes individuals came on their own, such as Lorraine Williams, an African-American schoolteacher from New York City. Most of the volunteers were white high school or college students. At Koinonia these young people worked in the fields, the kitchen, or wherever they were needed. Just as important, they shared in picnics, celebrations, Bible study, and at other times of fellowship in the life of the community.[10] In doing so they gained a taste of what it was like to live in a complete community, sharing not only ideals but resources, work, and worship.

While many of Koinonia's friends came to work on the farm, most helped from afar, offering varying types of assistance depending on their circumstances and the kind of influence they could bring to bear. Individuals around the country acted on their own initiative to find ways to stop the violence by appealing to law enforcement and government officials to protect the community. Appeals to Governor Griffin and other Georgia officials did not have much effect. Other friends aimed higher and wrote to President Eisenhower, asking him to take a position on the breakdown of law and order in southwest Georgia. Jordan himself wrote to the president asking him for help. Attorney General Herbert Brownell replied that under the Constitution the federal government had no responsibility for violence committed against private citizens and passed Jordan's letter along to the governor of Georgia. As one observer put it, this put the plea back into the "lap of the oppressors themselves."[11] The FBI also dodged Koinonia and its friends' pleas for help for a time, asserting that until a federal law had been broken it could do nothing.

Other friends took a different angle, intervening at the local level. Bill Hinley, a friend from Chicago who had grown up in Georgia, organized one such effort. He planned to send people into Sumter county to call on ministers, teachers, lodge presidents, and merchants. Koinonia approved of the plan as long as the visitors were not self-righteous. Hinley visited many people and reported on opinion in the nearby town, but he failed to change many people's positions.[12] In another attempt to stop the attacks, ministers from around the country came to Koinonia to stand vigil. They tried to organize a twenty-four-hour watch, hoping that the local people would not shoot at clergymen. In addition to stopping the violence, the ministers hoped to gain a "sense of identification" with Koinonia and experience in practicing nonviolence.[13] The violence was slacking off by the time the plan went into effect, however, and although many ministers visited Koinonia, no extensive vigil took place.

The interventions of outsiders backfired. Bill Hinley's and others' surveys of local opinion revealed that whites in Americus not only disapproved of Koinonia, they resented the farm's outside support. One man suggested that there might have been people either for Koinonia or indifferent, but at least "30 per cent hate them and are so mad they can't think or talk about anything else." Those who were more neutral would not risk their own reputations to help Koinonians. Most whites accepted the grand jury's conclusions, even with reservations. As Frank Sheffield told Hinley, "I do not believe they [Koinonians] are doing the violence. I do not believe they are communist. But I wouldn't be surprised if they were being used by communists." Others pointed to the money flowing in to Koinonia from the outside as evidence that they might not be sincere. Local people, moreover, unanimously disapproved of the intervention of outsiders, such as Hinley himself. The outsiders would "pour fuel on the flame" and cause more trouble. People should not question and cast aspersion on the grand jury, who were all "good honest men." The mayor even attacked Hinley, asking questions about his background and motives.[14] The Koinonians' supporters may have been trying to help by intervening with the local people, but instead they hurt them by confirming suspicions about the farm's "connections."

The outside community was more successful in giving Koinonia the material succor it needed to break the boycott and to survive financially. The most direct aid was in cash gifts. Koinonia received $14,518 in gifts in 1956, $37,044 in 1957, and $12,685 in 1958. Simultaneously, however, they lost all their crop and egg income, so despite the gifts they had net losses of $11,500, $9,341, and $9,374, respectively.[15] Also, since Koinonians could not get the bank loans on which a farming operation depends, friends attempted to secure grants for them from nonprofit foundations. Others tried to devise ways to get them alternate loans. One woman tried to deposit $1,500 of her own money in the Citizens Trust in Atlanta to encourage that bank to lend to Koinonia.[16] The financial support was one way people could invest in Koinonia's interracial experiment and act on their belief in integration.

As the boycott tightened around Koinonia, crippling its operations, friends scrambled to find markets for the farm's produce and to buy the materials it needed. Koinonia had tried and failed to maintain an egg market in Albany. Someone suggested trying the same thing in Montgomery, through the Montgomery Improvement Association. Other friends tried to get Koinonia the supplies it needed for the farm. Several prominent businessmen wrote to the heads of oil and gas companies to pressure them to sell to Koinonia.[17] For seed and fertilizer Koinonia eventually turned to their friends with influence in the government. Seed and supply merchants had government contracts to deal with farmers using Agricultural Department purchasing orders. Because this was a federal program, the dealers were technically barred from discriminating. Yet Koinonia still had to bring pressure to bear on officials to have the orders honored. Eventually Eleanor Roosevelt intervened to get the official order for merchants to sell to them.[18]

Some of Koinonia's more daring friends "ran the boycott" to get them the supplies they needed. Individuals brought supplies in by night and took Koinonia products to places as far away as St. Petersburg, Florida. One women drove all the way from New England with three bags of fertilizer in the back of her station wagon. Koinonia cryptically referred to this operation as the "airlift at Shangri-la" in their newsletter because they were afraid to reveal the names and locations of their customers and suppliers. Koinonia's coconspirators in this operation felt the consequences. When the Reverend Robert McNeil tried to buy some fertilizer for Koinonia in Phoenix City, Alabama, the Board of Deacons of his church charged him with making the purchase under false pretenses, which they considered a traitorous act.[19] Yet people braved the scorn or reprimand of their peers, because supplying the farm was the most direct way to keep Koinonia alive.

One of the most creative ways in which people helped Koinonia was by signing up to support the Christian Brotherhood insurance plan. The program was a response to the most dangerous aspect of the boycott, the farm's inability to get insurance. By February 1957 it risked losing its mortgage if it did not find new coverage.[20] To solve this problem, while tapping into the wealth of support being offered, Koinonians devised their own insurance plan. In this program supporters could pledge fifty dollars or more; in the event of loss, Koinonia would call in a percentage of the pledge to cover it. Koinonians recognized that the pledges did not represent a legal commitment and asserted that anyone making a pledge would be free to pull out later. They expected, however, that their friends would be willing to make good on their promises. By the end of May, Koinonia had received fifteen hundred pledges for a total of $75,000.[21]

Besides the practical benefits of providing coverage, the Christian Brotherhood insurance plan appealed to Koinonians philosophically and strengthened the bonds between them and their network of supporters. Koinonians had been uncomfortable depending on for-profit companies to provide insurance. Earlier, while they debated the nature of community, they had argued against having life insurance policies because they believed that they should trust the group to take care of each member as part of the economic sharing. In addition, their Christian faith told them to trust that the Lord would provide. But their supporters in the ideological community were left out of this economic sharing and sense of mutual responsibility. The Christian Brotherhood plan separated Koinonia from commercial insurance and thus relieved its concerns about dependence on such a profit-motivated enterprise. Moreover, the plan allowed the wider community to participate in economic sharing with Koinonia, giving people a way to join in the farm's struggle and have a stake in its survival.

Another device Koinonia used to circumvent the local boycott was the mail-order business for its products. It started after the roadside market was bombed, when Koinonia needed to get rid of its damaged products quickly. The members put an advertisement in the newsletter to sell scorched hams at low cost, and the response was overwhelming. Because there was such a demand, Koinonia decided to make the sale a regular feature of its business. When the boycott tightened and destroyed Koinonia's ability to produce enough to make the business work, it had to find a new product. At that time, an elderly couple from Albany, Salvatore and Antoinette Tavollaci, were planning to retire from their pecan-processing business. They sold their equipment to Koinonia and taught the members how to shell and grade the nuts. The plant could operate despite the boycott because the power supply came from a Rural Electrification Administration line and thus could not be cut by local officials. Koinonians could bid for the pecans anonymously because they were sold by auction, and they could market the nuts through the mail and not have to depend on local customers. To get the new operation off the ground, Koinonia asked for loans from its friends of twenty-five dollars each at 4 percent interest and began marketing the nuts through the newsletter.[22]

The pecan business was very much like the Christian Brotherhood insurance plan in that it joined Koinonia to the wider community through economic sharing and common effort. Through the loans people helped Koinonia to set up the business and shared the risk that it might fail. By purchasing, and more important, by reselling the products, Koinonia's friends kept the operation going. The latter activity was more significant because by selling the nuts, people were participating in the business. The financial benefits of this operation for Koinonia were great. Perhaps most important, it blurred the boundaries between the inner Koinonia community that shared work and resources completely and the external community that heretofore had only shared ideas. The results included an expanded idea of economic sharing, a way for people to invest financially in Koinonia's witness, and a demonstration of Koinonia's ability to adapt to new circumstances while maintaining its basic principles.

By the middle of 1957, so many groups and individuals had rallied around Koinonia that there needed to be some kind of coordination of efforts. John Thomas of Ringoes, New Jersey, had been informally organizing the efforts to fulfill Koinonia's financial needs. Con Browne suggested that Koinonia give the mailing list and fund-raising duties to a group of friends, so that Koinonia itself could concentrate on internal matters and work. Jordan hesitated because he believed it was important to keep in close touch with all of Koinonia's supporters.[23] They compromised. Koinonians would recruit more members so they could do the work themselves, while allowing an organization to form to help them in the meantime. In March 1957 about twenty-five people, including Jordan and Harry Atkinson, met in Pittsburgh to make plans for the formation of a council to handle clerical work and act as a clearinghouse for Koinonia's supporters. The Friends of Koinonia (FOK), as it was called, would be a contact point for people interested in helping Koinonia, would handle the farm's correspondence, and would keep people informed of the community's needs. In addition, they helped individuals in various states set up Koinonia committees or local chapters of the FOK to "mobilize interest and support of this dynamic witness to justice and brotherhood."[24] The FOKs gave institutional form to the ideological community. In the process they shaped the network into a so-

cial movement with an organizational base and coordination, a purpose—
to help Koinonia maintain its witness—and various methods for acting.

Some of the groups that came to the farm's aid were civil rights organizations, attracted expressly by its identification as a witness for integration.
The members of these groups saw Koinonia as part of a broader social
movement in which they were all working for better race relations. The
Congress of Racial Equality called on its members to support Koinonia, for
example, because of its like-mindedness in pioneering "nonviolence in
combating racial discrimination." The farm's dilemma, according to the
spokesman of the Macon Council on Human Relations, was an immediate
problem which had to be solved in the pursuit of the longer-range goal: better race relations.[25] To aid Koinonia, regional and national groups such as
the Southern Conference Education Fund, Americans for Democratic Action, and American Civil Liberties Union publicized the situation, invited
farm members to speak at their meetings, and circulated requests for gifts
or pledges. Several Human Relations Councils voiced support. The Southern Regional Council helped by providing legal advice, advertising the insurance program, and coordinating supply operations.[26] Koinonia worked
most closely with the Highlander Folk School. The cooperation began with
the summer camp and continued with joint efforts in sponsoring workshops. Koinonians helped choose the speakers for some of these meetings at
Highlander, and individual members led sessions. The cooperation made
the two groups, in Koinonia's words, "blood cousins."[27] However, as CORE
pointed out, the interest of these organizations was "strictly in the race relations field," and they did not share the Christian emphasis of the farm or
the commitment to complete sharing.[28] Koinonians welcomed the relationship with these organizations, although they began to feel uneasy about
the narrowness of its base.

The relationship between Koinonians and the outside community had a
variety of meanings for the people involved. While Koinonians benefited
materially and psychically from its membership in the wider fellowship,
their supporters gained moral reinforcement and a sense of participation in
a common struggle. Many people who were fighting individual battles
against race prejudice felt isolated and turned to Koinonia for the reassurance that they were not alone. Requesting the opportunity to visit, one
young man wrote: "We want to believe that there are some solutions [to the

race problem], some who are not afraid to put their dreams into the reality of the world."[29] The very fact of Koinonia's existence and witness gave solace to many, reassuring them they were not the only "white southerner who feels this way."[30] This affirmation helped people strengthen their convictions and rededicate themselves to acting on their beliefs. One visitor wrote after his departure, "I left in an inspired daze." He then met a young woman in South Carolina who was upset at the way southerners were "degenerating" into animals. After having visited Koinonia he felt he could confidently assure her that there were open minds and positive witnesses in the South.[31]

In addition to moral reinforcement, Koinonia gave to people an opportunity to do something about their beliefs. In particular, friends outside the South looked to Koinonia for ways to participate in the struggle for racial equality. There had been a few outlets for direct action in the North. For example, the Catholic Worker group engaged in yearly civil disobedience against air-raid drills to protest the arms race. In addition, CORE had been attacking discrimination in public accommodations in the upper Midwest. Yet by 1957 the latter organization's energy was dissipating, in part due to its success in combating segregation.[32] By this time the *Brown* decision, the Montgomery bus boycott, and the violence in the Little Rock schools drew the attention of white liberals to the South as the arena for civil rights work. Koinonia's friends felt frustrated by their distance from the action and, although they were not on the "front lines" in rural Georgia, wanted to do something to help the nonviolent movement of African Americans. One woman declared, "Many of us in the 'pristine' North are not 'leaving the South to settle its own problems'"; they were looking for something to do. For many of them helping Koinonia to maintain its witness was not merely goodwilled charity, it was a way to act on their beliefs in racial justice.[33] By giving people some way to express their sympathies, Koinonia helped a loose network of white, primarily religious but also some secular, liberals coalesce into a movement for supporting early integration efforts.

During this time Koinonians and people in the civil rights community developed reciprocal supportive relationships. Koinonians had a long-standing friendship with the African-American leaders in Montgomery. During the boycott they wrote to the white Lutheran minister who was helping the Montgomery Improvement Association, saying, "We are in complete sympathy with the work you are doing . . . and think of the people in Montgomery often." After the boycott Ralph Abernathy and Martin Luther King Jr. asked Clarence Jordan to speak at their churches in the hope that he would help the people of Montgomery to "take new courage and be inspired to do greater work."[34] Because Koinonians knew so many sympathizers of civil rights, people turned to them for help in publicizing their own efforts. Jordan used the Koinonia mailing list to try to drum up subscriptions and other material aid for his friend P. D. East, editor of the *Petal Paper,* who was being ostracized for his integrationist views. Anne Braden asked Jordan to be a petitioner for clemency for her husband after his conviction for contempt of the House Un-American Activities Committee. Sarah Patton Boyle, an advocate of school integration in Virginia, summed up the debt of these civil rights activists when she wrote to Clarence Jordan, "I haven't told you how much your unconscious witnessing did for my inner being."[35] This close cooperation was based on shared concern about race relations and justice. However, it masked the differences in overall philosophy and approach. This misunderstanding would influence the farm over the next decade, as Koinonians considered their debt to these friends in decisions about their future, and supporters meanwhile expected members to participate in particular ways in the civil rights movement.

The relationship between Koinonians and their outside supporters also created tension within the community as the members debated how to relate to their friends. Early in the crisis they were unsure whether to accept help from outsiders at all. At that time Florence Jordan had called for self-sufficiency, and Clarence Jordan had argued that the long-range objective was worth cooperating with others.[36] As the crisis continued, and people on the outside saw Koinonia only as a witness for racial brotherhood, the overall meaning of the experiment was in danger of being lost. Individuals wanted to join the farm only to work on improving race relations. One group explicitly asked if it could come "with a concern about helping the community because of their interest in the race problem while differing on the economic arrangement and with the full intention of leaving after a specified period."[37] Koinonia discouraged such seekers. They reminded their friends that "we are not witnessing to brotherhood alone. It [Koinonia] is a total reorientation of values—nonviolence, complete sharing and complete openness."[38] Harry Atkinson worried that depending so much on people with no interest in community jeopardized Koinonia's spiritual fellowship. Others at Koinonia preferred for people to come interested in sharing work, resources, and all aspects of life but would not turn away those only interested in race.[39] Eventually they found themselves debating whether it was even worth the risk to life and property, not to mention Christian fellowship and their broader philosophy, to stay in southwest Georgia.

Koinonia's participation in the community of civil rights advocates in the late 1950s had short- and long-term consequences for its history. The material aid in a very real sense enabled the farm to survive. Members were willing to adapt their way of life and work to incorporate aid from outsiders who wanted to help. Because of their reliance on outsiders, however, Koinonians felt a debt to them. When it came time to decide whether to stay in southwest Georgia, Koinonians considered whether they could abandon the witness their friends had contributed so much to protect.

For the longer term, the relationship with outsiders raised a dilemma which would plague Koinonia for nearly a decade. The wider community saw Koinonia as an experiment in integration and thus a demonstration for civil rights. The outsiders did not understand Koinonia's Christian communalism, which included along with interracialism total sharing and the effort to live as a disciple. Civil rights advocates, focused as they were on legal and political reform, also did not truly understand Koinonia's challenge, through its cooperatives and effort to build African-American self-sufficiency, to the economic support of the caste system. This misunderstanding of the nature of Koinonia's approach for bringing about change would cause conflict between the community and the civil rights movement and would shape Koinonia's participation in it. More important, the relationship to supporters forced Koinonians to face differences between their own goal of Christian interracialism and the more secular liberal goal of civil rights. How could they support the movement for rights while being true to their own broader principles?

7

To Bear Witness

IN LATE 1957 the crisis at Koinonia reached its climax as the tensions caused by local opposition, violence, and new relationships with the wider community came to a head. The longer the group had to endure violence and economic attack, the more exhaustion, strain, and short tempers weakened its inner fellowship. By the fall of 1957 the attacks had diminished its ability to fulfill its goals and, more important, had damaged the Koinonians' communal spirit to the point that some thought it might not survive. Koinonia had repeatedly been forced to respond to pressure from hostile quarters to move out of the area. Now friends and even members urged the group to abandon the dangerous situation. It seemed to face a choice: stay in southwest Georgia to stand up for the right to live and work with African Americans or go somewhere else to establish a Christian fellowship in peace. The dilemma brought to the surface tensions within Koinonia related to fundamental questions about its identity and purpose: Was it a Christian community dedicated to the complete reordering of life according to the New Testament, which included accepting all Christians as brothers and sisters? Or was it a witness for integration? Complicating the question was Koinonia's relationship with, and sense of responsibility to, the external community. This relationship, as well as the Koinonians' desire to be in southwest Georgia to witness during the civil rights movement, tilted the balance in the debate.

The events leading to the discussions of priorities began in early 1957, when Koinonians decided to send some members to Hidden Springs, New Jersey, to develop a community there. This experiment grew out of the need to get the Angry family away from the danger in Georgia. Rufus and Sue Angry and their children had been living at Koinonia since 1954 and were on their way to becoming the first African-American full members. Once the violence started, however, Rufus Angry's friends and relatives became frightened that something might happen to him and pleaded with him to leave the community. When he became so tense that his wife feared he might have a breakdown, Koinonians decided to send the family on a vacation. Friends in Kentucky and at Hidden Springs offered to take the Angrys in. Sue Angry decided to go to New Jersey to be near her kin in the Northeast. Koinonians expected that because there was no overt racial crisis in New Jersey, the family could live there undisturbed. Not wanting to send the Angrys alone, they arranged to send another family. The Atkinsons volunteered to go because Allene was suffering from the anxiety at the farm.[1] By mid-February, Koinonians had made the arrangements and both families had arrived at their new home.

As soon as the Atkinsons and Angrys arrived in New Jersey, they began to try to create a koinonia there. The previous owners had developed Hidden Springs, a 120-acre plot in Branchburg Township, for cooperative farming. At first the two families lived apart because of a housing shortage. The Angrys stayed briefly in two rooms in the big house on the property, then moved into an adjacent apartment. Until they could arrange something better, the Atkinsons lived with John Thomas, a friend of Koinonia's in nearby Ringoes. To make up for the distance between their residences, the group worked out communal dining and work arrangements. At the same time, the Koinonians began building bridges to the local community. They sent their children to the local schools, where the Angrys were the first black students in the district. The Koinonians had a friend on the school board who forestalled any negative reaction by building sympathy for the family as refugees from the South. The newcomers also joined the local Baptist church, having been assured that the Angrys would be welcome in the formerly all-white congregation. Harry Atkinson started negotiations to buy the Hidden Springs property, and by early April, Koinonia gave him instructions to complete the purchase. By then, the Atkinsons and the Angrys had established themselves in their new home and were preparing to "operate a community" there.[2]

But was establishing a community the purpose of this excursion into the Northeast? Before it started, the trip was supposed to be only a brief vacation from the tension in Georgia. Almost as soon as the refugees arrived in Hidden Springs, however, Koinonians started talking about establishing it as a permanent outlet for their products and as a refuge for people to get away from the violence. In this scenario the purpose of Hidden Springs was essentially to help the Georgia farm survive. Throughout the term of the New Jersey group's existence, Koinonians always referred to it publicly as a colony. On the other hand, at one point Koinonia privately proposed that Hidden Springs could become a future sister community, which would "be integrated financially" with its Georgian counterpart so that the two "would be one Koinonia, working closely together."[3] For a brief period Koinonians considered setting up a system like the Brüderhof's, in which several colonies were physically separate but spiritually and economically one community. The difference between this private speculation and the public pronouncements showed that from the beginning there was confusion about whether the New Jersey colony was a sister community of equal status or a survival strategy for the Koinonia in Georgia.

For a time, however, this question remained in the background as the Hidden Springs group worked toward both becoming a community and funneling aid to the Georgia group. The people who had been living on the Hidden Springs property joined the community. In addition, the farm sent some of its members, including John Gabor and Chris and Jeanette Drescher, so that by July there were twenty people in the new colony.[4] With the hope of becoming economically self-sufficient, the group immediately started farming and set up a leather-working shop. Meanwhile, the members began making contacts to get support for the Georgia group. Harry and Allene Atkinson spoke at several local churches and at special women's group or brotherhood meetings. The local press interviewed the Angrys, the only black family in the township, thus publicizing both the New Jersey Koinonia and the Georgia situation from which the family had fled. The *New York Times* covered the story as well, referring to the farm as "a community under fire because it includes Negro families" and making it familiar to a wider audience. The publicity won some sympathy for the Hidden

Springs group, and they began meeting with both their new and longtime supporters, especially in the Friends of Koinonia.[5]

Very soon after the establishment of the New Jersey colony, however, opposition to it began building among the local people. The Angry family, being the first blacks in the township, aroused suspicion. Their neighbors were afraid that Koinonia would bring in large numbers of African Americans. To their dismay Koinonians, like later civil rights activists, found that while northerners might criticize southerners for their racial practices, they did not necessarily support integration in their own backyard.[6] The opposition to the community's interracial fellowship took a legal form. In late spring 1957, the community found out that zoning laws restricted commercial business in its area. These laws meant that Koinonia could not sell anything but its own farm products, ruling out the leather business and the processing of Georgia pecan products. In addition, building codes prohibited further housing expansion. The New Jersey group petitioned the local zoning board for an exemption, but at the public hearing neighbors confronted it with hostile questions. This local opposition influenced the board to turn down the community's request.[7]

Left by the zoning decision without an independent means of support, the New Jersey group scrambled to find ways to pay its bills. It seemed the Koinonians in the North faced the same problem as the Georgia farm: opposition to their racial beliefs undermined their economic viability. At first the men contracted themselves out to work for a prefabricated housing business. The group also rented a processing plant in Newark so that it could prepare and market Georgia pecans. Some members moved back to Georgia, hoping to alleviate some of the economic stress at Hidden Springs. By the late autumn only the Atkinsons and Angrys remained in New Jersey. Yet, despite all the efforts to find a stable economic base, the New Jersey Koinonia's financial status continued to weaken. The Friends of Koinonia in Philadelphia and the community in Georgia helped it with donations, so the two families could get by for a while and pay for processing equipment. But in December, when they were unable to make the first payment on the property, the financial problem reached a crisis.[8] The boycott in Georgia had left that group unable to carry the New Jersey community. By the end of the year local opposition along with legal and financial trouble forced Koinonians to decide whether it was possible for the New Jersey group to continue.

The fate of Hidden Springs sparked a larger discussion because, instead of admitting defeat and moving home to Georgia, the people there fought to keep their colony open and to change the Georgia Koinonia's priorities. The Atkinsons, Dreschers, and Gabor considered the New Jersey Koinonia to be a budding community and wanted more time and support so that it could develop. The Atkinsons, speaking for the group, argued that they had "poured heart and soul into starting a new Koinonia here" and had believed that had been the intention of all the members. They accused the Georgians of undermining their attempt to build a community. From their point of view, the New Jersey group had generously sent the Dreschers and Gabor to help with the harvest at the farm in Georgia, leaving the Atkinsons and Angrys alone to deal with the legal problems. Moreover, they charged that Koinonia had undercut the northern processing and marketing operation by not shipping nuts and other supplies. To them, the New Jersey group was as important as Koinonia Farm and deserved as much attention and resources as it needed to survive. They reminded their friends in Georgia that Koinonia had not been self-supporting for years and asked that they be allowed to exist for a while on the help of friends and by the grace of God.[9]

Despite these pleas for a chance to continue, the Georgia Koinonians decided that Hidden Springs was too much of a financial burden and moved to close it. They denied sabotaging the operation. On the contrary, they asserted that they had done their best to keep the colony alive. They had invested more than $15,000 in the project and sent some of the best people there to keep it going. The legal situation, however, seemed to prevent Hidden Springs from ever becoming self-supporting; thus, it could never be more than a burden on the Georgia group. In December, Clarence Jordan went to New Jersey to announce the decision that the group there should not continue as a community, leaving open the chance that they could find a way to keep it as a place of refuge.[10]

The closing of the Hidden Springs colony had profound consequences for Koinonia. Most obviously, Koinonia Farm lost its outpost in the Northeast and the close contact with its supporters there that the New Jersey group had established. The closing also deprived the farm of its potential market outlet and refuge for members. More important, when Hidden Springs was abandoned, Koinonia lost some of its members. The Angrys refused to return to the farm in Georgia because Rufus could not stand the pressure, and Sue did not want to subject her children to the poor, segregated Georgia schools.[11] When the family decided to move to Pennsylvania, Koinonia lost two of its African-American members, which was a blow to its self-identity as an "interracial community." The Atkinsons also refused to go back to Georgia. Allene Atkinson hesitated to face the violence again. Moreover, the couple had deep concerns about the community spirit at Koinonia, which they believed suffered from the tense situation in Sumter County. The Atkinsons warned that unless Koinonia took drastic steps to solve these problems, they would leave the community and go to the Brüderhof. To rescue their Christian fellowship, they asserted, Koinonians needed to move out of southwest Georgia.

The Atkinsons' suggestion opened a far-reaching debate and brought to the surface long-standing uncertainties about Koinonia's priorities. The decision over whether Koinonia should leave Sumter County involved a larger question: What was the purpose of the community? Those who urged Koinonia to leave did so because they believed it was the only way to preserve the community's Christian fellowship and sharing. Those who wanted the group to stay in Sumter County argued that it was vital that the community preserve its witness for the principle of racial brotherhood. The New Jersey Koinonia debate also raised the question of identity. Was Koinonia more committed to the principle of racial brotherhood or to the fellowship of total Christian community? One observer stated the choice bluntly: "Is the community working for desegregation . . . or is the purpose to demonstrate what genuine Christian community can be? If it's the former, then you should stay in Americus, if it's the latter, then you could do so anywhere."[12]

There was no doubt or disagreement that the community in Georgia was in danger in many ways. Gunfire threatened people's lives, economic survival was far from certain, and the fellowship of the group suffered from tension and overwork. Margaret Wittkamper complained that "we are so busy with survival we don't have time to minister," and the whole group agreed that the members needed more opportunity for worship and prayer. By the summer of 1957 almost all the members admitted to a lack of unity and despair at the possibility of improvement.[13] The farm began losing long-term members, some due to personal problems exacerbated by the inability of the group to solve them. John and Iola Eustice had marital trouble, for example, and the community had not been able to help them with it. John considered leaving because he felt Koinonia was being too rigid, too fundamentalist. For her part, Iola left because she could not abide Koinonia's opposition to divorce and its insistence that it knew God's will for her. In another case Norman Long fought with Clarence Jordan and, over time, withdrew from community activities. Some at Koinonia suggested that his homosexuality affected his relationship with the group. They, and he, could not agree, however, on whether his sexuality was a group or individual "problem." Long left Koinonia with the issue unresolved.[14] These personal problems would have taxed any community. They were made worse at Koinonia because members were too busy struggling for survival to have the time and energy to work them out.

The Atkinsons spoke for the group that advocated leaving southwest Georgia when they argued that preserving the Christian fellowship should outweigh all other concerns. They urged fellow members to strive to attain a maximum of openness in the relationship and unity in their beliefs. To accomplish that, they had to fix the damage done by the tension and address the reasons that people were feeling estranged. That meant focusing on relationships, not outreach. Harry Atkinson asserted that Koinonians put too much emphasis on individual interpretations of different parts of the Christian message, such as brotherhood, pacifism, integration, and service. Because of this attachment they were unwilling to submit to God's will or the group consensus.[15] With this argument Atkinson showed that at least some Koinonians recognized the tension inherent in their goals—too much focus on one could undermine the success of the others. Furthermore, he also got to the heart of one of Koinonia's major problems in the 1950s and 1960s: indecision about which area should have priority. Should they be primarily an inward-looking community focused on relationships or an outward-looking witness with particular goals to accomplish? Atkinson was one who believed that it was not Koinonia's role to be involved in particular social issues, not even the fight for integration. The community was far too weak to do that by itself. Moreover, the witness could have no effect because "goodness is never forced on anyone who does not want it."[16] Koinonia's purpose, therefore, was to be a Christian community, sharing completely not only in finances and work but in spirit. If they had to leave Sumter County to preserve that, they should.

For the Atkinsons, Dreschers, and John Gabor, it was easy to envision leaving southwest Georgia, because they were already physically and, to an extent, emotionally estranged from the farm. First, they felt separated from the Georgia location, having been in New Jersey for a few months and having spent energy developing a community there. In addition, before they had gone north, they had spent less time at Koinonia than some others had. Chris and Jeanette Drescher had joined Koinonia, after earlier extended visits, in December 1956. That same month John Gabor had arrived for his intended permanent stay at the community. Although the Atkinsons had originally come to Koinonia in 1944, they had moved on and off the farm several times. Besides having less time and energy invested in Georgia, this faction also had prior doubts about the success of the community there. John Gabor would have preferred Koinonia to be more spartan and withdrawn from the world. For example, when Koinonia bought a television, which he considered a sinful toy that distracted people and gave visitors the impression that the community was not serious, he threatened that either it or he would have to go.[17] The Atkinsons had long-standing doubts about the community's openness, unity, and ability to solve its interpersonal problems. They had been among those who wanted to model Koinonia on the Brüderhof pattern. In the Hidden Springs controversy, they continued to look to the Brothers for help in reviving Koinonia's spirituality. Thus, the group that urged Koinonia to leave southwest Georgia already had felt separated from both the land and the community there before the Hidden Springs debate began.

Some friends in the wider community agreed with this faction and pleaded for Koinonia to move out of Georgia and save itself. They were realistically concerned for the safety of the people at the farm. The Brüderhof, for example, urged Koinonians to come north if things got worse. Some of their friends were victims of the misconception that race was a southern problem from which they could run away. Gross Alexander of California suggested that they relocate to the West because they would not find there as much "racism and prejudice as in the deep South." After all, their friends reminded them, Christ had instructed Paul that if he found he was not received in one locality, he should go to another.[18] Other communities in history have pulled up roots and departed when local hostility threatened them, including the Shakers, Mormons, and Koinonia's sometime role models, the Brüderhof and Hutterites. Friends urged Koinonians to follow these examples and focus on preserving the Christian fellowship rather than on the issue of race relations. Some even argued that Koinonia could not be effective in the fight for integration because people would soon stop supporting a group that seemed near collapse. Moreover, the issue of integration would be solved "slowly and legally," they said, and thus Koinonia should not commit itself to stay in that location to work on it.[19]

Excepting these few voices, however, most of Koinonia's friends considered the farm to be primarily a witness for racial brotherhood and supported it as such. One friend said, "It [Koinonia] attracted enemies in part because it was a demonstration, long before the segregation [*Brown*] decisions, that integration works. It has become a rallying point for those who want to retard desegregation as it has for those who want to see desegregation advanced."[20] Because these friends saw the farm as an important experiment in integration, they tried to keep it alive, in particular by donating large sums of money. Others gave their time and energy to work on the farm and help it survive. The cash gifts, insurance program, and volunteer labor tied the network to the community and gave people around the country a stake in Koinonia's future.

The Koinonians who stayed in Georgia were tempted to escape. Earlier in the year they had debated whether to leave because of local pressure. At that time Allene Atkinson had proposed leaving if things got worse while Margaret Wittkamper called it a testing time and insisted the witness go on. Jordan, for his part, showed a desire to stay but was open to the will of the group. The consensus had been to wait and see but leave open the option of moving as a body. A few months later they considered deeding their property to the National Council of Churches or the American Baptist Convention so that they could escape, though they did not follow up on that plan.[21] By the summer those still at Koinonia continued to express some reservations about staying. Con Browne admitted that they worried "whether we are letting the integration issue control our witness" too much. With so many African-American friends breaking their ties with them because of the violence, their fellowship was scarcely interracial anyway. Furthermore, they worried that as the physical and spiritual tensions at the farm made people leave, the population would drop so low that it could not sustain itself economically. More important, could they call themselves a community if only a few people remained?[22] Clarence Jordan considered moving the community elsewhere because he took to heart Christ's admonition to his disciples that they should leave places where they were not accepted. While they debated the issue, Koinonians made preliminary investigation into other sites in California, Florida, and Michigan, where they thought prejudice would not be as great.[23]

Just as the Atkinsons, Dreschers, and John Gabor had reasons for feeling estranged from the Georgia locale and being willing to relocate for the sake of community, others had experiences and concerns that inclined them to stay. The main spokespeople for the Georgia group were the Jordans, Brownes, Wittkampers, and Ross Anderson. The three families had invested years in the farm; the Jordans had lived there since the beginning, the Brownes since 1949, and the Wittkampers since 1953. Margaret Wittkamper spoke for her family when she said they just did not want to move again. Con and Ora Browne had built bridges to the local white community and, once the shock of isolation wore off, steeled themselves to fight to get them back. Moreover, they believed in sticking with a problem and working it out. The sense of obligation to their friends and the witness for equality weighed particularly heavily on the Jordans. Lastly, Ross Anderson, a new but influential member, was especially concerned about Koinonia's social witness and wanted to stay where the action was.[24]

Beyond these individual reasons, the Georgia Koinonians stayed because they recognized their significance in the racial struggles of Sumter County and the South. They felt some responsibility to continue to witness to their neighbors. In part they remained to "be agents of reconciliation among these people divided by racism."[25] Moreover, they were concerned about the effect of their decision on the blacks and whites around the South who were taking a stand against discrimination. Almost against their will they had become a rallying point. Even if their effort for change in the South was small and faltering, they did not want to give up and let anyone down.[26] They wrote to the Atkinsons that whether they liked it or not, "every one of the nonviolent movements in the South looks to us as an example of some white folks who care." They were unwilling to flee and "hide their light" because of their sense of obligation to the civil rights network and their own belief in racial progress.[27]

The Koinonians who remained in Georgia did so, in addition, for their own spiritual well-being, which they felt would have been lost if they had sacrificed their principles. Their desire to live in "full Christian brotherhood" was too strong for them to give up the fight so easily.[28] Even if conditions made it impossible for the time being for the members to live and share completely with African Americans, the group decided that it must remain as a witness for the ideal of racial brotherhood and the hope that someday people could live together as Christians regardless of race. To give themselves the strength to endure in the meantime, Koinonians focused on their Christian purpose. To Koinonians belief meant "by-life"; to really practice their faith they must act on their principles in daily life, sacrificing everything if they must. And if things should get worse, "Well, we're not the first Christians who would have died for what they believe," Florence Jordan once said, "and we won't be the last."[29]

The crisis was a turning point in the life of the community, with the debate over Hidden Springs as the fulcrum. The pressure brought out the inherent strains within Koinonia's program, making it increasingly difficult to balance the different goals. The attacks undermined its activities, including the agricultural coops and vacation Bible school. The violence forced many of the African-American residents to leave, lessening the interracial character of the community. The internal fellowship of the remaining whites was also weakened by sheer exhaustion. As Atkinson pointed out, the focus on particular issues—in this case integration—was undercutting the unity of the group. Koinonians would have to sacrifice either the health of their inner fellowship or their witness on race relations. Even though they had discouraged their supporters from seeing them only as an integrationist movement, when the chips were down Koinonians dedicated all their resources to preserving their interracial witness. They chose this direction because of their commitment to racial brotherhood and sense of obligation to others who shared that belief and because of their desire to stand up for their Christian principles.

Although this seemed to settle the question for the short term, the debate had made clear the potential incompatibility of their goals and the remaining problems between members. Some Koinonians left, including the Atkinsons, Angrys, and others.[30] On the other hand, those who remained were strengthened in their resolve to maintain their interracial life as much as possible in the face of violence. Even those who stayed, however, continued to show some ambivalence about the decision. In their minds they were not completely giving up the ideals of Christian community. "We feel that it is still a community witness and that things are at this time focusing on this particular aspect [race] of our witness, just as it focused on pacifism during the last war," wrote Con and Ora Browne.[31] In other words, the issue was not resolved. Koinonians went into their next decade still uncertain about their identity and how to act upon their at times contradictory goals.

The events of this period raised the issue of the relationship between community, interracial brotherhood, and civil rights. Koinonians realized the difficulty of maintaining an interracial community and balancing a viable fellowship with an interracial witness, under pressure. As important in raising this issue was the nature of the friendship between Koinonians and civil rights activists. Although based on a shared goal of racial justice, their cooperation masked significant differences. Specifically, Koinonia's friends did not understand or relate to the farm's communalism or pacifism. Koinonians and their friends were able to work together and reinforced each other in the hostile climate of the post-*Brown* years. And Koinonia's sense of indebtedness kept the members from leaving southern Georgia when the pressure was at its most intense. But although Koinonia signaled its intention to stay in the South and work with the civil rights community, the members had not reconciled their differences in philosophy and method, nor had they decided for themselves how they could cooperate within the confines of their beliefs. As the movement picked up momentum around them and focused on other issues such as voting rights, Koinonians were left to decide what role their community would or could play.

Part 3

New Challenges,
New Directions,
1958–68

8

Wandering in the Desert

THE KOINONIANS' decision to remain in southwest Georgia left many of the questions raised by the crisis unresolved. In just a few years, their lives and program had been drastically changed. When the farm was first founded, members had pursued a well-defined outreach program, based on then contemporary models in agricultural extension and Christian missions, relatively unhindered by outside pressures or financial limitations. Now, African Americans could no longer safely work with them, and local hostility had put an end to the Monday evening agricultural classes, vacation Bible school, and interracial summer camp. Besides, their program of interracial fellowship and agricultural education no longer addressed African-American needs, nor was it enough to bring about better relationships in the climate of the new decade. Finally, the Koinonians' financial situation prevented them from doing very much of their own farming. Once the crisis began to cool down, they turned their attention to reviving both their external outreach and inner community. In doing so, they faced problems in finances, member transience, relevancy of their program, and contradictions between communalism and interracialism. The two basic issues with which they wrestled were how to live together as Christians while cooperating with friends in civil rights and peace movements, and what place their own social concerns had in their common life. Through the early 1960s Koinonians confronted this dilemma by prioritizing their goals and eventually making major changes in their life together.

As the violence abated, Koinonians tried to resurrect their early program of agricultural education and aid for African Americans, Christian missions, and living in community. In the first area they confronted both their own financial difficulties and changes in the rural economy around them. Their first task was to rebuild the farm financially and physically. During the worst years of the crisis, the destruction of property, start-up costs of the mail-order business, investment into Hidden Springs, and legal fees had put them over $30,000 in debt. During that time gifts and loans from friends had not been able to cover all their losses. In 1959 the situation improved a little when they showed their first profit and could pay back some of their debts. In order to put themselves on a more viable economic footing, Koinonians experimented with a combination of new products and agricultural schemes. By 1961 the transition from poultry to pecans had been completed, and Koinonia began earning as much from selling nuts as they previously had from eggs. The farm also expanded into new areas of agriculture, such as pine trees and cattle. To develop a herd by 1968, they invested in replacing row crops with coastal Bermuda grass and laying an irrigation system. The Koinonians' problems were far from over, however. Most of these new ventures would not yield profits for several years. In the meantime they continued to operate in what Jan Jordan later called "a survival mode."[1]

The Koinonians' struggling effort to revive their agricultural program took place in a much changed economic climate. The agricultural extension work, which was so successful in the early years, never recovered to its pre-crisis level. In part, the members simply lacked the time and energy to organize classes in farm techniques because they were too busy just trying to stay financially afloat. More important, economic and social changes in Sumter County rendered the earlier farm program obsolete. Sharecropping and tenantry had declined significantly after the Second World War and were replaced by "agribusiness." As a result, according to census data of 1960 and 1970, the number of black men engaged in agricultural work declined by half over the course of the decade. In addition, Americus and Sumter County were trying to shift from agriculture to industry.[2] Koinonia's program seemed increasingly "out of step with the economic life of the time."[3] As one friend said to them, "The technique you devised to do good for one particular time may not necessarily still be valuable."[4]

Although they gave up much of their former agricultural education work, Koinonians were still able to provide material aid and some independence to African Americans. They began to reestablish contact with their neighbors by providing charity to poor families. At first, many local African Americans continued to fear association with the farm. In early 1958 only one black family visited regularly.[5] But later that year the thaw in hostility against them allowed Koinonians to have relations with their neighbors in relative safety again. They visited elderly couples, took food and water to a man who was paralyzed and a woman with a broken leg, and built a stove for a local family. In their monthly newsletter Koinonians declared that "being able to work with these people again without reprisals is a relief and a joy."[6] Koinonia's outside supporters bolstered the charity work. During the crisis they had publicized the conditions of their African-American friends. As a result, a flood of donations of food and clothing came in from across the country.[7] The most significant part of their material outreach during this time was the farm's dairy cow distribution project. Because of contracts made during the crisis, Koinonia became the distribution center for the Church of the Brethren's Heifer Project in southwest Georgia. Koinonia received shipments of heifers, arranged to have them tested by a veterinarian and inoculated, and then gave them to poor families.[8] Ironically, the attacks on Koinonia had the positive result of putting them in touch with a broad base of support and increasing their ability to funnel material aid to their neighbors.

Koinonians did not want only to provide charity, because that would not challenge the caste structure or benefit people in the long run. With the demise of the agricultural training and farming, Koinonians addressed the economic needs of African Americans by providing jobs. The pecan plant required more seasonal full and part-time labor than the members of the farm could furnish. Black women from the neighborhood gladly took jobs in the factory. Alma and C. J. Jackson's mother, Gussie, was one of the first; Carranza Morgan's wife Maize soon joined her. As the mail-order business grew, the work became more regular, until Koinonia could give full-time employment to about fifteen people. The women worked there despite

questions and antagonism from the white community because it was a secure job at a high wage. Money was only one benefit. Willa Mae Champion
remembered that Jordan was the first person ever to thank her for a day's
work and the first boss who asked her opinion on things.[9] The mail-order
business, then, replaced the agricultural education and cooperative work by
giving jobs with high wages, respect, and some economic stability to
African Americans in rural Sumter County.

Koinonia's mission outreach to local African Americans went through a
similar transformation. The vacation Bible school and youth program
could not be reinstated as such, although Koinonians did start a nursery and
day care center for the neighborhood. Because of the lingering danger, they
did not risk visiting African Americans in their homes, which undercut
their ability to build relationships based on common worship. To make up
for the loss of their traditional program, Koinonians tried other ways to
reach African Americans. Con Browne stepped into the vacuum and increased the contact with African-American ministers and church leaders. In
1959 black pastors in Albany approached Jordan about leading a training
program. Browne took the responsibility and for three years taught extension classes for the Interdenominational Theological Center in Meigs,
Thomasville, and Albany, Georgia. Toward the end of his tenure at the
community, Browne hoped that Koinonia would develop this educational
work with rural black ministers further.[10] This effort to train African-
American ministers harkened back to one of Jordan and England's earliest
goals for Koinonia.

The change in circumstances made Koinonians turn their attention to a
different mission field. Before, they had focused on teaching their interpretation of the Word to rural African Americans. Because they were now limited in that area, Koinonians began spending more time taking their
message to white audiences around the country. As more people learned
about Koinonia's ordeal, the number of invitations for speaking engagements grew. As in his early career, Jordan was a popular favorite on the
church and youth group circuit. He often traveled far from home, speaking
in Hawaii, Minnesota, and Ohio. Surprisingly, some southern church
groups and colleges continued to invite him. He also appeared at African-
American schools in the region, such as Howard University and the North
Carolina College at Durham.[11] On his various trips he spoke about the

Koinonia Farm story or some aspect of Christian race relations. In addition he often gave lectures on his translations of the New Testament. The other men at the farm, most of whom had been to seminary, shared the responsibility for spreading the Word. Sometimes the women of the community also went along on trips to meet with various groups.[12] With all these speaking engagements, the Koinonians' interpretation of the New Testament and their prescription of how a Christian should act with respect to violence and racism became known to more people, in particular to a new generation of young Christians.

Jordan also carried on Koinonia's mission work through his writing. On one of his speaking trips he gave a lecture on Ephesians at an American Baptist Convention in Detroit. Soon after that hundreds of people requested copies of the speech. In response Koinonia started printing copies of his translation of that book. Publishers responded quickly, with Harper and Row agreeing to distribute Jordan's work. Through the early 1960s Jordan translated the New Testament, setting the gospel story in modern Georgia. His aim was to make the ideas in the Bible understandable to twentieth-century people and make Christ's teachings more real to them.[13] These "Cotton Patch" translations of the Gospels, as they became known, and Jordan's speeches based on them enhanced Koinonia's mission to outsiders and became an important moneymaking product of the farm. Moreover, the outreach to a wider audience foreshadowed later efforts to go beyond witnessing and into teaching discipleship.

With their Christian missions to the local people reduced, Koinonians searched for other ways to serve. For a while they tried to help visitors who came to them with mental or emotional trouble. In the late 1950s they had taken in local men with problems such as alcoholism. As Koinonia had become more famous, friends around the country asked it to help people who might benefit from life in community. For example, Koinonians gave a home to Gene Gulinson, a young boy from St. Louis who had been in some trouble with the law. They hoped a wholesome environment and stable family situation might put him back on the right track.[14] Koinonia's faith in the healing power of community and the ability to serve anyone who came to it was tested when it was joined by men with more severe emotional problems. One, Paul Goodman, came to Koinonia to explore the possibility of joining the community. In 1959 he was arrested in Albany for protesting, naked, against the missiles at bases there. By late summer his parents had sent him to a veteran's mental hospital in North Carolina, but Koinonians continued to have contact with him. They tried to get him released in the custody of either Koinonia or the Brüderhof at Forest River, North Dakota. His parents, they argued, were unsympathetic with his interest in Christianity and so living with a foster community might help him more than his family.[15]

The experience with Goodman made Koinonians aware of the limits to their service. Some members wondered if Koinonia was equipped to deal with real emotional troubles. Were there some illnesses that "living in community" could not heal? Moreover, they doubted that the eight adult full members remaining at the community could adequately provide for these troubled people's needs. The effort to find a new form of service made Koinonians face their weaknesses. While they had some success in reinvigorating their program, they could not minister to their neighbors as they had before the crisis. They found some ways to reach out through charity, to take advantage of the resources of the external community, and to create jobs for some African Americans who had been hurt by changes in the rural economy. They were frustrated, however, in their inability to focus their efforts and accomplish more. They realized they had neither the resources nor the energy to devote fully to a new program. If they wanted to initiate more successful outreach, they needed to strengthen their membership and iron out their communal problems.

In the third area of their program, living in community, Koinonians suffered from instability caused by a transient membership. In order to bolster their internal fellowship, Koinonians needed to attract new members and incorporate them into the group, minister to visitors, and reach out to African Americans. Having heard about Koinonia's crisis, people came from all around the country to the farm, bringing their ideas and experience. But the reasons people came, and left, reveal the confusion over the farm's purposes as well as the Koinonians' internal problems of finance and relationship. One couple attracted by the situation was Don and Jeanette Devault, who came to Koinonia as part of a spiritual pilgrimage. Don Devault, a professor of chemistry and physics at the College of the Pacific, was an admirer of Gandhi and had spent time in prison during the war for draft resistance. The couple had been active in peace causes in Chicago and California. They heard a taped speech by Jordan during the height of the crisis and were intrigued by the Koinonians' nonviolent response to their ordeal. Then, during Devault's sabbatical, the couple contacted the farm and asked to join for a year. The Devaults differed from earlier Koinonians in their single-minded concern for nonviolence and their intention to be only temporary members. They also differed in their understanding of pacifism. They came to believe that Koinonia was too passive and wanted to take a more active stand on peace issues. This eventually led the couple to leave the farm to participate in vigils at nuclear installations.[16] The Devaults' experience represented the new members the farm attracted in the late 1950s and early 1960s. They came intending to stay a short time rather than becoming full members of the community. In addition, they were primarily interested in making an outward witness on only one aspect of Koinonia's principles.

Unlike the Devaults, John and Joan Veldhuizen resembled Koinonia's early population in personal history, interests, and intentions. Joan Veldhuizen had grown up in the Baptist and Methodist Churches and had participated in both denominations' youth groups. After college she went to California as a missionary to young Hispanic boys and girls and ran a program similar to that of the Baptist Fellowship Center and Koinonia Farm. John Veldhuizen originally intended to work in agricultural extension. Like Jordan, during college he changed his mind and went into the ministry. In the late 1950s he grew dissatisfied with being a minister. At the same time he heard Jordan speak at a pastors' convention. He soon wrote to the Jordans that he was resigning his position to come to Koinonia, "because I feel I'm living a double standard—God's and the institutional church's." The Veldhuizens fit in well with the other Koinonians and for a time were fully part of the shared life on the farm. Like the Devaults, though, they did not stay long. They could not bring themselves to complete the membership process because they were uncomfortable with the commitment. As John Veldhuizen wrote in his diary, "If my word and actions were not sufficient my signature would not be sufficient either." While they shared Koinonia's desire to live a Christian life and had intended a long-term stay, their discomfort with the emphasis on commitment to community above all and uncertainty about the farm's future convinced them to move on.[17]

Dorothy Swisshelm, who came to the farm in 1958 and lived on and off there for several years, exemplified the transient nature of the new membership. Swisshelm belonged to a church in Cincinnati whose pastor was Maurice McCrackin, a longtime friend of Koinonia's. McCrackin brought Jordan to speak to his congregation, where he greatly impressed Swisshelm. She was getting tired of her job as a psychiatric social worker at a local hospital and was interested in peace and civil rights issues, so she decided to go to the farm. Her experience reflected the mixed purposes and goals that people brought with them to Koinonia. For the next four years she moved in and out of the community, traveling to other places in the South to engage in social work. She spent a year in Miami as a social worker and sent her wages back to Koinonia. Then she relocated to Biloxi, Mississippi, to work with blacks and whites there under the auspices of the United Church of Christ. While she was at the farm, she participated in marches and wrote letters in support of activists. Despite moving in and out, she never severed her relationship with the farm or renounced the commitment she signed in 1959. Only when family responsibilities called—she needed to help her sister in Ohio—did Swisshelm depart for good. By then her fear that the farm could not support all its members, combined with her sense of family obligation, forced her reluctantly to leave.[18]

The question of how to blend these new people into the community consumed much of the Koinonians' time in the first years of the new decade. During the crisis the farm had lost many of its first generation, the group that had established the community's system of working and living together. In their place came the Veldhuizens, Devaults, Swisshelm, and a number of other individuals and families. The remaining older Koinonians had long discussions about whether to welcome these newcomers and whether they were ready to accept the farm's definition of Christian life in community.[19] The arrival of new people exacerbated the uncertainty over the farm's purpose. The newcomers helped the farm through some rough spots with their labor and energy, but they also brought with them their own ideas about outreach and community. They differed from earlier Koinonians in several ways, including the fact that they had heard about the farm through the network of liberal Christians and came to the community often only intending to stay a limited time. Moreover, as the Devaults, Veldhuizens, and Swisshelm illustrate, they often were interested in particular issues, wanted to make a more active social witness, or were ambivalent about commitment to community for its own sake. They forced Koinonians to confront the balance of outreach and community. Many of them left after a short period due to frustration and a desire to be more involved in social issues. Other people came to live at the farm for long periods, even up to a year, without ever intending to go through the membership process. This made it difficult for the people at the farm to develop their inner relationship, because they were never quite sure who should be included in the community.

The attacks against the farm also drew to it an increased number of short- and long-term guests who came to help or to visit and learn. Koinonia had always had visitors, but now it received 800 to 1,000 people a year, who came for an hour, a week, or a month. The sojourners were a diverse lot. A group of beatniks from Atlanta excited the young people on the farm. Joan Veldhuizen was intrigued by the "Children of Light," a missionary group who traveled around being "a sign to the people" and occasionally pitched its tent at Koinonia. Foreign visitors—including a former member of the Japanese Parliament—and learned people—such as the dean of the Harvard Divinity School—engaged Koinonians in stimulating conversation and kept the level of intellectual activity high. All the activity made Koinonia, in Jan Jordan's words, a "happening" place to be.[20]

The guests enlivened the community but also added weight to the members' already heavy burden. Visitors required attention from the more permanent residents, many of whom themselves were new to community. Though they were barely members, people like Swisshelm and the Veldhuizens shared the responsibility with the Jordans, Brownes, and Wittkampers to welcome people and make them feel a part of the group. Doing so had its rewards but also took time and energy away from farmwork and their own community building. The strain took its toll as Koinonians increasingly found themselves unable to deal with the responsibility. Swisshelm expressed her concern for these visitors to a friend: "We're so busy with housekeeping and making a living we can't give them much attention. . . . We'd like to give them a taste of the way of Christ, but are understaffed so to speak."[21] Such preoccupation with guests' needs kept Koinonia from developing its inner fellowship.

One part of community living that had been especially hurt by the crisis was the relationship to African Americans. No blacks became members or even novices in the late 1950s or early 1960s. To some extent this was related to Koinonia's inability to attract many new members at all. In addition, there was still some danger for African Americans who associated closely with the community. Therefore, Koinonians, for the time being, did not hope to regain the interracial character their community had when the Jacksons, Bobby Engram, and the Angrys were integrated into its life. Instead, they pursued what relationships they could through work and friendship. Local African Americans still came to work there, especially in the pecan plant. In addition, Koinonia had good friends in the black community. Slater and C. B. King and their families came over from Albany on weekends to visit. And, during the height of the civil rights movement in the area, larger groups of young people came to Koinonia for picnics and recreation. As part of the outreach program, Koinonia invited groups of African-American women to Koinonia for quilting parties and to talk about their experiences and troubles.[22] Thus, even while struggling to hold the community together and adjust to its transience, Koinonians continued to work to make it an interracial fellowship to whatever extent was possible.

An underlying factor in the Koinonians' inability to carry on a program to their satisfaction or to stabilize their inner fellowship was the continued uncertainty about their priorities. They were tired, financially burdened, and confused about their future. The questions raised by contact with the external community remained unsolved. Particularly in light of changing circumstances, their mission became increasingly unclear. What kind of outreach should they attempt? How much should they be involved with the social movements of the day? How should they relate to their growing network of supporters, particularly those who were active in civil rights and peace work? During this period Koinonia turned to its friendships with other communitarians for strength. But that relationship also led the members to reevaluate their commitment to community. Was communal living really their call? Perhaps it had become obsolete and should be abandoned. By the mid-1960s its inner troubles pushed Koinonia to the very brink of a fundamental change in its way of life.

For years Koinonians had suffered from indecision about the nature and extent of their outreach. Having refused to give up their witness under pressure, Koinonians now asked how far should they take it. Throughout their history they had not demonstrated or protested to push their views. Rather they had lived as an example, a "demonstration plot," of their beliefs and tried to bring change through their own lives, relationships, and work in a local area. What the members had done in agricultural reform and sharing with African Americans on their farm and in the local area was a radical departure from social custom and had made them pioneers when there were no mass civil rights or peace movements. But with new conditions in the rural South, changing needs of African Americans, and the growth of such movements in the early 1960s, Koinonians had to decide whether to stick to their own way of doing things or join others. Some new Koinonians argued that the community should get involved not just in helping its neighbors but in reaching out and providing leadership to people in the whole South. Ross Anderson wrote eloquently about the potential for Koinonia to be a guide in nonviolence to the burgeoning social movements of the time. He wanted the farm to join with the Fellowship of Intentional Communities in working with people in the sit-in and antinuclear movements, helping them to mature in their satyagraha. He believed the group should make a testimony against social evils by sending itinerant ministers to other social movements to reach out to "the thousands living in darkness—especially in regard to bringing world peace."[23]

As in earlier debates, however, other Koinonians continued to emphasize community as the priority. "This is a Christian community—making the word flesh in our lives and communal witness," Jordan wrote to a potential member. "The social witness and ramifications of this are by-products." Moreover, Jordan stressed that the farm's "interracial character" was not activism for integration but an offshoot of its loyalty to Jesus.[24] Other members agreed that the mission that Anderson called for was not worth sacrificing their "church/community." These Koinonians were willing to allow individuals to make whatever witness they chose, as long as it was not as a representative of the group. For example, Jordan criticized Anderson for publicizing his tax resistance, saying it should be something an individual does on his or her own.[25] Koinonians allowed Anderson his freedom to act on his conscience but did not sponsor him as a group. In short, the community came first. Individuals were free to act, but the group would not.

Despite their insistence on their community as the priority, however, Koinonians welcomed visits from, and maintained contact with, groups and individuals engaged in social justice causes. Many of the young people who came to the farm did so to work for better race relations.[26] When they requested an invitation to visit, they cited their civil rights credentials. As one young man from Florida said, "I am 18, a college sophomore, CORE member, been arrested for a sit-in, worked at an AFSC [American Friends Service Committee] camp on an Indian reservation, [and] engaged in a hunger strike to protest segregation at lunch counters."[27] These sojourners arrived expecting to do civil rights work and assuming that Koinonians would do the same; they were often disappointed when that did not happen. Some Koinonians went out to work with other groups. For example, Joan Veldhuizen went to Atlanta for a meeting of the Women's League for International Peace and Freedom, and Ross Anderson crisscrossed the country participating in marches and vigils protesting the arms race.[28] Finally, Koinonians worked with CORE and Peacemakers because they believed "we as Christians should not separate ourselves from groups interested in the same goals, even though some people in them are not Christian."[29] Although ambivalent about their own level of activism, Koinonians pledged to support others who "are standing for Christian beliefs [in race relations] under attack."[30]

The seeming contradiction in the Koinonians' debates, pronouncements, and actions reflects their inner conflict over reconciling activism and community. The expectations of their supporters about how they would act in contemporary social movements did not match their views of themselves and their priorities. Koinonia as a whole could not agree on the proper balance between their goals. Individual members were even personally conflicted because they had certain goals and wanted to find ways to pursue them within the parameters of their Christian and communal principles. These tensions had short- and long-term results for the community. First, the farm lost potential members who wanted to do more in the local or national arena.[31] Moreover, the situation created a misunderstanding in the broader community. Outsiders looked to Koinonia to promote peace and antisegregation activism, such as that proposed by Anderson. But most Koinonians shunned public demonstrations. This misunderstanding and its resolution would be a significant factor in Koinonia's relationship to the civil rights movement in southwest Georgia. Meanwhile it caused increasing frustration as Koinonians tried to figure out their purpose and stay alive as a community.

The tension, uncertainty, and frustration eventually pushed Koinonians to consider broad changes in their communal life. As they had in earlier times of internal crisis, Koinonians turned to other Christian communities for support and advice. In the early 1960s they renewed their friendship with the Brüderhof at Forest River and became acquainted with the Reba Place Fellowship, an urban community in Evanston, Illinois. In June 1960 members of the groups met for a three-day conference to talk about their beliefs and the possibility of cooperation. All of the communities were having trouble and thought they could help each other with spiritual or material aid and advice. Clarence Jordan opened the meeting with a discussion of what they had in common. During the conference the groups affirmed their belief in brotherly love, support for a witness against prejudice and violence, and commitment to sharing as a way to witness against greed and economic injustice. With that agreed upon, the communities discussed practical ways they could work together to express their beliefs. In particular, the conference participants talked about setting up a referral system so that together they could take care of the needy people who kept coming to the farm.[32] This gave Koinonians some confidence that with a little help they could manage their burden.

But further cooperation only brought out disagreements, and over the next few years the relationship disintegrated. When they continued to discuss ways to work together, and even the possibility of unifying with Forest River or Reba Place, complications arose. Jordan hesitated because of the different affiliations of the communities: Koinonia still worked primarily with Baptists, Reba Place with the Mennonites, and Forest River with the Hutterites. In addition, when the Wittkampers visited Forest River, the family encountered a number of problems, ranging from the children's behavior to disputes over money. By the summer of 1963 it seemed that although Reba Place, Forest River, and Koinonia Farm agreed in principle on most things, in practice they could not get along. They were incapable of sacrificing particular goals for the good of a unified group. The final straw was that they could not decide who should give up their location. Forest River had great expanses of fertile land, Reba Place a mission to the city, and Koinonia the witness to racial equality.[33] Reba Place announced it thought Koinonia should dissolve. As one member put it, "We are not sure God wants Koinonia to revive. We think he wants Clarence free to write, translate, and preach. We should figure out how to free Clarence, then what to do with Koinonia."[34] The intercommunity problem paralleled Koinonia's internal trouble: an inability to set priorities among inner relationships, farming, ministering to an urban population, and witnessing to the race problem. Koinonians were obviously not going to find solutions for their problems with these other groups.

Meanwhile the farm's financial situation continued to deteriorate. By the beginning of 1962 Koinonia seemed on the brink of collapse. There were not enough members with good agricultural experience to run the beef herd and general operations. In addition, the price of pecans, Koinonia's main moneymaker, was falling. Friends suggested that they choose one productive enterprise and stick to it, so that they could limit investment and learn the operation well enough to succeed. Another proposal was for Koinonia to give up production and live off donations. Perhaps supporters would pay for Koinonia's work with the needy and its availability as a base for social activism.[35] Jordan added an option: lease the operations to individuals and families and shift to a wage-earning system instead of the common purse.

For the first few months of 1962 Koinonians debated the benefits of giving up complete economic sharing. Jordan's position was quite clear. He had come to believe "the community of work is not possible, even in a committed Christian group." This was a complete reversal of his position at the founding of Koinonia. Over the years he had realized that complete sharing required people to do work they were not interested in, led to problems of authority and tensions over the allocation of jobs, and did not favor the efficient management of the business.[36] Although the other members agreed on the need for a change, they expressed reservations about the effect that it would have on their communal spirit. Would they be giving up their spiritual values by stressing working for a living instead of out of love? They wanted to maintain flexibility and their fellowship.[37] Significantly, at this time the effect of full economic sharing on internal race relations did not seem to be a factor in the decision making. Primarily Koinonians were seeking to create a new structure under which the members would experience less strain over financial matters and be freer to share in other ways.

Koinonians devised a new economic system and, after consultation with Forest River and Reba Place, agreed to implement it as of the first of March 1962. They divided the community's operations into several categories, including farm management, processing, mail order, and "miscellaneous."

The latter involved maintenance, the newsletter, scheduling of outside lectures, and care of guests. Each family became responsible for an income-producing enterprise. Then the individuals worked as hard as they wanted to maintain a standard of living of their own choosing. They could hire as they saw fit, pay their own bills, and earn their own living.[38] The Brownes took over sales and marketing, the Jordans the farm management, and Wittkampers the garden. They continued to work out the details such as whether the miscellaneous duties would be paid work or carried out by all members voluntarily. For the time being at least, in addition, the community would continue to own the means of production and the families would lease it.[39] Koinonians hoped this new system would solve their financial troubles and let them get on with the more important business of strengthening their spiritual community.

The restructuring marked a sharp departure from Koinonia's original philosophy of shared resources and distribution according to need and meant the members were no longer living in what they would have called "complete community." They felt driven to this change by necessity. Because they were going to fail economically, something had to give in order for them to keep on living together, sharing spiritually, and maintaining a witness. By this time Jordan no longer felt that economic sharing was essential to spiritual sharing. In fact, he argued that by freeing people of financial dependence on each other and the tensions that could cause, they would have more openness and voluntary sharing.[40] This episode demonstrated Koinonia's underlying priorities. It maintained its primary goal of creating a Christian fellowship which included interracial relationships. Danger had reduced the latter to a witness, but Koinonians were willing to give up almost anything to preserve at least that. Now, when conditions threatened the spirit of Christian community itself, Koinonians gave up the common purse to save it. Significantly, Koinonians did not think they were giving up community completely. Rather, by giving up the full economic sharing, they preserved the most important parts: the witness and the spiritual sharing. This redefinition of Christian community stood until after Jordan's death, when Koinonia passed into new hands.

This new system might have reconciled Koinonia's goals of sharing fellowship and witnessing on race relations if it had been in a more stable position materially or was starting fresh without built-up tensions. Instead of solving the problems, however, the new system raised a host of questions. The Internal Revenue Service informed it that the members would now have to pay self-employment tax and social security. How would older members, like Will Wittkamper, be paid their benefits? A larger problem was how to distinguish among family, enterprise, and community money. The Jordans wanted a separate bank account to keep their personal income, which the sale of the Cotton Patch translations supplemented, separate from farm money. For their part the Wittkampers, whose job was to tend the garden, felt that the new system did not make operations clear. How should they separate garden tools from farm tools? Was their teenage son an employee or family member? Because Koinonians had been accustomed for years to think of all resources and property as shared, it was hard for them now to separate things in their minds. On top of this other disputes arose. The group could not agree on whether to keep the mail-order business going and whether those proceeds should go to pay past debts or have another use. Clarence and Florence's seeming aloofness—they had begun to miss important meetings—further strained personal relations.[41] Years of hard work, uncertainty, and economic troubles were taking their toll. Not only were material troubles wracking the community; the members seemed unable to agree or cooperate on anything.

Despite the restructuring, in the summer of 1963 Koinonians were forced to take another extreme step to lighten their economic burden. They decided one family should leave, while the other two would carry on until a clearer calling came. The Wittkampers could not go because Will was too old to get a job elsewhere. Jordan was willing to leave, but Con Browne pointed out that he was the only one who knew much about farming. Furthermore, Con did not want to run Koinonia, and the Brownes were thinking about leaving anyway. The couple had been disheartened by the group's failure to get along with other communities. Con Browne felt something was missing, that "we didn't have the whole thing" in terms of communal spirit. Just then, Myles Horton of the Highlander Folk School asked Con to come there to take his place when he retired. Browne accepted the job at Highlander because he saw it as a place where he could put in his "two cents." At first the Brownes' departure was considered to be a year's leave of absence, with the option of returning if Koinonia's situation improved. Once they were gone, however, their exit became permanent.[42]

The departure of the Brownes, one of the last of the pre-1950s families, marked the end of a long era in Koinonia's history. Browne had envisioned Koinonia as an effort to live a complete Christian life. Con and Ora had been with Koinonia when it was primarily a mission, when it switched to an emphasis on Christian community, and through brutal attacks and the effort to rebuild. Now the strain on the community of trying to witness to all these various areas—service, racial harmony, nonviolence—was too much. The Brownes' departure symbolized the end of the effort at complete Christian life in community. And it left the Jordans and Wittkampers to decide what to do next.

At the end of their rope, the remaining two families agreed to look for a way to dissolve Koinonia. They believed after all this struggle that perhaps God was telling them that their call was no longer to live in community. This was the height of Jordan's disillusionment and conviction that as he entered his fifties, maybe he would better serve as a writer and preacher. The two couples made preparations to get rid of the farm. They had three proposals. They thought a church group, perhaps the Mennonite Central Committee, could take charge of the property and use it as an "interracial retreat or training center for Christian leadership in the South." They predicted that in the wake of the civil rights movement, the South would need direction. In particular they wanted someone to guide the young people who were changing the South by using nonviolence. An alternate idea was that churches could send families to live on the Koinonia Farm property and run the businesses, somewhat like a progressive, Christian colonization of the area. Their last idea was that the farm could be converted into a "rehabilitation headquarters for the dispossessed and oppressed." It could provide employment and housing to blacks in the area who might have lost their jobs or farms.[43] Jordan spent that fall looking for takers on these proposals and considering other jobs. It seemed clear that Koinonia Farm was about to fold.

But not yet. In December 1963 Jordan wrote to the Reverend Seido Ogawa that he saw a "light dawning" in southwest Georgia and wanted to be there to greet it. "I want to be around to clasp in love the hands of those who have despised and rejected us. I was born among these people and want to walk in the newness of life" with them, he declared.[44] By that time the fight for civil rights in southwest Georgia had begun. As much as the remaining Koinonians insisted their purpose was broader than simply activism for civil rights, they could not turn their backs on that struggle. The Jordans and Wittkampers wanted to lend their support to the movement and be there when it brought changes in race relations in Sumter County. Many of their problems remained unresolved. The population was down to two permanent families plus guests and workers. Koinonia as a community barely existed. The members' fellowship was frayed, the economic sharing was limited, and financial problems still remained. The burgeoning civil rights movement gave them a reason to hold on. During the years of the movement in southwest Georgia, the Koinonians' relationship to it added to their turmoil but also provided the glue that kept the remnants of the community in place long enough for them to test their understanding of beloved community and to discover a way to marry interracialism and sharing.

The entrance to Koinonia Farm in October 1958. (Courtesy of Leonard Jordan)

Clarence Jordan, founder
of Koinonia Farm,
ca. 1965. (Courtesy of
Leonard Jordan)

Koinonia's welcome sign, vandalized during the height of the Sumter County movement, 1963. (Courtesy of Leonard Jordan).

Civil rights activists gathered at a SNCC meeting on the farm, 1964.
(Courtesy of Leonard Jordan)

Collins McGee (on tractor) and Greg Wittkamper working together at Koinonia,
ca. 1965. (Courtesy of Leonard Jordan)

9

Koinonia and the
Movement

W HEN CIVIL RIGHTS protests swept across southwest Georgia in the early 1960s, the students, ministers, and activists—both black and white—who came to the area to participate stopped at Koinonia Farm. The desire to help these people kept Koinonia from folding but also forced members to decide how to act on their beliefs in the new environment. They had never considered themselves a protest organization, nor did they consider legal and political avenues to be the proper channels toward human equality. But now, with demonstrations for legal integration and political rights all around them, how would they respond? Could they adapt their basic philosophy and belief in brotherhood to the new environment? Having stayed in southwest Georgia for the sake of their witness and in order to see the movement through to its conclusion, between 1962 and 1965 the remaining Koinonians carved out a niche for themselves in the Albany and Sumter County movements that suited their belief in brotherhood, nonviolence, and "incarnational evangelism."[1] Their participation clarified the nature and extent of their Christian approach to racial equality, as well as the relationship between their commitment to community and interracial brotherhood, on the one hand, and to the demand for civil rights, on the other hand.

While Koinonians focused on recovery from their own crisis, activism for integration and civil rights increased around them. African-American communities pressed for the enforcement of the *Brown* decision. And in 1960 black students started a sit-in movement which swept across southern cities. Meanwhile, Koinonia's friends in the secular and religious network responded by putting their energy into three tasks: surveying conditions, preparing communities for desegregation, and supporting those under attack for their civil rights activities. In 1958 both the Southern Regional Council and the Southern Conference Education Fund did a regionwide survey of voting conditions and the response to desegregation, with Carl and Anne Braden traveling and interviewing over two hundred people. Church leaders in communities like Athens, Georgia, and Rock Hill, South Carolina, worked to smooth the way for school integration. Even in Mississippi white liberals worked below the surface to lay the groundwork for change. The community that had helped Koinonia Farm now rallied to support the sit-ins and individuals who were under attack. The SRC, for example, sent legal and other aid to churchwomen, ministers, and others.[2] During this period, then, the main issue in civil rights was integration, and the main task for white liberals was to prepare for it and help those pursuing it.

The relationship Koinonians had developed with both black and white activists during the 1950s laid the groundwork for cooperation with the movement. Koinonians for a long time had maintained a friendship with the congregation of Vernon John's church in Montgomery. When the bus boycott began, Norman Long and Eddie Johnson went there to attend mass meetings and lend moral support. Later in the decade members of the farm attended meetings of liberal groups and helped civil rights workers when they could. Long attended the Conference on Christian Faith and Human Relations in early 1957, for example, and the farm provided a temporary home for one of the staff of the *Racial Equality Bulletin*.[3] Meanwhile, Koinonians strengthened their friendship with African Americans who would soon be leaders of the Albany and Sumter County movements. The Barnum family, owners of the funeral parlor that was Americus's most important black business and leaders of the local African-American community, became acquainted with Koinonia in the fifties. C. B. and Slater King and their wives Carol and Marion also traveled to Sumter County from Albany for dinner.[4] These friendships not only satisfied Koinonia's desire to build fellowship between white and black, they forged a bond between it and the African-American community that shaped its involvement in the civil rights struggle.

As the African-American direct action and protest movement spread in southwest Georgia, it seemed that Koinonians would have enough in common with it to inspire continued cooperation. Besides friendship and mutual support, Koinonians obviously shared with activists the goal of African-American equality. Moreover, Koinonians appeared to agree with the movement on important points of philosophy. To begin with, the civil rights movement had a spiritual base, drawing its strength from the religious beliefs, institutions, and music of the African-American community. Indeed, Charles Sherrod, the leader of the Student Nonviolent Coordinating Committee (SNCC) in Albany, was, like Jordan, a Baptist preacher with a radical vision of Christianity.[5] In addition, Koinonia, Martin Luther King Jr., and SNCC espoused nonviolence as the means by which to fight for equality. Most important, however, Sherrod, Jordan, and King each put forward a vision of the beloved community. Koinonians were trying to inaugurate a true interracial fellowship based on Christian sharing. King believed the movement was building a genuine intergroup life with personal, social, and even economic relations based on love. For his part Sherrod claimed that during the early 1960s SNCC was working to create a society where people could live unalienated, in brotherly love. According to Vincent Harding, community was a central theme throughout the movement, from the songs about sitting at the welcome table to the effort to build a new political community in the Mississippi Freedom Democratic Party. In other words, the movement was about building an authentic community in which people could work together to achieve their full potential.[6] This common religious spirit and vision were the basis of cooperation between Koinonians and the movement.

The correspondence in ideas between Koinonia and civil rights activists masked points of difference, however. For one, Koinonians considered themselves distinct from the growing movement in overall goal and approach. They insisted that their witness was for a complete Christian way of life, which included racial brotherhood as one element. Integration by itself was not enough without the bond of love that Christian fellowship called for. Bringing people together was not done for its own sake but for the spiritual enrichment of both. Jordan would ask, if you integrated a group of devils, would that bring about the Kingdom?[7] In other words, Koinonians wanted to change the basis of relationships, and integration was only the first step. In addition, Koinonians did not actively pursue political or legal change. Jordan declared that the answer to racial conflict "lies in God and in Grace, not in government and law." God blows away our prejudices, "not the Supreme Court, but God."[8] This difference in approach extended to the issue of demonstrations. Sherrod and other SNCC leaders recognized that militancy could inspire self-respect and thus break the hold of fear and intimidation on rural, Deep South blacks, making the act of demonstrating both empowering and liberating.[9] Moreover, demonstrations and protests could unify the black community, an important function in a city like Albany where there were large class differences. Unfortunately, at least from the Koinonia perspective, this increased unity did not extend to the white community.[10] Koinonians believed demonstrations were disruptive and created disunity. Differences over tactics would later be the seed of a rupture between the farm and the movement.

Perhaps most important, the surface similarity of the visions of beloved community was misleading. Koinonians had what they believed was the basis of an interracial Christian community on the farm and wanted others to join it. At the time of the beginning of the movement, the Koinonians' understanding of community was still fairly rigidly defined and included complete economic and spiritual sharing. Although during these years Koinonians gave up the common purse, they still held to the idea of total commitment to the community as part of a complete Christian life. Civil rights activists, on the other hand, envisioned community in a more fluid way, as the sum of mutually supportive and loving relationships. Furthermore, SNCC believed it was building community within the movement through organizing, mass meetings, and cross-class cooperation and sacrifice. This difference meant that although Koinonians and movement leaders used the same words, their visions would be hard to reconcile.

The Koinonians' opposition to demonstrations and aversion to political avenues for change did not mean they believed it was necessary to sit and wait for God to change prejudices. Christians could start to bring that about through their daily actions. The Koinonians approached working for human equality by living what they considered to be a Christian life and by providing economic support for African Americans. Jordan had preached that the best method of evangelism was incarnation; the best method of teaching is to be. Thus, first and foremost a Christian should labor to live according to Jesus' lessons about brotherhood and nonviolence and to be an example for others. That included opening Christian fellowship to all believers and creating interracial relationships. So members visited African Americans in their homes and invited their neighbors to the farm for recreation, Bible study, meals, and quiet conversation. Koinonians hoped that bringing whites and blacks together for worship would help both groups learn to understand and live with the other. By doing so in their own lives they were making a start, which they hoped others would follow.

The other element of Koinonia's method for bringing about racial harmony was economic development. Jordan asserted, "Lincoln emancipated the Negro politically but not economically. He remains an economic slave, and he doesn't want to vote as much as he wants to eat."[11] Through their agricultural education program Koinonians had begun to work to free African-American farmers economically by helping them to be more productive. After the crisis wrecked that effort, Koinonians focused on giving their black neighbors jobs where they would get good wages and respectful treatment. In Koinonia's first brochure it had proclaimed its intention to live in Christian community according to certain guidelines, one of which was racial inclusiveness, while helping the oppressed. Everything the members did fell within the parameters of those goals. Their program could seem spiritual and otherworldly in its reliance on God's grace for a change in the heart of white southerners. But at the same time it was quite radical, in the sense of going to the root, in its call for immediate change in daily life, and materialist in its emphasis on economic emancipation.

Events in southwest Georgia soon tested how Koinonians would support the civil rights movement while being true to their distinctive philosophy and approach. The scene of the first movement into which Koinonia was drawn was Albany, Georgia. In the fall of 1961, Charles Sherrod and Cordell Reagon of SNCC arrived in Albany and started working with some of the local youth. Then on the first of November they, in coordination with nine members of the local NAACP Youth Council, protested segregation at the Trailways bus terminal. Shortly thereafter, police arrested Freedom Riders for obstructing traffic and failing to obey an officer. Throughout the next year the movement in Albany called for the release of the Freedom Riders and others and for the desegregation of public facilities. In early demonstrations several hundred students protested the jailing at city hall and Albany State College. To accompany the demonstrations, blacks organized nightly mass meetings at the local churches. Civil rights workers also began to target segregated public facilities of all kinds, including the library and buses.[12] In the summer college students poured into the city, and the range of targets for desegregation increased to include parks, swimming pools, lunch counters, tennis courts, and all public facilities. Meanwhile, African-American leaders gave daily workshops on nonviolent techniques to ensure that the swelling movement stayed peaceful.

Koinonia's involvement in the Albany struggle demonstrated its support for civil rights, while underlining its commitment to interracial fellowship and community. Some members attended marches and mass meetings.[13] In her diary Lora Browne described a visit to a mass meeting in June. Voter registration had begun in Albany, and Koinonians had been invited to hear Martin Luther King Jr. speak. In excitement she, her father, and Jan and Clarence Jordan dressed in their Sunday best and went to the black church. Lora was profoundly moved by the prayer and music, particularly the uplifting twenty-verse rendition of "We Shall Overcome," which the assembly sang with clasped hands.[14] In moments such as these, Koinonians experienced the fellowship with African Americans that they hoped and worked for. One member wrote, "It was a terrifically exhausting emotional experience to see and hear hundreds of Negroes praying and singing (all at the top of their lungs) for freedom, for treatment as human beings."[15] After these meetings the congregation welcomed the Koinonians and asked them to return. Koinonia maintained that by attending they demonstrated their support for the African Americans' pursuit of freedom. As Lora later exclaimed in her diary, "I think it is real important for Negroes to know there are some white southerners who support them!"[16]

In addition to sharing fellowship at mass meetings and showing their support, some adult Koinonians took behind-the-scenes roles in the movement. Though already friendly with significant participants, including C. B. and Slater King and their wives, at these assemblies Jordan and Browne forged stronger ties with the local leadership. After the gatherings some Koinonians would stay and talk with the executive committee of the movement. Although they did not want to take overt leadership roles because they believed blacks had to head the movement, Koinonians did give their opinions. Sometimes differences over tactics arose during these meetings. Carol King remembered that when they were discussing the proposed boycott of white merchants, Koinonians objected. Although they had supported a boycott in Montgomery, now that they had suffered from one and witnessed its coercive nature, they did not want to be part of it. They did not try to talk the Albany leadership out of the move, however; they simply stated their reasoning and intention not to participate.[17] This was one case when Koinonians walked a thin line, trying to balance support for the movement while abiding by their own separate beliefs.

The Koinonians' more important institutional role was to provide a refuge at the farm. They began by opening their doors to people from Albany who needed rest and recreation. They hosted frequent social events and became a nursery for the children whose parents were arrested. In addition, the scores of "ministers, priests, rabbis, and lawyers" who headed for Albany from across the nation stopped at Koinonia along the way. When college students started arriving in the summer of 1962, and housing was in short supply in Albany, the overflow bedded at the farm.[18] More than just a place to stay, however, Koinonia was a source of comfort. It was a place where people could relax and enjoy the fellowship of those who shared their principles. Frances Pauley, a white woman activist with the Georgia Council on Human Relations, attributed the survival of herself and others to Koinonia. "Koinonea was my haven because if it hadn't have been for Clarence, I don't know whether I would have been able to have existed. . . . It was just the way he was. And I would always leave there like I could keep on, always."[19] Though their own fellowship had been weakened by the attacks and their aftermath, the Koinonians' activity in providing a refuge gave them a way to create, if only temporarily, an interracial community within the movement at the farm.

One group that took advantage of Koinonia's hospitality was the Student Nonviolent Coordinating Committee. When the first members arrived in the area, they came to the farm. Charles Sherrod, head of SNCC in Dougherty County, visited the farm with Marion and Slater King and quickly established a close friendship with the Jordans and Brownes. He went to Koinonia on Sundays to join in its worship service, share a meal, and then sit back and talk about social and theological issues. As a seminarian he particularly enjoyed discussing Jordan's Cotton Patch translations. When more students arrived, Sherrod sent them to visit, making the farm's guest list look like a who's who of the organization. As the Brownes remembered, because many of SNCC's leaders at that time had religious backgrounds, there was a spiritual union of sorts between them and Koinonians. Organizers for the student group on occasion stayed on the farm, sharing living quarters and meals. In late 1962 SNCC held a several-day retreat on the property. They brought bedding and slept on the floor of the community building and other spare rooms. Between them, Koinonia and SNCC worked out a cooperative cooking and dining arrangement. While at the farm, in addition to having their own meetings, SNCC students worked in the fields. To that extent they participated in the life of the community. Koinonians believed that this experience gave the activists time to draw together, relax, and enjoy the fellowship of community.[20]

In 1963 Koinonia's attention shifted closer to home, from Albany to Americus. The next three years saw organizing efforts by civil rights workers, punctuated by periodic bursts of demonstrations and protest activities. The movement in town began when SNCC sent Don Harris and John Churchill to live at Koinonia and begin a voter registration drive. Over the course of the spring, the activists worked slowly, contacting black families and getting to know people. They also developed a local leadership by convincing the Reverend J. R. Campbell, of an Americus African-American church, to be president of the fledgling Sumter County movement.[21] Through 1964 and 1965 the movement focused on voter registration, community building, and desegregation. During this time C. B. King's campaign for Congress helped canvassers bring the number of African Americans on the voting rolls up to 25 percent of the eligible population. Activists also organized educational programs for local blacks, such as a day camp at Koinonia, freedom and literacy schools, a library center, and films. In the meantime individuals tried to desegregate the local schools, including Sammy Mahone and Collins McGee, two African-American youths with ties to Koinonia who applied to Georgia Southwestern College and South Georgia Trade and Vocational School, respectively.[22]

In the summers of 1963 and 1965, movement activity shifted to large-scale demonstrations and protests. First, in 1963 the movement attempted to desegregate public facilities, beginning with the Martin Theater. Concurrently, SNCC held mass meetings at the local churches, as had been done in Albany and elsewhere. In early August, when a group of about thirty people at a meeting decided to march to city hall, they were met by police. The officers immediately arrested Don Harris, Ralph Allen, and John Perdew of SNCC and Zev Aelony of CORE and charged them with attempting to incite insurrection. In response, the movement sponsored a flurry of protests and letter writing urging the release of the four men. To clamp down on demonstrations, the city passed an ordinance prohibiting pickets.[23]

In early August 1965 the arrest of four women during the justice of the peace election sparked a second wave of protests. On election day voters had lined up in three queues: white men, white women, and "colored." Mary F. Bell, who was a candidate, Mamie Campbell, Lena Turner, and Gloria Wise decided that if white women did not have to wait "all bunched up with a gang of men," neither did they. They entered the white women's line and were arrested by the deputy sheriff.[24] The Reverend Mr. Campbell, a leader in the Sumter County movement and husband of one of the prisoners, demanded that town officials have the women released. Failing to get satisfaction, he called the Southern Christian Leadership Conference for help. The incident triggered a monthlong series of demonstrations. Two hundred blacks held an unscheduled march to the jail, then followed it with a midnight vigil and picketing of the courthouse. Nearly every day after the march there were demonstrations by civil rights workers and teenagers.[25]

Throughout this period Koinonians worked closely with civil rights organizations, serving as a base of operations for the movement in Sumter County and providing aid. SNCC's leaders visited and boarded at the farm. Moreover, as during the Albany struggle, the community opened its doors to the organization for training sessions and retreats. For example, in October 1963 Robert Mants Jr. of the student organization held a workshop and discussion of the movement at Koinonia, where he organized a group of Americus youth to start a boycott and a voter registration canvass.[26] The young people at Koinonia became particularly involved. The Wittkampers' sons, Billy and Greg, attended mass meetings, and Greg participated in at least one march, against his parents' wishes. Moreover, after an attack on demonstrators by the police, he assisted Aelony in collecting signed affidavits from witnesses. Both boys worked on voting rights and even had to stand up to the sheriff and insist on Billy's own right to register. Greg also helped organize young blacks who wanted to go to Americus High School.[27] Other Koinonia youth attended meetings and worked on the *Voice of Americus,* which was produced in the farm's offices. The paper's stories about cooperation, Jordan's work, and Koinonia events revealed the symbiotic connection between the farm and black activism.

Koinonians also developed a close relationship with the Congress of Racial Equality through its representative, Zev Aelony. In 1959 Aelony had visited the farm for an extended period. He came back in the early sixties to help the community and organize black farmers. Along with Collins McGee, a black man from Americus who moved onto Koinonia, he ran the farm's vineyards and experimented with turning the grape business into a co-op. As a result of that partnership, McGee became a member of CORE, further cementing the bond between Koinonia and the organization. Aelony also led classes in nonviolence at the farm, which were attended by most of the black youths in the movement.[28] When he went to jail on the insurrection charge, Koinonia mobilized to gain his release. Swisshelm wrote letters to Representative Jimmy Carter and church officials, seeking support in the case. During his imprisonment one of Aelony's main concerns was that CORE would continue his work at Koinonia and maintain the relationship with the community.[29]

At the time people on both sides of the Sumter County struggle recognized Koinonia's role in it. Indeed, as soon as the movement started in the area, the farm was quickly associated with and even blamed for it by local whites. One opponent of Koinonia asserted that Jordan and his "camp" were responsible for the county's "racial difficulties." Others called it the "breeding ground for trouble."[30] On the other hand, Sumter County activists credited Koinonia for what it had done. Mabel Barnum remembered that during Koinonia's crisis years, "When people saw that little group wasn't going to let the Klan run them off, they knew from that time on that you don't have to be scared of the Klan." Lena Turner added, "Koinonia had demonstrated to young Negroes of Americus something everything else in their world has denied: that white and black can live and work and build together."[31] Here was evidence that Koinonians had at least partially succeeded in their essential goal: to bring white and black together and to witness to the possibility of interracial life and cooperation.

Underneath Koinonia's cooperation with the movement ran a current of ambivalence toward its philosophy and tactics and, by 1965, an increasing discomfort with the direction it took. This discomfort stemmed from the Koinonians' increasing recognition that their understanding of Christian interracialism could not be reconciled completely with the actions of movement activists. In the beginning Koinonians had recognized a kinship with Martin Luther King and the leaders of SNCC in their Christian beliefs, adherence to nonviolence, and vision of community. By the mid-1960s, however, Jordan and others had developed strong misgivings about the tactics civil rights activists used to achieve their goal, particularly protests and demonstrations. Jordan's son Lenny remembered that his father preached that "you needed to live life day-to-day in an honest and fair and equal way," thereby making your whole life a demonstration. But "to force the issue was never his way."[32] Jordan would eat and work with his black friends, and if some opposition arose, he would "fight till the end and never back off" from his right to do so.[33] An incident with his daughter illustrates the point. When Jan Jordan wanted to go to a march with her friend Lena, her father responded: "If you and Lena in the course of your friendship went into a drug store and were arrested, I'd fight it all the way to the Supreme Court. But if you go to the demonstration you are on your own."[34] His beliefs put Jordan into a somewhat awkward position. He did wholeheartedly endorse the goals of the movement and wanted to support it in any way his conscience and interpretation of the New Testament would let him. His ambivalence made him an ardent spokesman for civil rights who in the local movement most often stood on the sidelines.

The other adult members of Koinonia also had mixed feelings on the tactics of the movement and debated whether to endorse or engage in demonstrations. This debate was part of their ongoing discussions about how active they should be in the new social movements around them and how much they should adapt others' tactics on shared goals. Some individuals, like Ross Anderson and Dorothy Swisshelm, did participate in marches. But longer-term and more established Koinonians did not approve of such demonstrations. Con and Ora Browne complained that the tactics sometimes involved breaking the law. Margaret Wittkamper said protests were all right if the group got a permit first, but she objected to some of SNCC's marches because they went ahead without one. They were also unsure of whether their children should take part in marches. They feared the young people already had enough to handle with the pressure they endured at school because of their parents' support for integration.[35] Ora Browne remembered, "We talked it over and the community decided each person could feel free to go to meetings and participate in demonstrations but we weren't doing it as Koinonia because some people didn't agree."[36]

A major component in Koinonians' misgivings about the civil rights movement was their interpretation of nonviolence. In particular, Jordan became disappointed with Martin Luther King Jr. and by the mid-1960s began criticizing him, calling him a political rather than a spiritual leader. He especially faulted the civil rights leader for accepting military protection during the march on Selma.[37] A parable written by Jordan in 1965 made this point. In the story Jordan tells of a man of "no violence" who wanted to lead his oppressed people to freedom but was attacked by the man of some violence. For protection the no-violence people appealed to the man of great violence, who was at the time engaged in bombing and burning foreign villages. The man of great violence protected the people of no violence from the man of some violence. Thus, the oppressed were freed, but at what cost?[38] With the story Jordan registered his dismay that the "nonviolent" civil rights movement and its leaders depended on collaboration with the extremely violent United States government for success.

Basically, Jordan was concerned that the movement was not nonviolent enough, and that activists had the wrong idea about what nonviolence was in the first place. Jordan's nonviolence was akin to Quaker nonresistance, the main tenet being the refusal to respond to violence with violence or even hate. But that did not mean complete passivity. Jordan argued that nonviolence must include positive action as well. "My opinion is that nonviolence alone, unaccompanied by active good will and love, is not only sub-Christian but may be even anti-Christian, especially when it is conceived of and used as an effective strategy or technique."[39] He based his nonviolence, as most of his other ideas, on Jesus' words, which instructed Christians to do no harm to others and to "love your enemy." Jesus "did not advocate putting on a demonstration when someone hurts you." He advocated turning the other cheek. "You don't love your enemy because you want to convert him or because it is the practical thing to do. You love your enemy in order to be a son of God."[40] In short, nonviolence is not a tactic, it is a way of life that included positive, healing action.

This understanding of nonviolence was one factor in a growing split between Koinonia and SNCC. By the mid-1960s, when Jordan was announcing that nonviolence should not be seen as only a means to an end, SNCC was declaring that it should be. SNCC thought Koinonia was too passive, refusing usually even to use the courts.[41] And Koinonia believed SNCC took nonviolence too lightly, considering it just one of many possible tactics. To try to address these differences, Jordan, Will Wittkamper, and Dorothy Swisshelm met with leaders of SNCC to discuss nonviolence.[42] Other matters added to the tension in the relationship, however. Koinonians felt pressed by the responsibility of providing facilities for retreats, particularly during a time of their own instability. The lifestyle of the SNCC students also bothered older Koinonians. Ora and Con Browne noted that there was a "sexual revolution" going on, and older Koinonians did not approve of the personal and sexual ethics of the young people. This difference diminished the bonds between SNCC and Koinonians. The final straw, as far as Koinonians were concerned, was SNCC's move toward Black Power.[43] The departure from beloved community into separatism and black pride went against Koinonia's ideas that all people were the same in Jesus' eyes and should live together as such and their credo that whites and blacks should cooperate to bring about change. By 1965 their feelings about protest tactics, SNCC's attitude toward nonviolence, and the direction the movement was beginning to take led Koinonia to break its ties with organized civil rights activity.

Despite their growing differences with the civil rights movement, however, Koinonians continued to cooperate in areas on which they could agree, particularly on economic issues and the desegregation of the church. More than twenty years after establishing their agricultural training program in the county, Koinonians looked around them and saw that African Americans were still poor and dependent on whites for jobs. The civil rights struggle perhaps had helped to open access to public facilities and to secure voting rights, but it had not helped people to afford decent homes or the necessities of life. As one man on the street in Americus said of his newly acquired rights, "That shit don't help me none." The majority of African Americans in town continued to live in shacks on dark, dirty streets. They faced job discrimination and when they were able to get a job were paid low, nonunion wages.[44] In their newsletter Koinonians declared that "the long struggle which lies ahead is not so much for civil rights as for economic emancipation." Blacks should have education, their own businesses, their own land and homes. Moreover, whites should cooperate with them in order to ensure that they obtained these goals. In some ways the movement had made the situation worse because in strife-torn cities African Americans who participated in civil rights activity were the victims of economic reprisals. This left people in "desperate need" of short-term assistance as well as long-term development.[45]

Koinonians tried to address these needs by funneling financial aid from their vast network of friends to local African Americans. For example, Koinonians discovered a group of four people, the Freedom Medical and Housing Corps, who helped blacks in Albany improve their health care and housing. Because Koinonians saw this as a "positive and practical task," they asked their friends to send money to help them. Jordan also solicited donations for Operation Freedom, on whose board he served. The organization, "the Red Cross of the civil rights movement," gave economic aid to people engaged in the front lines of desegregation battles. In a similar vein, Koinonia Farm served as a distribution center for the National Sharecroppers Fund. A donation to the farm from the involvement fund of the Women's Missionary and Service Auxiliary of the Mennonite Church in Illinois inspired Koinonia to set up a loan fund to help small African-American businesses. Members developed the involvement fund into a system by which concerned people could send money to help south Georgia blacks and Koinonians could distribute it. In the course of a few months, the fund grew to over $1,200.[46] This program borrowed from Jordan's food pantry idea at the Baptist Fellowship Center in Louisville, allowing people to put resources into a pot to benefit those in need. This investment fund was also an important precursor to Koinonia's later financial involvement with the black community.

By the mid-1960s some groups affiliated with the civil rights movement were, like Koinonia, turning their attention to rural economic issues. Members of the SRC expressed growing concern about farmworkers and other people displaced by changes in agriculture. A series of conferences sponsored by the National Sharecroppers Fund and others drew together farmers, teachers, ministers, and CORE and SNCC activists to discuss co-ops, credit unions, and other economic options for the rural South. The main goal of these meetings was to provide black farmworkers with access to information and programs in rural economic development. One result was that by 1968 there were forty cooperatives involving 12,000 black families in the Deep South.[47] These organizations brought blacks together in farming and other enterprises, marketed crops, secured loans, and in other ways promoted economic development and benefits for their members. In southwest Georgia, Sam Wells, an old friend of Koinonia's, founded Southern Rural Action to start co-ops among blacks. Randolph Blackwell started a community center on land donated by Koinonia and built prefab homes. Finally, Charles Sherrod worked with the Kings and others to start New Communities, Inc., a farming cooperative designed to provide homes and employment for blacks from Albany.[48] These enterprises represent a basis for further cooperation between Koinonia and other activists in their shared interest in economic paths to justice for rural blacks.

Koinonians developed this area of mutual interest by working with civil rights groups, especially CORE and SNCC, to bring about structural changes that would give blacks more financial independence. In June 1963 Aelony wrote to CORE that farmworkers in Sumter County, who were victims of the decline of rural conditions and reprisals, had begun meeting every other week to talk about solutions to their problems. He proposed that Koinonia and CORE organize a producers' cooperative at the farm, in which local people would own and operate the productive enterprises. This would both free Koinonia of some of its burden and give African Americans a measure of economic independence. Moreover, the Koinonia co-op could serve as a training ground for workers who would go out of the area and set up similar enterprises elsewhere. Aelony, Collins McGee, and others at Koinonia wrote a constitution for the cooperative and solicited loans from the Rural Areas Development Agency. The effort failed to reach expectations because of the hesitancy of local blacks to take the responsibility of ownership and the transience of the staff, but the project set the precedent for black-white economic partnership, on which Koinonia built later.[49]

Koinonia and Aelony also wanted to help African Americans to get better jobs off the farm. Aelony recognized that staying in agriculture might end up hurting blacks because as farm mechanization progressed, their jobs

would disappear.[50] Koinonia joined with Aelony and SNCC to organize workers in the area, beginning with notoriously underpaid African-
American women domestics. In the summer of 1963 the *Voice of Americus*
carried an invitation for "all maids, domestic workers, and cooks" to come
to a picnic at Koinonia. Besides socializing, the agenda included speakers
from Atlanta, Albany, and Americus and a discussion of creating a union.
At the picnic there was also an opportunity for women to show their quilts
and arrange to market them cooperatively. By the next summer Aelony announced that the quilt co-op was going well, and the International Ladies
Garment Workers Union had sent a representative to organize the maids.[51]
Koinonia played an indispensable role in these activities because it provided
African Americans a place where they could meet and not be harassed. The
organization efforts also promoted Koinonia's overall goal of helping
African Americans assert themselves economically.

While Koinonians continued to work to give African Americans economic independence, they also labored to break down barriers in worship.
Jordan had always felt it was a shame and perhaps a sin that the church was
one of the most segregated institutions in the country. With the movement
making race relations a public issue, he and other Koinonians made overt
efforts to end the segregation of the church. In one case a group of Koinonians, including Collins McGee, went to a special service at a local Southern
Baptist church. Although the group entered the church and got past the
usher, they were soon expelled and threatened with arrest for "disturbing di-
vine worship."[52] Jordan also criticized the arrest of a longtime friend, Ash-
ton Jones, who was detained for blocking the entrance of the First Baptist
Church in Atlanta. Jones had responded to the church's ejection of blacks
by standing outside the church and announcing, "Step right in, folks; worship a segregated God in a segregated church." Koinonians circulated several pages about the case and appealed for help from their friends. In
addition, Jordan broke with his usual practice and joined a group of ministers at a convention in a protest against the First Baptist's minister.[53] The
Koinonians' effort to open the doors of the church grew out of their long-
held determination to bring whites and blacks together in Christian fellowship. Thus, the areas in which Koinonians continued to cooperate with
the movement by the mid-1960s were extensions of Jordan's original approach to better race relations: economic cooperation and shared worship.

In most areas, however, by 1965 Koinonians began to break from the civil rights movement and go their own way. As Koinonians became more disenchanted with the direction of the movement, Jordan joined other liberal ministers in expressing concern for a reconciliation between white and black. "From where I sit," he wrote, "it seems the intense, bitter phase of the racial revolution . . . is largely behind us. The stage into which we are entering will be the slow tedious one of mopping up, of rebuilding bridges, of learning to live together in the new order."[54] In the heat of the movement, black and white had moved apart. In SNCC the philosophy of beloved community and coming together was being replaced by black power and separatism. White liberals were disenchanted with the turn of the movement and felt pushed out. Moreover, they were turning their attention to the Vietnam War. Other whites were pulling away from civil rights advances in reaction to the series of riots in the long hot summers. Finally, the average churchgoing white person—in Will Campbell's words, the one being revolted against—was being left out of the revolution and was struggling to learn how to live in the new reality. Campbell and other liberal white ministers in the newly formed Committee of Southern Churchmen began looking for ways to begin to bring people together, believing that after desegregation "integration is the next step, the positive acceptance of desegregation and the glad welcoming of Negroes in the full range of human activities."[55]

At this point Jordan began calling for whites and blacks to unite in a "God Movement." The weakness in the civil rights movement, Jordan declared, was that it had focused on legal and political issues and neglected the human, spiritual side. Rights activists had looked for strategic and tactical rather than spiritual answers to racial problems. Jordan had always believed race division was a problem of spirit, not power; the problem was alienation between people who should be united in Christ. Therefore, the solution was to bring people together and create fellowship and common devotion to God. Political actions could not accomplish this. Another problem was that the movement had disintegrated into a divisive struggle. Rather than working for the overall redemption of society, it had become an "us versus them" fight. Whites and blacks were more alienated than ever. Jordan called for a spiritual awakening among both groups of people.[56] Blacks and whites should work together in a new mass movement, a "God Movement," with a platform based on the Sermon on the Mount, to bring about a redemption of society. The God movement would be "a greater and deeper movement than the civil rights movement." It would be "the stirring of his mighty spirit of love, peace, humility, forgiveness, joy, and reconciliation in the hearts of all of us."[57] Between 1965 and 1968 Jordan began articulating the need for this new interracial partnership. He did not as yet, however, have a clear vision of the shape the partnership, or movement, would take.

Koinonia Farm's work had a significant impact on the local area. In its early years it was a pioneering example of interracial life, as it provided a chance for whites and blacks to meet and act together and to live harmoniously. One result was the very close relationships between Koinonians and local black families like the Jacksons and Morgans. Then, during the movement, it brought people together for a taste of living in community, while it provided refuge, services, and facilities that helped keep the Sumter County movement going. In the process Koinonians earned the respect of African Americans in both Sumter County and Albany. The farm also addressed a real economic need first with its agricultural education and later with its support for co-ops and employment of blacks in the pecan business. In addition, Koinonia contributed to the civil rights movement more broadly. In the mid-1950s it provided a focal point and example of integration that activists, particularly religious white liberals, could rally around. In more general terms Koinonia brought to the movement a focus on relationships and reconciliation that went beyond desegregation and equal rights.

In retrospect, however, it is clear that the method and philosophy of the Koinonians contained several damaging weaknesses. They would have brought about change very slowly, taking at least a generation in the economic realm and much more in the social arena. Another fault was that Koinonians had trusted that the demonstration of interracial living would sway other white southerners. They had underestimated the extent to which the goodwill of that audience had evaporated between *Brown* and 1960. Most important, Koinonians had underestimated, and thus did not reckon with, institutionalized racism and the real differences in social, economic, and political power between whites and blacks. Although Koinonians had some success in developing good relationships between whites and blacks, they could not have had more impact outside the local area without addressing the balance of power.

Asking what was wrong with Koinonia Farm's approach to changing race relations may be the wrong question. The more interesting queries are why

Koinonians pursued change the way they did and what their relationship with the civil rights movement reveals about the nature of their interracialism. The Koinonians' ideas about race relations were imbedded in a larger philosophy about Christian life, which included community, interracial brotherhood, and nonviolence. Jordan and those who joined him started out with specific goals, including living together and helping local African Americans in material and spiritual ways. In the early 1950s the group defined itself as a Christian community which held racial equality as one of its precepts. From that point on there had always been some ambivalence about how to balance concern for inner community with interest in racial change. When attacks against them threw a spotlight on their interracialism and forced them to set priorities, Koinonians chose to maintain their witness at all costs. But even then they saw their racial beliefs as interconnected with community and nonviolence. They could and would work with others who shared one of their goals but not all their beliefs. But Koinonians would not fully adapt the tactics of others in the civil rights movement when those actions went against their total philosophy. Members of the farm were limited in their participation in the movement by their differences over demonstrations and the meaning of community and nonviolence. Moreover, they were left behind when the movement emphasized rights and power. In a sense, however, Koinonians also left the movement behind. Uncomfortable with the focus and tactics of the movement in mid-decade, Koinonians searched for new ways to bring about economic cooperation and spiritual sharing between whites and blacks.

The farm's experience teaches us about the effectiveness of community in social change. Koinonians saw interracial fellowship in community as a way to bring about improved race relations. This was related to but not the same as striving for civil rights. Koinonians, of course, agreed on the goals of voting rights, access to education and opportunity, and the end of discrimination, as avenues to equality. They supported any effort to achieve these goals. But they believed they were not enough to solve the race problem. The more important goal, as Koinonians saw it, was reconciliation, the bringing together of whites and blacks as equals. By 1965 they thought that the movement was putting too much effort into individual rights and was using divisive tactics in the process. Someone needed to work for reconciliation, as they believed they were doing through community.

Unfortunately, to put it most simply, community as Jordan originally conceptualized it did not work. Koinonians failed to bring whites and blacks together as equals because they did not take into consideration differences in values and goals. They established a community guided by their own values and expected African Americans to join it in order to bring about reconciliation. In short, better relations depended on African Americans assimilating to Koinonia's standard. African Americans had been uninterested in turning over their possessions and signing the commitment in order to become members, however. As long as Koinonia was structured as it was in the 1950s, as a complete community, separation between whites and blacks continued. Moreover, even when there was interracial fellowship, as in the early years, it did not address real differences in economics and power. In order to move ahead with building an interracial fellowship which would effect greater change, Koinonians needed to alter the terms of community and the meaning of sharing. They had begun to do this when they dropped the common purse and pursued the development of cooperatives with local blacks. Jordan's conceptualization of a God movement would lead them further in this direction, toward a new vehicle for their beliefs.

In their own way Koinonians and individuals in the movement reinforced and supported each other. The farm provided moral and material support to the movement in southwest Georgia by opening the community as a refuge and base of operations. The civil rights movement served as a bridge for Koinonia between its past program, over its internal difficulties of the mid-1960s, to a new purpose. Koinonians stayed in Sumter County in order to see how things turned out and be there when racial strife diminished. During the movement they cooperated to the extent allowed by their overall philosophy of Christian community, interracialism, and nonviolence. Then as the movement reached its conclusion, Koinonians saw a new need they could fill. The strife had created antagonisms between white and black and had caused economic repercussions for blacks, which Koinonians felt they must address. Most important, the movement had revealed the need for a new dedication to a spiritual awakening that Koinonians believed they could serve. By keeping them busy and opening up a new field of work, the movement kept Koinonia Farm alive during its most precarious time. It also prepared it to face new conditions with a new program.

10

Partners

COOPERATION WITH the movement had given Koinonians a reason to carry on through their troubles of the early 1960s. Now that they started to go their separate way, breaking from the movement, their old problems resurfaced. Between 1965 and 1968 the farm was at its lowest point. Finances were unstable at best, membership had dropped to the lowest level since the early forties, and because people could not agree on how to proceed toward their goals, morale had sunk. Moreover, Jordan was becoming increasingly dissatisfied with Koinonia. He felt a restless need to do more about race relations, continued economic problems, and the Vietnam War. He had begun to talk about his disenchantment with community per se, as well as his vision of the God movement. The catalyst that spurred him to put these ideas into action was a visitor to Koinonia. Just as Martin England long ago had inspired Jordan to start Koinonia Farm, Millard Fuller helped him to redirect his experiment. The Koinonians' basic dilemma had long been that their liberal Christian vision included ideals about communalism, race relations, and nonviolence that at times were at odds with one another. For years they had tried to balance them as best they could. But their experience with the civil rights movement convinced them that if they were to be effective, they needed to find a new approach. In 1968, with the help of a few friends, Jordan and Fuller resurrected, redirected, and renamed Koinonia. In partnership Koinonians found a way to reconcile their various goals by changing the nature of sharing and making the overall program better equipped to take an active role in social problems.

By the time Jordan was ready to make these changes, the situation at the farm was in turmoil. In 1963 the remaining members had decided that the farm would continue to be the holder of all resources and pay for housing, food, medical expenses, and other necessities. But each family would "assume the responsibility for income producing enterprises," make all of the related business decisions, and in turn receive a living allowance or wage.[1] When the group accepted this plan, it broke from the complete koinonia of goods. At that time the remaining members justified the move by declaring, "We do not consider community of goods an absolute essential to the Christian life."[2] Economically, Koinonia had exchanged full community—complete sharing out of a common purse—for a less rigidly defined system. The members still sought to keep the spiritual and emotional aspects of community, however, and encouraged people to come live at or near Koinonia to seek "a more meaningful life."[3] Koinonians wanted to keep some semblance of community alive by emphasizing fellowship and hoping new people would come to keep the farm going.

Unfortunately, Koinonia Farm had more and more trouble attracting and retaining long-term members. Through the mid-sixties the resident population hovered around two or three families and one or two individuals. When the Brownes and Dorothy Swisshelm departed, only the Jordans and Wittkampers remained as permanent members. Although visitors swelled the number of people on the farm, particularly during the height of the civil rights movement, so transient a population was not enough on which to build a stable community. The outlook briefly brightened in 1965 and 1966 when Al and Carol Henry and George and Marty Hardins arrived. At that time the farm's newsletter carried the hopeful declaration that with its core of families, numerous guests, and 10,000 friends on the mailing list, the Koinonia movement was growing. Not long afterward, however, both new couples left, the Hardins for unexplained reasons and the Henrys so that Al could take a job working with civil rights groups in Atlanta. Jan Jordan and her new husband Farrell Zehr came to the farm to help for a year in 1967.[4] The mood at Koinonia by that time was pessimistic. Clarence Jordan was bearing more and more of the weight of responsibility for the farm. According to Florence Jordan, they decided that if someone else did not come to help carry the burden, they would have to give up the community.[5]

People did continue to express an interest in coming to visit or stay at Koinonia. Those from outside the region often wanted to get a "first hand knowledge of what's going on in the South, to do civil rights work, or to make a Christian witness to southern whites."[6] A few sought community. The late 1960s were a time of stirring among young people who were hoping to overcome alienation and make a more meaningful connection to others. Finally, as always, Koinonia attracted people who needed help or a place to live. Ever since their very early work with alcoholics, Koinonians had a reputation for welcoming people in need. For example, in 1966 a longtime friend asked Koinonia to take in a young woman with cerebral palsy who had no family.[7]

For a number of reasons the Jordans regretfully discouraged people from coming to the farm. They were hardly in the position financially or emotionally to help people with severe problems. Moreover, large groups of visitors took time and energy away from farm work and could cause problems for Koinonians with their neighbors. Florence Jordan told one group from Ohio that visitors would have to provide for themselves; Koinonia had no room for a lot of inexperienced workers, and the Jordans could not spend all their time training people to do farm labor. Furthermore, she wrote, "we would feel that any contact with the larger outside community would have to meet with our approval. For anyone staying at Koinonia is, in the eyes of the county, a representative of Koinonia."[8] Clarence Jordan also discouraged potential guests by telling them the environment was hostile, the farm's residents had little outside social life, and, most important, "we barely have a community and are uncertain about the future." He also asserted that newcomers would have to find outside jobs to support themselves and doing so might be difficult.[9] By this time Jordan was seriously considering leaving or closing Koinonia. Perhaps he did not want the responsibility of new members. For whatever reason, by 1967 Koinonia not only was not getting new residents, the Jordans did not seem to want them.

As Koinonia Farm's situation deteriorated, Jordan became more concerned about social ills and convinced that community could not address them. The weaknesses he saw in the civil rights movement and the escalation of the Vietnam War caused him to focus more than ever on pacifism and related issues. Jordan spoke out against the war and encouraged young men to register as conscientious objectors. More often he preached about the broader implications of pacifism. He asserted that a pacifist should go beyond merely not hurting to helping: to practicing active goodwill and addressing social conditions, particularly economic inequality. Jordan believed nonviolence was linked to antimaterialism. He wrote, "A pacifist has to be willing to share with the less privileged—or be stuck with using coercion to defend his possessions."[10] By the mid-1960s Jordan had begun to envision a "God Movement" which would have nonviolence as its lifestyle, central philosophy, and means of action and which would replace the civil rights movement. Yet at the same time he was increasingly convinced that Koinonia Farm, as it was presently organized, could not handle the task of initiating such a movement. In 1966 he wrote to his son Jim that he did not doubt the basis of the Koinonia experiment and believed the message to be still relevant. But because Koinonia seemed "unable to break the 'people barrier'" and gather enough members to be a vital community, it needed to change direction and approach.[11]

Between 1966 and 1968 the Jordans and Wittkampers surveyed their options for the future. In his letter to his son, Jordan suggested they might turn the farm over to Collins McGee. Or, if they could find outside employment for him and others, they might liquidate the agricultural program altogether. Jordan also proposed moving closer to Atlanta, so that he could be near an airport to facilitate travel to his speaking engagements. Because they did not want to sell the property and divide the income, they looked for ways to give it away. Jordan meanwhile considered other jobs. Ann Morris of the School of the Arts in New Jersey asked Clarence and Florence to accept teaching positions and supported the offer with letters from the children pleading for them to come. The Church of the Brethren asked Jordan to take a pastorate, and Sam Emerick talked to the Yokefellow Institute about giving him a fellowship.[12] These opportunities appealed to Jordan because he wanted the freedom to write and speak. But he would not accept anything before he had settled the fate of the Koinonia experiment.

A number of factors complicated Jordan's desire to give up the farm. For one, the Wittkampers did not want to move. When Margaret pondered what God wanted them to do, she felt sure he had called her to remain at Koinonia. Besides, there were few if any options for her and her husband; Will was seventy years old and would have trouble finding a job as either a farmer or a minister. In later years Greg Wittkamper attributed the fact that Koinonia survived long enough to be reborn to his mother's unwillingness to leave. Jordan felt responsible for the Wittkampers and would not abandon them there alone. The two families had trouble disposing of the property, anyway. They even tried to give it to the Disciples of Christ and the American Baptists, but no one wanted it.[13] The final factor convincing Jordan to stay was the assassination of Martin Luther King Jr. King's death left Jordan more convinced than ever of the need for a God movement to overcome the polarization between blacks and whites. The assassination also left him more aware of the importance of staying "to be in the South as white people witnessing to the faith of Jesus Christ."[14] In part because of the lack of options but more importantly because of the desire to keep the witness going, no matter how small, Jordan once again stayed in Sumter County.

The extra energy and input that inspired Jordan to translate his discontent and ideas about the God movement into a new program for Koinonia came in the person of Millard Fuller. Fuller was an unlikely inspiration for antimaterialists like the Jordans and Wittkampers. When they first met him, he was a millionaire businessman and lawyer, whose firm had defended the men who beat the Freedom Riders in Montgomery. But he was also a Southern Baptist in the midst of a spiritual and marital crisis. Fuller's devotion to his business had taken a toll on his health and marriage. In 1965 his wife Linda left to seek counseling, and he abruptly realized he had to change his life in order to keep her. He flew to New York City to meet her, and together they agreed to start down a new path for their lives.[15]

On the drive back to Montgomery from New York, Fuller remembered that his friend Al Henry was living on a farm in southwest Georgia. The couple stopped at Koinonia for a brief visit, toured the farm, and had lunch with the community. During the meal Fuller listened as Jordan answered theological questions from other guests. The answers impressed him so much that he decided to share his and Linda's story. The loving and supportive response convinced the Fullers to stay at the farm for a month. During that time they helped prepare pecans for shipment and spent a lot of time talking about God. The experience led them to reorient their lives. Millard Fuller came to the conclusion that he wanted "to express his discipleship to Christ in selfless service to blacks." While at Koinonia they liquidated their assets and prepared for a new life.[16]

Over the next few years the Fullers and Jordans kept in touch while they searched for God's purposes for them. While Jordan held Koinonia together and searched for a new direction, Millard Fuller worked as a fund-raiser for Tougaloo College and kept his mind open to guidance from God. "We are in the hand of God. I can feel it," wrote Fuller. "Whatever decisions we make will be in accordance with his will."[17] Gradually the Fullers began to feel called to do something more. The way of life they experienced at Koinonia and the feeling that Jordan was on the verge of leading a great spiritual revival continued to pull at them. In the spring of 1968 Millard Fuller resigned from his fund-raising job and wrote Jordan a short letter asking, "What do you have up your sleeve?" Jordan, who was ready to try something new himself, arranged to meet him for a few days at the Oakhurst Baptist Church in Atlanta.[18]

The Atlanta meeting initiated a series of discussions about how to build a new movement based on the Koinonia message. Fuller's willingness to join Koinonia and help resurrect it gave Jordan the reassurance that he did not have to carry the full weight of responsibility himself. Fuller injected some needed energy, giving Jordan a moral and spiritual boost. The two men emerged from their first talk certain that the Holy Spirit was guiding them and determined "to throw every ounce of our weight into helping men to radically restructure their lives so as to be in partnership with God."[19] Immediately they began consulting with friends and getting advice on how to structure a movement. In August 1968 they assembled a group of associates to plan the new venture. The men they invited came from various parts of the circles in which Fuller and Jordan moved. There were long-time friends and supporters of Koinonia including Bob Swann, John Miller of Reba Place, and Sam Emerick. Some of Koinonia's local friends also attended, including Slater King of Albany and Doc Champion, whose wife Willa Mae worked at the pecan plant. Fuller invited men who might bring a different perspective because of their distance from the old Koinonia: Ned Coll, the founder of "the revitalization corps"—a domestic peace corps—and Ladon Sheats, an executive of IBM who was in the process of reorienting his life for Christ. The gathering also included businessmen, ministers, and church officials.[20]

Jordan opened the conference by encouraging the group to "think big . . . this is not a time for spiritual pygmies."[21] Excitement and hopefulness were audible in the men's voices as they spoke about their vision. They considered many ideas about how to tap into the energy on campuses, give people spiritual inspiration, and show them some way to act on it. The group came up with a general outline for action: "preach, teach, and heal." All the men gave top priority to freeing Jordan from other responsibilities so that he could spread his message. The group also agreed on the need to teach on the campuses, to get people discussing Jordan's ideas. But what to do next— what would they encourage people to do with their new understanding? Some suggested organizing people into service projects. Others, such as Millard Fuller and Ladon Sheats, argued that people could serve where they were, by changing their own lives and in turn preaching to others. For his part, Jordan advised against too much structure. He did not want to constrain the movement of God's spirit. The consensus by the end of the first discussion was to focus in the short term on preaching and teaching through Jordan's lectures and discipleship schools, then later work out a formula for healing.[22]

Throughout the discussion and Jordan's ruminations about the God movement, the concept of "partnership" kept coming up. In his Cotton Patch translations Jordan called the disciples "partners" to emphasize their role in helping God and Christ accomplish their goals for the redeeming of the world. At the August 1968 conference, he argued that the "alienation, estrangement, loneliness, anonymity, competitiveness, racial pride, and all the fragmentation of man from himself and God" made it necessary for people to learn to be partners.[23] To do that, first one had to listen to God's will and do his work. The second step was to be partners with your fellow humans, working with others as equals toward a common goal. Millard Fuller gave an example: partnership meant that an ex-millionaire lawyer with education and business experience like himself should work as an equal partner in an agricultural enterprise with an uneducated, poor, African-American sharecropper like Bo Johnson.[24] Such a partnership would bridge the gaps of race, class, and educational opportunity and unite people in common work. The concept of partnership became the driving force in Koinonia's new program.

Partnership also addressed structural economic problems that concerned Jordan. As he pointed out, poor farmers in southwest Georgia had to produce about 3,500 bushels of corn in 1968 just to pay the interest on their land. Most had little hope of owning their land outright unless they inherited it.[25] In addition, most underprivileged people could not amass the capital needed to start their own businesses. The result was they were then stuck in debt or working for low wages. Jordan and his associates envisioned a number of ways to put his ideas to work against the problems he saw. Koinonia could provide land to poor farmers and capital for small industries, encouraging workers to run the enterprises cooperatively. The workers would have control over their business and not be subject to exploitation by an employer. Jordan and Fuller hoped these arrangements might replace the competitive spirit with a sense of cooperation in God's work and at the same time restore dignity to the workers.[26]

Partnership was a modification of community. It shared community's goal of breaking down barriers and bringing people together to work and live cooperatively. But partnership distilled the outward-looking social purpose of the earlier philosophy. Put another way, partnership was an activist way to accomplish what Jordan had hoped community would but did not. The primary difference between the two was that partnership focused on work rather than on lifestyle. The people who came to live at Koinonia would not be part of a full Christian community sharing out of a common pot as they had until the early 1960s. Instead, families would work in separate partnership enterprises, while still living together and sharing socially and spiritually. The change of name was significant. Koinonia Farm was a place where people lived in community. Koinonia Partners was a group of people working in partnership and living together at a particular place. With this shift Koinonians completed a cycle. In the 1940s they had focused on ministering to African Americans, and only in the 1950s did they start paying attention to defining community and "unity." Through the 1960s they unsuccessfully struggled to have both an outreach and a strong inner fellowship. With the shift to Partners, Koinonians returned to their original arrangement of living together to accomplish goals. In doing so they found a balance between their various ideals. They got cooperation, blacks and whites working together, and the spiritual and emotional satisfaction of living together. At the same time they were relieved of the tension caused by the effort to live in complete community, and they lowered the barriers that full sharing had erected to black participation.

Race relations were still a central part of Koinonia's philosophy, and the essentials of its approach to changing the racial caste system were carried over in the partnership program. When Jordan talked about breaking down barriers between people, he spoke in terms of race and class. Partnerships would bring whites and blacks together to work. Moreover, when partnership addressed economic problems, it continued Koinonia's long attention to development and cooperation. Jordan recognized that without access to land or capital, African Americans would be trapped in poverty. Koinonia's partnerships aimed at providing this access. The main difference between community and partnership with respect to race relations was that Koinonians did not expect African Americans to participate in the full economic sharing of a common purse or accept their definition of community living. They hoped that the blacks who worked in the partnership farming and industries would share socially with the whites, joining in meals, worship services, and recreation. By dropping what had seemed most objectionable to African Americans—the full sharing—and replacing it with cooperation, Koinonians hoped to be able again, as in their very early years, to promote economic change and Christian social fellowship.

At the August 1968 meeting Jordan, Fuller, and their associates created a three-part program to give concrete expression to the idea of partnership and the perceived need for a new movement. First, there would be preaching. Jordan would tour the country to deliver his message while Koinonia produced tapes, records, and books to distribute. These efforts would spread the word about partnership with God. Second would be the teaching phase. Koinonians would follow up Jordan's speeches by organizing discipleship schools around the country. These would be intense one- or two-week sessions where people would come to "keep alive the new spirit" that Jordan inspired by further reading and study. The participants would be charged with establishing partnerships in their own lives and neighborhoods, nurturing the seed of Jordan's message to grow into a broader social movement.

The third and most important part of the new program would be healing through partnerships. Fuller and Jordan's ideas about partnership would be put to practice in industries, farming, and a new venture, housing. To begin, the Wittkampers, Al Zook and his family, who recently moved to Koinonia, the Bo Johnsons, and others would start partnerships in farming and other enterprises. The capital for the enterprises would come from the Fund for Humanity, a loan fund established by Koinonia. The fund borrowed from Jordan's very early work with the pantry at the Baptist Fellowship Center. Well-to-do people made contributions into the fund and thus shared their excess resources; the money was given to the less-well-off as capital for starting businesses. This extended partnership to the relationship between people in the external network and those working and living at Koinonia. Then the local people involved would work in and run the businesses together, as equals in all decisions, and share the proceeds. Jordan hoped that the new partners, having learned the value of voluntary sharing, would then contribute part of the profit back to the fund.[27]

The proposed partnerships had roots in Koinonia's ongoing work. By early 1968 Koinonia had developed some of the industries that would soon become partnerships. For example, the community had established a sewing shop for local women, providing the space, machines, patterns—the "capital" so to speak—and letting the neighbors use it.[28] Earlier there had been some cooperative agricultural adventures, such as Zev Aelony and Collins McGee's experiment with a vineyard. The third proposed area of partnership was in housing. Koinonians would provide land and help people build homes on it. This, they hoped, would address the problem of substandard housing in Sumter County. In 1967 and 1968 they had begun setting aside land when some local African Americans had come to them asking to buy a little plot of land on which they could build a house. Since Koinonians were not doing much farming anyway, they cleared half-acre and acre lots and offered them for a decent price.[29] Plans for building homes on the plots were in the works when Koinonia went into its transition.

The proposals for the new partnership program reflected contemporary trends in race relations and poverty work. By the late 1960s civil rights activists and organizations in Georgia turned their attention to improving the lives of the rural poor. This activity often took place in conjunction with the War on Poverty and the Great Society, as activists tried to provide rural blacks with access to these programs. White liberals in the Georgia Council for Human Relations (GCHR), still quite active in southwest Georgia, worked on welfare rights and the minimum wage. The Cooperative League tried to help southern farmers by forming twenty-six co-ops in the southern states and founding the Southern Federation of Cooperatives. Most significant, like Koinonians other liberals showed increasing interest in the problem of low-income housing for rural and small-town areas. Several groups, including the GCHR, SRC, and Georgia Advisory Committee to the United States Civil Rights Commission recognized the need for more housing for the very poor. Besides pressuring city governments for aid, these groups supported the Self-Help Housing Project. This was a program in Thomas County which provided technical help and training for people to build their own homes. The founders' goal was to provide better housing and education for rural people as a step toward better jobs and wages.[30] When Koinonia launched its cooperative businesses and housing project, it was tapping into this current in civil rights activity.

The renewed interest in economics as a basis for equality brought Koinonians and other activists back full circle to the actions and goals of the late 1930s and early 1940s. Coming out of the Depression, liberal white southerners had seen poverty as the root of rural and racial problems and had sought solutions that addressed economic inequalities. Koinonians at that time had been part of a broader movement in agricultural reform and cooperatives. In the 1950s and early 1960s, as race became defined as a moral problem with integration as the main solution, economic development and cooperation had lost priority. Disabled by their communalism and interpretation of nonviolence from participating fully in the civil rights movement, Koinonians had struggled to find a niche in which they could pursue their own approach to improving race relations. By the late 1960s activists who were looking for a basis of power for the black community sought it in economic independence. Meanwhile white liberals recognized the importance of addressing poverty. With this trend Koinonians once again found themselves in sync with a broader movement, this time focusing on rural employment and housing.

Koinonia Partners' strategy had an auspicious beginning. Almost immediately the preaching and communication created excitement and drew a new wave of people to the farm. Jordan's speaking schedule increased as he traveled to youth meetings, college campuses, and conventions. In early 1969, after attending their son James's wedding in South Africa, the Jordans traveled through four African countries on a missionary tour. While there, they made a $500 Fund for Humanity loan to a small businessman in Ghana.[31] During this time Koinonia also organized discipleship schools. Ladon Sheats, who had helped organize Koinonia Partners at the August conference, arranged several sessions in New York City. There were also schools on the West Coast and at Koinonia itself. At these sessions twelve to fifteen committed Christians learned the meaning of radical discipleship. The curriculum emphasized Bible study, but the sessions were loosely structured in order, as Jordan put it, to "leave plenty of freedom for the moving of God's spirit."[32] Students at discipleship schools at Koinonia toured the farm and joined in community recreational activities. People who came to the schools journeyed from Oregon, New Jersey, Georgia, Alabama, Ohio, and even Ontario.[33] Eventually, the resident population of the farm started rising, too.

Partnership industries and farming likewise got off to a good start. The partnership program put a lot of emphasis on shared work and new economic arrangements, and so Koinonians hoped that the industries would be the most successful part of their program. Mail orders picked up 50 percent in the next year, expanding enough to employ twenty-five people. The people working in the pecan plant, fruitcake bakery, and candy kitchen drew a salary and diverted profits back into the fund. Al Zook and Bo Johnson started a farming partnership growing corn and peanuts. Technically they were employees of Koinonia Partners and paid themselves a salary. Lenny Jordan, the youngest Jordan child, raised steers with his black classmate Thomas Woods. Koinonia provided the land free of charge, and the boys shared the proceeds and paid separate personal income tax. They were also encouraged by Koinonia to donate back into the fund.[34]

Although Jordan and Fuller had hoped the enterprises would be run on a completely cooperative basis, in the long run it did not work out that way. The low-income people from the area hesitated to enter into cooperative ventures. According to Millard Fuller, "We discovered people like Bo wanted a guaranteed income. They didn't want to take any risks. . . . They wanted a paycheck at the end of every week."[35] Perhaps the idea that they would be furnished land, work it, then divide up or share the profits sounded to African Americans a little too much like the sharecropping system from which they had just escaped. In both farming and the mail-order industry, the African-American workers wanted a job at good wages and in a pleasant environment. But they did not agree with Koinonia's vision of cooperation and sharing. Because of that, rather than working and dividing up the proceeds equally as had been originally envisioned, the employees made a set salary while the extra profits were diverted back into the Fund for Humanity.[36] This reflected a long history of divergence between white and black views at Koinonia, but now the whites accepted the differences and worked it into the overall program. This acceptance was reflected in the variety of flexible paid, sharing, and cooperative arrangements in the partnership enterprises.

The partnership housing plan, meanwhile, met and surpassed expectations. By the end of the summer of 1968, Koinonians started applying donations to a fund to go toward building four-room homes for local families, designated forty-two half-acre plots, and cleared a four-acre park. They proposed to sell twenty sites outright, as they had earlier, and to build homes on twenty-two along a partnership model. The Fund for Humanity would pay for the construction; then the homeowners would pay it back over twenty years in $25-a-month installments. The intent was to build housing for any poor family, but since most of the underprivileged in southwest Georgia were black, most of the people who applied for Koinonia housing also were black. In December, Koinonia started building the first house for Bo Johnson's family. Volunteers arrived to help with the houses, clear land, and layout the park. Koinonia hired a black contracting company for the construction, in order to give some local people steady employment. By May 1969 two houses were almost complete, and work was beginning on a third and fourth.[37]

Jordan did not witness the completion of the houses. On October 29, 1969, he died of a heart attack. He had been feeling poorly for a few days and was anxious to make progress on his writing. So he retired to the peace and quiet of a shack on the property which served as his office. He was interrupted briefly by Lena Hofer, a little girl visiting from the Hutterites. After a few minutes he reached out to give her a good-bye hug, and his body jerked. Lena ran off to get help. By the time Florence and others were summoned, Lenny Jordan had discovered that his father was dead. Fuller moved the body into the house and called the coroner. Ironically, or perhaps fittingly, he had trouble getting any town or county officials to come out to look at or pick up the body.[38]

The community decided to bury Jordan on his demonstration plot. That night Jack Singletary and some others dug a hole at Picnic Hill. Fuller was chosen to say a few words. Daunted, he asked Florence's advice. She told him to read some Scripture, which Jordan so dearly loved. The passage he chose came from Jordan's own translations: "In order that you all, too, might be our partners, we're plainly telling you about something that's real, something that we ourselves have heard, that we have seen with our own two eyes. The darkness is lifting and the true light is already dawning." After the service Faith Fuller spontaneously burst into a chorus of "Happy birthday, dear Clarence."[39] The audience was touched and felt this appropriate because Jordan would see his death as a rebirth. At the time of Jordan's passing, Koinonia was embarking on its own resurrection from its low point in 1965–67. It was a different Koinonia. Jordan was not there in the flesh to help guide it, and the three-pronged program underway diverged from the early work. But to a remarkable extent it perpetuated Jordan's original vision.

By the end of 1969, streams of young people were pouring new energy into the life and work of the community. Students from Antioch, Defiance, and Beloit Colleges, a young Quaker from Washington, D.C., and the Young Life area director from Philadelphia joined Koinonia. Some came to volunteer and others to live there. Work camp groups from as far away as Vermont came through in the summers. Indeed, there were so many helpers that Koinonia Partners decided to organize a permanent volunteer program. The newcomers fixed up the farm, painting and renovating older buildings, cleared the park and set up the playground, and most of all worked in the new housing program.[40] Participation in Koinonia's program gave the young people a sense of Christian agency. One young woman wrote to a friend that "living at Koinonia has made me feel I am part of a movement that is trying to relate to these needs—both spiritual and physical. I am beginning to sense that deep inner peace and freedom which comes with being able to give of one's self in a program dedicated to promoting the spirit of love among all men, regardless of race and creed."[41] At the same time the new partners and volunteers energized Koinonia and gave it new life.

The new vehicle of Partners preserved the Koinonians' beliefs in sharing, interracialism, and nonviolence but in forms shaped by white and black needs, circumstances, and evolving philosophy. Before he died, Jordan had given up the idea of full sharing. He had organized Koinonia Partners so that while newcomers still turned over their assets either as a gift or loan, they now worked for a salary in one of the partnership enterprises.[42] Koinonia had moved toward this level of individual responsibility because material circumstances, specifically the economic realities of the farm and the area around it, had required increased efficiency and liquidity. In the early 1970s, however, as more young white people moved to Koinonia, the economic arrangements were modified. These educated middle-class newcomers were excited about living in full community and pushed Koinonia back in that direction. Eventually a common fund provided for most necessities of those who wished to become full partners, and each then received a spending allowance. Although it was not the full sharing of the 1940s and 1950s, the new members had taken Koinonia back in the direction of "holding things in common."[43] But Partners had room for local blacks to be part of Koinonia, without participating in the full sharing, by working in the enterprises, earning a wage, and turning the profits back into the Fund for Humanity. This economic arrangement, then, was a compromise between the young idealists who flocked to Koinonia for full community and the needs of the local African Americans for a regular paycheck.

The actions of the partners in the realm of sharing reflected the difference between the concepts of partnership and community. The essential elements of cooperation were carried over. Moreover, Partners continued to stress shared work and economic development as a way to change race relations and the situation of African Americans in the Deep South. But the philosophy and approach of partnership differed from that of the Koinonia Farm community. Full community had failed as an economic operation and as a vehicle for social change. Jordan and Fuller wanted to address social problems in a more direct way. As a result, partnership was more activist and outward-looking. Jordan and Fuller saw Koinonia Partners as the seed of a God movement, which would spread as people heard the message and set up partnerships in their own areas. The new concept of partnership caused the changes in Koinonia's structure and program. Most importantly the economic structure was loosened to allow people to establish different kinds of work partnerships. In essence, the change from community to Partners put the long-held beliefs in sharing, nonviolence, and working for brotherhood in a vehicle that was both more flexible and activist.

Like sharing, nonviolence continued to be a major point of Koinonia's philosophy. By the end of his life Jordan was preaching against the Vietnam War and the draft. His oldest son registered as a conscientious objector and did alternative service.[44] As always, the members of Koinonia did not participate in anything that supported war and preached against violence. The partners also acted on Jordan's admonishments late in life and stepped up their active goodwill toward the surrounding community. They did so through outreach to their neighbors in the form of child care and house building. The new members differed from the former Koinonians somewhat, however. Early Koinonians defined nonviolence as a refusal to respond to attacks against them with anything but love and viewed demonstrations or protests as too aggressive. New partners, on the other hand, in addition to gestures of love and goodwill toward their neighbors, participated in demonstrations against nuclear weapons and the death penalty, something earlier Koinonians would not, as a whole, have approved. The change was due to the differences in the new members' experience. The Koinonians of the 1970s were far more comfortable with public demonstrations and protests as a means of action than those who had lived there in the 1950s and 1960s. They were part of a generation that had grown up watching civil rights demonstrations on television and had marched against the Vietnam War. Such tactics therefore were not foreign or unreasonable to them. Koinonians were still advocating nonviolence but in a way that was more active and suited to the circumstances of their era.

Finally, in the area of race relations, Koinonia Partners took many of the ideas of Jordan and his early associates and acted on them in a different way. Koinonians had set out to minister to African Americans' spiritual and economic needs. The zealous Southern Baptists who first peopled the farm wanted to take their message to the blacks of the rural South. The outlets for that energy had been vacation Bible school and home visits. In addition, however, the young Koinonians had also wanted to worship alongside, and get to know, African Americans as equal disciples of Christ. Koinonia Partners continued to work with neighborhood children, although the emphasis was more on education generally and less on Christian mission. The idea that the group needed to, or even should, "take the word" to African Americans had faded because the new members benefited from their upbringing in a time somewhat less plagued by, though not freed entirely from, the paternalism of an earlier day. The white partners also continued to include their neighbors in worship services, inviting elder Ludrell Pope or Doc Champion to lead the prayers. A few partners eventually started to attend

African-American churches. In these informal ways white partners tried to keep alive Jordan's dream of white-black Christian fellowship.

Koinonia Partners also adapted the early goal of agricultural training and economic development for African Americans to the conditions of the late 1960s. Koinonians had begun working on economic development for blacks as a way to give them independence. Their original agricultural program had gotten off to a successful beginning before falling prey to the attacks against the farm in the 1950s. Emerging from the boycott and violence, Koinonia found that agricultural conditions had changed. As agribusiness displaced sharecropping and even small landowners, poor blacks in southwest Georgia moved off the farm. By the end of the 1960s, Koinonia needed a new economic program to address the needs of the black community. The members worked on cooperatives and unions and employed as many neighbors as possible in the industries. The jobs created in the partnership industries gave employees a voice in the process and an egalitarian work environment. In addition, Koinonia provided land to a few farmers, although over time this became less important as an economic enterprise. Most importantly, Koinonia Partners turned its attention to Sumter County's housing crisis. The partnership housing program combined the Koinonians' beliefs that land was held in trust from God and that people should work cooperatively. Koinonia provided land free of charge, and partners and potential homeowners built the houses together. The agricultural demonstration plot had worked for its time. In the new times Koinonia turned to demonstrating "the economics of Jesus" in housing.[45] In both cases the goal was the same: providing economic independence for African Americans.

When Koinonia became Koinonia Partners, the transition put old wine into a new skin. Koinonia had been on the verge of disintegration. The lack of members, financial stability, and sense of direction plagued it. Jordan, moreover, was increasingly uneasy and frustrated with Koinonia's inability to address social ills. Koinonia Farm's structure and program had been molded by the culture of midcentury Southern Baptism and by the perceived needs of rural African Americans in the 1930s and 1940s. But the original structure was now inadequate to keep the organization going or to address the needs of either the white members or their black neighbors in the late 1960s. In addition, over the years the Koinonians' effort to balance their desire to live in community with their outreach goals had caused uncertainty and inner tension about their purpose. By the 1960s both their community structure and outreach were on the brink of collapse. They spent the decade looking for a new purpose, direction, and way to act on both their beliefs and goals. Together with Millard Fuller, and with the advice of friends, Jordan devised a new program. Although different in the amount of structure, economic arrangements, and form of outreach, the new Koinonia mirrored the old in basic philosophy. This program allowed it to reconcile its disparate goals of spiritual fellowship and material aid for African Americans into a program which was appropriate in the new environment. In doing so Koinonia Partners established a structure in which relationships between whites and blacks would be based on shared work and fellowship and in which members could both live a Christian life and take action on problems of race, economics, and militarism.

Epilogue

K OINONIA HAS EXISTED as a Christian, interracial cooperative community in the Deep South for over fifty years. Its history raises several questions, including: how did its members' philosophy arise out of southern culture, how did the farm survive through such adversity, and, most important, how were the elements of community and interracialism reconciled? In the hope that this narrative has answered those questions, I close my tale of Koinonia Farm. Interestingly, Koinonia Partners' history is the story of how Koinonians continued to explore their central beliefs and act upon them. In the early 1990s the Partners engaged in a several-year process of reevaluating the community's structure and purpose, weighing, as did former generations, the relative importance of inner fellowship with outreach and service. This is an ongoing process, demonstrating the Koinonians' continued struggle to act on religious beliefs, reconcile the contradictions between the goals of sharing and improving race relations, and respond to changing circumstances.

This history has attempted to answer certain questions about the nature of Koinonia's liberal Christian beliefs and approach to social problems, particularly regarding race. To begin, Koinonia Farm was an organic outgrowth of southern, and especially Southern Baptist, culture. The members had been trained in southern Protestant institutions, where they learned the importance of personal salvation, living a moral life, and evangelism. Through their lives in church organizations Koinonians developed a worldview and way of acting which they shared with other southern white Protestants. In these organizations Koinonians learned to think of the church as a community and a fellowship of Christians. They were also influenced by the southern progressive minority, which taught that African Americans should be included in that fellowship. Jordan and other Koinonians combined ideas about community and interracialism in ways that went further than most of their early contemporaries. When they were excommunicated from the Rehobeth Church, it seemed they were being rejected by their religious culture. But even during their crisis Koinonians were supported by a community of liberal southerners and elements of the southern church. Moreover, in the 1960s and 1970s, when Koinonia lost much of its particularly Southern Baptist flavor, the farm was still part of an ecumenical, progressive Christian network. Indeed, the conflict over these ideas was within the southern church, not between it and Koinonia.

Being supported by elements of the culture does not guarantee a community's survival, however. The farm was able to accomplish its work and continue to function over the years despite such hostility because the members never lost sight of their overall purpose and principles. Essentially, Koinonians have always believed in living a Christian life, including sharing and living in peace and equality with fellow Christians. And they held that working cooperatively with, and providing economic support to, African Americans would improve race relations. Today's partners would recognize the early Koinonia plan and program because it is their own, in slightly different form. The Koinonians' ideology has been a compass which has guided the members through various crises. For example, when population pressures and other developments caused problems, they organized their lives together based on their Christian communal principles. Their refusal to yield their witness on race relations kept them in southwestern Georgia during the storms of the late 1950s. And their beliefs provided the blueprint for the rebuilding of the 1960s. At times over the years the Koinonians' philosophy hampered them. Their nonviolence made it hard for them to respond to the attacks and boycotts against them, for example. More important, their communalism and pacifism kept them from participating fully and effectively in the civil rights movement of the early 1960s. Although their inflexible hold on their principles limited their options and complicated their reactions, however, it also served to keep them functioning as a group until they could find a new, more effective way to act.

Koinonians combined this commitment to ideology with flexibility in matters of form. They changed their community's internal structure, focus, and modus operandi according to the circumstances at different times in their history. They started out living together without much official structure so that they could accomplish certain outreach goals. When internal problems required attention, they shifted their focus inward and organized themselves. Later, when they were under attack and struggling to rebuild, Koinonians made adjustments in their financial arrangements, outreach program, and even the nature of their community. They were always willing to adapt to changes in their environment. For example, when the economy around them shifted, they replaced agricultural cooperatives and education with partnership industries and housing. This adaptability kept their message relevant to people interested in joining Koinonia, to social issues, and to the needs of local African Americans.

The primary issue raised in this history of Koinonia Farm, however, is the nature of the members' beliefs and the relationship between communalism, interracialism, and civil rights. The constant element in Koinonia's story was its commitment to improving race relations through two basic strategies. First, as Jordan saw it, African Americans needed economic independence before they could achieve equality. For that reason Koinonians worked to provide economic aid to blacks and to include them in cooperative endeavors. At different times those ventures took the form of agricultural education, jobs, and housing. In addition Koinonians sought to create an interracial community. They believed that personal relationships built by living and working together would bring blacks and whites together. In the early years Koinonians accomplished this through their mission activities. Later they sought to achieve it through recruiting African-American members into the community.

This strategy for improving race relations had mixed results over the years. In the 1940s the Koinonians were part of a movement for rural rehabilitation which included biracial cooperation. Their early agricultural education made a contribution to the economy of the area. Moreover, Koinonians developed strong friendships with local black families. In 1950 when they defined community as full sharing and commitment, they set up barriers to African-American participation. Then the attacks against the farm undercut the Koinonians' economic programs. For a decade they struggled to combine their desire for fuller relationships within community and interest in outreach and race relations. They tried, unsuccessfully, to bring blacks into membership. During the movement they temporarily established an interracial community in the refuge of the farm, but disagreements over tactics with activists broke it apart. In the late 1960s attention shifted to the economic base of equality, and Koinonians found a new niche in the partnership program. Over the years Koinonians had moved back and forth between emphasizing community or interracialism, often having to give up some of one or the other. They hoped that the partnership idea would combine the essence of both goals. Koinonia Partners continued to struggle with interracial relationships, however, and the state of race relations at the community lay at the root of the further restructuring of the mid-1990s.

Koinonia's experience reveals much about the role of community in bringing about better race relations. Community has long been part of the rhetoric of civil rights. Indeed, like Koinonians, Martin Luther King Jr. and others in the movement had sought to create an interracial "beloved community." On the surface the history of the farm would seem to lead to the conclusion that interracial community does not work. At the root of the problem in this case lies Koinonia's definition of community at the eve of the civil rights movement. In the early 1950s the members had narrowly defined community, expecting full consensus, commitment, and sharing. Then they expected African Americans to accept that definition in order to join. In addition, for many years, including at a crucial point in the movement, Koinonians were unsure whether their inner relationship or work in race relations was more important. This uncertainty hampered their ability to act effectively. In order to have a role in social change, community has to be a meeting place between groups, a place where blacks and whites can bring ideals, goals, and cultural values to share. In this definition community is an open, flexible relationships based on common goals. Moreover, it is constantly developing and growing rather than being statically defined by a particular commitment or ideal. The concept of partnership that Koinonians adopted in the late 1960s was a step in this direction. How successful it will be in bringing the races together, not just in work but in fellowship, is still being worked out.

Events in Koinonia's later history illustrate the way the partners continued to deal with these themes and issues. On the one hand, the success of the partnership idea in the realm of economic reform was demonstrated by the expansion of the housing program. In the late 1960s a few African Americans had approached Jordan about buying a little of his land on which to build houses. Koinonians leased the land and built modest homes, letting the new owners pay them back in small amounts over the years. Then, when Koinonia Partners began, the partnership housing industry took off. In the mid-1970s Millard and Linda Fuller went to Zaire and, with volunteers from the United States and Canada, built 114 homes. The experience so energized the Fullers that they decided to launch a larger housing project than Koinonia Partners could handle. In 1976 Koinonia Partners and Millard Fuller founded Habitat for Humanity (HFH) to build houses on the partnership model around the world.[1] As of 1993 there were 707 affiliates of HFH in the United States alone, and over 15,000 houses had been built worldwide. Meanwhile, Koinonia Partners continued its own building program in Sumter County, reflecting its dedication to working locally. The partners' goal is to replace all the substandard housing in the county. The housing program was celebrated at the April 1992 jubilee weekend with an emotional mortgage-burning ceremony.

While the housing program illustrates the success of the economic side of Koinonia's work, more recently the partners have been confronting problems in their interracial relationships and communal structure. In February 1990, in response to requests from the African-American employees, Partners held a retreat to discuss race relations. The workers had declared that "the present situation here at Koinonia is one that makes our hearts bleed, because we as employees see things that are in total conflict with the philosophy of Koinonia and the Christian philosophy." Worst of all, "Koinonia has turned into just another Southern business." They complained that they did not share in business decisions, were taken advantage of because of the lack of benefits, and, in the most cutting criticism, did not feel a part of the community.[2] A group of partners decided that in order to begin to heal this situation, they would organized a series of events for their annual retreat month. They watched videos and listened to guest speakers from interracial ministries, held conferences and social events with employees, and participated with workers in a three-day session led by Lillie Allen, a professional counselor who specializes in coordinating intimate meetings about racial feelings. The white partners followed up these events with a questionnaire to the employees and had brain-storming sessions to try to come up with some solutions.

Koinonia Partners learned a lot about the racial situation in its community during the monthlong retreat. Most importantly, the partners realized they could not rest on the laurels of Koinonia's historic effort to promote interracial fellowship. With the help of their black employees, the white members recognized the power imbalance between partners and workers, which resulted in the lack of decision-making power and benefits for the latter. Increasingly, the partners understood that voluntary downward mobility and the willingness to give up possessions and financial security in order to join the community was a white middle-class phenomenon. "It makes no sense to require a people who have been given few economic/social/political options to reduce the gains achieved for the sake of community.[3] The partners could not expect local blacks to give up what they had in order to join them and perhaps should consider allowing them an alternative path to membership. By the end of the conference, the members of Koinonia Partners began taking action on a few specifics which had been requested or endorsed by the employees. For one, they included longtime employees in the guest house's directory to the Koinonia community. They also began a search for one word that would designate all the people at Koinonia: full members, workers, people who lived on the property in partnership houses, volunteers, etc. Finally, they agreed to look at alternative authority structures, to have frequent meetings with the employees, and to commit themselves to a consistent effort to improve the situation.

Over the next several years Koinonia underwent major changes that fundamentally altered the structure and mission of the community. First, Partners disbanded the common purse. In small part, economics led to the decision. Moreover, some of the white partners felt that giving up complete sharing would relieve the tension in their relationships. Most important, however, was the recognition that the shift back to the common purse since the early 1970s had divided the white partners from the black employees. By giving up the sharing and having everyone who worked at Koinonia earn a salary, Partners hoped to equalize the status of whites and blacks. Along with the new wage system, Koinonia also restructured authority. It ended the rotating system of office-holding by full partners and replaced it with an executive director and paid positions in various ministries. In late 1994 a longtime African-American employee became the executive director of Koinonia Partners, with other positions held by white former partners or black former staff.

These changes brought into question the mission of Koinonia. In the five-year period after the 1990 retreat Koinonians rethought their purpose and rewrote their mission statement. During this process partners and employees met separately, and in 1992 each contributed a draft statement. The differences were striking. For the employees Koinonia was a service organization whose role was to be "a model of equal justice" and to provide programs in jobs, housing, day care, and paralegal assistance.[4] The partners, on the other hand, envisioned Koinonia as a "demonstration plot for the Kingdom of God." Their plan included outreach programs and a just livelihood for the workers but also a commitment to sharing of worship, prayer, and resources.[5] The compromise version portrayed Koinonia as a Christian service organization dedicated to providing service in an atmosphere of sharing. The differences in the original drafts, however, illustrated the distance between black and white that fifty years of "living in community" as Koinonia defined it had not healed.

At the time of the fiftieth anniversary, Koinonia Partners was concerned with the same issue that had long confronted the members of the farm: how to reconcile a Christian life of sharing, interracial fellowship, and commitment to social change. The experience of the anniversary period revealed that the struggle over those issues continues. By mid-decade the partners were working on sharing authority and understanding cultural differences. With these changes, the remaining question was whether Koinonia was fulfilling or abandoning its past. According to most of the residents in the summer of 1995, Partners is completing Jordan's task by reaching out and helping the local people. A few, however, see the end of the true Koinonia in the loss of the common purse.[6] These differing perspectives alone demonstrate that the building of a beloved community is an ongoing process. Looking back on the history of Koinonia Farm, I propose that Partners is fulfilling its history by experimenting with ways to equalize the status of whites and blacks, in the process empowering African Americans; to share Christian fellowship; and to reach out to the local community. In these efforts, the Partners' program continues to incarnate Jordan's vision.

Appendix

Notes

Bibliography

Index

Appendix

Koinonians

This list includes individuals who played an important role in my history of Koinonia Farm either as members, neighbors, or laborers. It is not an inclusive list of people who associated with the community. Koinonia was home, for varying lengths of time, to hundreds, perhaps even thousands of visitors, guests, and long- and short-term members over the years. I do not mean to imply that people not on this list were not important. Married couples are listed together except when they arrived separately. The dates indicate the approximate times when the individuals were at the community. It should be noted, however, that many people came and went over the years, making it hard to establish the period of their involvement. Moreover, documentary evidence on exact dates of arrival and departure is rare.

1940s

Allene Griffin Atkinson, 1949–57
Harry Atkinson, 1944–57
C. Z. Ballard, [?]–1951
Willie Pugh Ballard, 1947–51; in area until 1953
C. Conrad and Ora Browne, 1949–63
Mabel and Martin England, 1942–44
Jesse (Bobby) Engram, 1949–52
E. Millard Hunt, 1948–5[?]
Chester Jackson, [?]–1950
Bo Johnson, 1941–51, 1967–present
Joseph (Candy) Johnson, 1942–47
Marion Johnson, 1950–56
T. Howard Johnson, 1949–56
Clarence Jordan, 1942–69, and Florence Krueger Jordan, 1942–87
Norman Long, 1949–57
Denice Olman, 1944–49
Gene and Jack Singletary, 1948–51; remained in the area and in close contact

1950s

Rufus and Sue Angry, 1954–57
Alan and Edna Baer, 1958
Gilbert Butler, 1948–56
Marguerite Reed Butler, 1953–56
Cliff and Peggy Campbell, 1959
Don and Roberta Devault, 1958–59
Chris and Jeanette Drescher, 1955–57
Iola and John Eustice, 1953–57
John Gabor, 1956–57
Alma and Mary Jackson, 19[?]–56
Billie and Claud Nelson, 1952–55
Juanita and Wallace Nelson, 1958
Ann and Lee Peery, 1955–59
Ann and Cliff Sanford, [?]–1951
Joan and John Veldhuizen, 1959–60
Margaret Wittkamper, 1953–9[?], and Will Wittkamper, 1953–[?]

1960s

Ross Anderson, 1957/8–1962
Linda and Millard Fuller, 1965, 1968–7[?]
George and Marty Hardins, 1966
Al and Carol Henry, 1965–67
Collins McGee, mid-1960s
Dorothy Swisshelm, 1958–63
Farrell and Jan Jordan Zehr, 1967
Al and Ann Zook, 1968

In the 1960s a number of the children who grew up at Koinonia took important roles in its activities. They include:
Lora Browne
James Jordan
Jan Jordan (later Jan Zehr)
Lenny Jordan
Billy Wittkamper
Greg Wittkamper

Notes

Abbreviations

ATR	*Americus Times-Recorder*
CORE reel:file	Congress of Racial Equality Papers, 1941–67; and Addendum, 1944–68
EV box:folder	Emory Via Papers
FP box:folder	Frances Pauley Papers
FSC box:folder	Fellowship of Southern Churchmen Papers
HB correspondence	Henlee Barnett Correspondence, appendix of Barnette, "Clarence Jordan: A Prophet in Blue Jeans"
KFN no.	Koinonia Farm newsletter
KP Min/FM Min	Minutes files at Koinonia Partners
KP tape collection, no.	Koinonia Partners Tape Collection
KPA	Koinonia Partners Archives
MLK box:folder	Martin Luther King Jr. Papers
MRM folder	Morris R. Mitchell Papers
MS 756 box:folder	Clarence Jordan Papers, MS 756
MS 2340 box:folder	Clarence Jordan Papers, MS 2340
MS 2341 box:folder	Clarence Jordan Papers, MS 2341
SRC reel:file	Southern Regional Council Papers, 1944–68
Wilkins box:folder	Josephine Wilkins Papers

Introduction

1. Other scholarly work on Koinonia includes Chancey, "Restructuring Southern Society"; Chancey, "A Demonstration Plot for the Kingdom of God"; Deatrick, "Koinonia"; Lee, *Cotton.*

2. On southern religion generally, see Hill, *Southern Churches in Crisis,* "The Southern Accent in Religion"; Hill, *Religion in the Solid South.* On Southern Baptists, see Ammerman, *Baptist Battles;* Queen, *In the South the Baptists Are the Center of Gravity;* Kelsey, *Social Ethics among Southern Baptists;* Rosenberg, *Southern Baptists;* Yance, *Religion Southern Style.* On Southern Baptists and the Social

Gospel, see Eighmy, "Religious Liberalism"; Valentine. *Historical Study of Southern Baptists and Race Relations.*

3. Mathews, *Religion in the Old South;* Hall, *Revolt against Chivalry.*

4. White, *Liberty and Justice for All;* Luker, *Social Gospel in Black and White.*

5. Dunbar, *Against the Grain;* Martin, "The Fellowship of Southern Churchmen"; Martin, *Howard Kester and the Struggle for Social Justice;* McDowell, *Social Gospel in the South.*

6. Connelly, *Will Campbell and the Soul of the South;* McNeil, *God Wills Us Free;* Hall, *Revolt against Chivalry.*

7. Martin, "The Fellowship of Southern Churchmen"; Taylor, "On the Edge of Tomorrow."

8. For recent reviews of civil rights historiography, see Steven Lawson, "Freedom Then, Freedom Now: The Historiography of the Civil Rights Movement," *American Historical Review* 96 (2) (April 1991): 456–71, and Adam Fairclough, "State of the Art: Historians and the Civil Rights Movement," *Journal of American Studies* 24 (3) (Dec. 1990): 387–98. On "local people" and women, see Dittmer, *Local People;* Crawford et al., *Women in the Civil Rights Movement;* Giddings, *When and Where I Enter.*

9. Dunbar, *Against the Grain;* Glen, *Highlander: No Ordinary School.*

10. Krueger, *And Promises to Keep;* Reed, *Simple Decency and Common Sense;* Sosna, *In Search of the Silent South;* Sullivan, "Gideon's Southern Soldiers." For an assessment of white liberals, see Chappell, *Inside Agitators;* Egerton, *Speak Now against the Day;* Patton, "Southern Liberals and the Emergence of the New South"; Newberry, "Without Urgency or Ardor."

11. Kramer, "Criteria," 45.

12. I have chosen to retain the word *brotherhood* rather than use a more gender-neutral term because it is the word that Koinonians themselves used and to them best sums up what they were seeking.

1. Roots

1. This definition of southern Protestant faith is described most fully in Hill, "The Southern Accent in Religion."

2. Bailey, *Southern White Protestantism,* 2.

3. Ammerman, *Baptist Battles,* 42 and chap. 3.

4. Queen, *In the South the Baptists Are the Center of Gravity,* 7. For more analysis of Southern Baptist and southern Protestant influence on southern culture, see Ammerman, *Baptist Battles;* 43; Yance, *Religion Southern Style,* 5; Hill, *Religion in the Solid South,* 41–42; Hill, *Southern Churches in Crisis,* chap. 1.

5. Queen, *In the South the Baptists Are the Center of Gravity,* 10; Kelsey, *Social*

Ethics among Southern Baptists, chap. 1; Ammerman, *Baptist Battles,* chap. 2; Mc-Clellan, "The Shaping of the Southern Baptist Mind," 2.

6. See, for example, the *Christian Index* (Atlanta) for January 1920, all issues; on Southern Baptist women's mission work, see Sorrill, "Southern Baptist Lay-women," 21–28; on missions, see Rutledge, *Mission to America.*

7. Kelsey, *Social Ethics among Southern Baptists,* 11.

8. Yance, *Religion Southern Style,* "Relevant Religion: Southern Baptists and Social Concern," and "The Social Reluctance/Awakening of Southern Baptists."

9. Interview with William Wallace Finlator, 4-30-91.

10. Lee, *Cotton,* 16.

11. Hill, *Southern Churches in Crisis,* chaps. 5–7; Hill, *Religion in the Solid South,* 32–34; see also Valentine, *Historical Study of Southern Baptists and Race Relations;* Kelsey, *Social Ethics among Southern Baptists,* chap. 8.

12. Interview with Willie Pugh Ballard, 10-20-90.

13. Ammerman, *Baptist Battles,* 61.

14. Interview with Howard Johnson, 11-24-90.

15. Interview with William Wallace Finlator, 4-30-91; letter from Con Browne to author, 9-23-93.

16. A number of historians have found evidence of the Social Gospel in southern denominations. See Eighmy, "Religious Liberalism"; McDowell, *Social Gospel in the South;* Taylor, "On the Edge of Tomorrow."

17. See McDowell, *Social Gospel in the South,* for the story of the Social Gospel among Methodist women between 1886 and 1939.

18. Eighmy, "Religious Liberalism," 362.

19. See White, *Liberty and Justice for All;* Luker, *Social Gospel in Black and White.*

20. For a recent analysis of white liberals in the history of race relations, see Chappell, *Inside Agitators.*

21. See White, *Liberty and Justice for All,* chap. 10, for a case study of Edgar Gardner Murphy.

22. For more information on Methodist women in the interracial movement, see McDowell, *Social Gospel in the South;* Knott, "Bound by the Spirit, Found on the Journey."

23. For the story of Methodist women's antilynching efforts, see Hall, *Revolt against Chivalry.*

24. Minutes of Meeting with Representatives of Local Committees, 1-10-48, in the papers of the Southern Regional Council on microfilm, reel 64, file 1989.

25. Resolution of the Georgia Interracial Commission, 4-20-45, and Report of the State Director, 4-19-48, SRC 64:1989.

26. See Ellis, "The Commission on Interracial Cooperation." For a critique of the failure of the CIC, see Chappell, *Inside Agitators,* 40–41.

27. Lillian Smith was also on the forefront of white criticism of segregation. I have not listed her here because she is not as clearly shaped by her religious beliefs, nor does she put her opposition to Jim Crow in distinctly religious terms. For information on Smith, see Brewer, "Lillian Smith: Thorn in the Flesh of Crackerdom."

28. On the Fellowship of Southern Churchmen, see Martin, "The Fellowship of Southern Churchmen," and portions of his *Howard Kester and the Struggle for Social Justice.* On the STFU, see Dunbar, *Against the Grain;* Jacklin, "Mission to the Sharecroppers," 311.

29. For a description of the mood on southern white campuses, see Lynn, *Progressive Women.*

30. Interview with William Wallace Finlator, 4-30-91; see also description of student YWCA in Lynn, *Progressive Women.*

31. Meeting of Intercollegiate Interracial Councils, 1948, SRC 23:802.

32. Yance, *Religion Southern Style,* 36; Eighmy, *Churches in Cultural Captivity,* 89–92, 155; interview with Foy Valentine, 10-8-90.

33. Valentine, *Historical Study of Southern Baptists and Race Relations,* 142, 149; Warnock, "Moderate Racial Thought," 46.

34. Eighmy, *Churches in Cultural Captivity,* 152–54; Kelsey, *Social Ethics among Southern Baptists,* 223 and chap. 8; Warnock, "Moderate Racial Thought," 33.

35. Maston, "Of One," 29; Valentine, *Historical Study of Southern Baptists and Race Relations,* 189, 203, 200, 194; "BSU Convention Stresses Christian Approach on Races," *Baptist Standard,* 10-23-47, p. 7.

36. Interview with Howard Johnson, 11-24-90; with Con Browne, 11-17-90; with Claude Broach, 4-6-91.

37. Interview with Gene Singletary, 7-10-90; with Willie Pugh Ballard, 10-20-90.

38. Interviews with Howard Johnson, 11-24-90, 7-20-92.

39. Interview with William Wallace Finlator, 4-30-91.

40. See Evans, *Personal Politics;* McAdam, *Freedom Summer.*

2. The Word

1. "Clarence Jordan Tells the Koinonia Story," n.d., in the Koinonia Partners tape collection held at Koinonia Partners, no. CJ56.

2. Bartley, *Creation of Modern Georgia,* 169.

3. Lee, *Cotton,* 6; "Clarence Jordan Remembered," photocopy in possession of author.

4. Interview with Frank, George, and Lillian Jordan, n.d., KP tape collection, no. CJ58D.

5. Lee, *Cotton,* 1; Talbotton Consolidated Monthly Report Card in MS 756, Clarence Jordan/Koinonia Farm Papers, box 9, folder 2, Hargrett Rare Book and Manuscript Library of the University of Georgia Libraries, Athens.

6. Interview with Frank, George, and Lillian Jordan, n.d., KP tape collection, no. CJ58D.

7. Buddy [Jordan] to Clarence Jordan, 2-4(?)-27, MS 756 1:1.

8. Interview with Frank, George, and Lillian Jordan, n.d., KP tape collection, no. CJ58D; Lee, *Cotton,* 6–7.

9. "Clarence Jordan Tells the Koinonia Story," n.d., KP tape collection, no. CJ56.

10. Lee, *Cotton,* 6–7; "Clarence Jordan Tells the Koinonia Story," n.d., KP tape collection, no. CJ56.

11. Clarence Jordan to Mom, 2-24-30, 3-17-30, Mom to Clarence Jordan, 11-28-30, Clarence Jordan to Mom, 4-29-32, MS 756 1:4, 6.

12. Clarence Jordan to Mom, 9-16-29, to "college friends," 8-14-31, MS 756 1:3, 15; Lee, *Cotton,* 11.

13. "Clarence Jordan Promoted," 1-28-32, clipping, MS 756 28:2.

14. Lee, *Cotton,* 13–14.

15. Interview with Claude Broach, 4-6-91.

16. D. B. Nicholson to the Jordan family, 3-4-33, MS 756 1:7; interview with Claude Broach, 4-6-91; Clarence Jordan, "My Call to the Ministry," 8-13-33, MS 756 1:7.

17. Hinson, "Southern Baptists and the Liberal Tradition in Biblical Interpretation," 16–20; Yance, *Religion Southern Style,* 36.

18. Clarence Jordan to Edward A. McDowell Jr., 5-29-64, MS 756 6:9. In this letter Jordan may be referring to the Commission on Interracial Cooperation and misremembering the name. See also Edward A. McDowell Jr., "The Minister: Key Man in Race Relations," published by the General Board of Education of the Methodist Church, April 1948, SRC 43:1478.

19. In his first two years at the seminary Jordan took the usual course work for an M.A. which included: New and Old Testament, Church History, Homiletics, Christian Ethics, Christian Sociology, and Theology. His professors included A. T. Robertson and William Hershey Davis in New Testament, J. R. Sampey, the president of the seminary, for Old Testament, and J. B. Weatherspoon for Christian Ethics. Interview with Claude Broach, 4-6-91.

20. "Clarence Jordan Tells the Koinonia Story," n.d., KP tape collection, no. CJ56.

21. Jordan, "Christian Community in the South"; Jordan, "What Is the Kingdom of God?" and "Thy Kingdom Come—On Earth," Sunday school lessons in *High Call,* Summer 1950, 29–32, MS 756 15:1.

22. Lee, *Cotton*, 26.

23. Clarence Jordan to Maurice Trimmer, 7-14-41, MS 756 1:12, H. Cornell Goerner to Henlee Barnette, n.d., in appendix of Barnette, "Clarence Jordan: A Prophet in Blue Jeans," speech presented to the Southern Baptist Theological Seminary, April 1983, on microfilm; Bob Herndon to Henlee Barnette, n.d., HB correspondence; Lee, *Cotton*, 25; Florence Jordan to Henlee, 8-26-82, in MS 2341 the Clarence Jordan/Koinonia Farm Papers, box 3, folder 8, in the Hargrett Rare Book and Manuscript Library of the University of Georgia Libraries, Athens.

24. Clarence to Mama, Oct. 1934, MS 756 1:8.

25. Interview with Claude Broach, 4-6-91.

26. Duke K. McCall to Henlee Barnette, 3-3-82, MS 2341 3:8; Lee, *Cotton*, 19–20.

27. Jordan to Lucile Lynch, 11-17-39, to "Fe," 11-20-39, MS 756 1:11.

28. Howard McClain to Arthur Barton, 4-11-41, MS 756 1:12; Clarence Jordan to "Baptist Colored Pastors," 1-19-40, to Rev. W. C. Fisher, 1-31-40, MS 756 1:11; news release announcing night of "Negro Music," 3-15-40, MS 756 24:4.

29. Clarence Jordan et al. to Women of the Advisory Board, 2-13-40, MS 756 1:11; "Summer Classes Begin at Fellowship Center," *Hand of Fellowship,* June 1939; Long Run Association Program, 1942, MS 756 15:2; Clarence Jordan to D. Swan Haworth, 11-15-39, to J. W. Thompson, 1-31-40, Long Run Committee on Negro Work to the Appropriation Committee, Baptist State Board of Missions, 11-28-39, Clarence Jordan to Personal Service Chairman, 2-22-40, MS 756 1:11.

30. Sorrill, "Southern Baptist Laywomen," 24–25.

31. Long Run Association program, 1942, MS 756 15:2; Clarence Jordan to Mrs. A. Hahn, 4-26-40, to Personal Service Chairman, 2-22-40, MS 756 1:11.

32. Long Run Association program, 1942, MS 756 15:2; Howard McClain to Arthur Barton, 4-11-41, MS 756 1:12.

33. Jordan quoted in David Morgan, "Alongside Us Caucasians," clipping [presumably from the *Biblical Recorder,* 11-6-40, p. 10, MS 756 29:unlabeled file [12A].

34. News release, 3-15-40, MS 756 24:4.

35. Marjorie Moore to Clarence Jordan, 5-31-41, MS 756 1:12.

36. W. C. Boone to Frank Leavell, 10-20-41, MS 756 1:14; Clarence Jordan to Frank Leavell, 5-12-42, Marjorie Moore to Clarence Jordan, 6-23-42, Clarence Jordan to "Cap'n Marge" [Marjorie Moore], 8-11-42, MS 756 2:2, 3.

37. Arthur J. Barton to Clarence Jordan, 4-8-41, Howard McClain to Arthur Barton, 4-11-41, MS 756 1:12.

38. Duke K. McCall to Henlee Barnette, 3-3-82, MS 2341 3:8; Lee, *Cotton*, 19–20.

39. Mary Nelle Lyne to Rev. E. F. Estes, 1-23-39, MS 756 1:11.

40. Willie Carrico to Clarence Jordan, 2-7-39, Frank H. Leavell to Clarence Jordan, 5-13-41, Juliette Mather to Clarence Jordan, 8-20-41, MS 756 1:11, 12; George

Tindall, "This Changing Scene," *Furman University Hornet,* 2-21-41, clipping, MS 756 28:7; Miller Jackson to Clarence Jordan, 2-21-41, Clarence Jordan to Michael T. Ray, 2-25-41, Edith Wells to Clarence Jordan, 3-28-41, MS 756 1:12.

41. Lee, *Cotton,* 27–28, reprint of letter from Martin England to Walt N. Johnson.

42. Deatrick, "Koinonia," George Stoll to Martin England, 9-30-32, MS 756 1:6; Lee, *Cotton,* 29.

43. Florence Jordan, "The Witness Was What Counted," interview by Pat Coy in *Round Table,* Summer 1984, 2–7, MS 2341 4:5.

44. Martin England to Henlee Barnette, n.d., MS 2341 3:8.

45. Martin England to Dr. Howard, 5-17-42, MS 756 2:1.

46. "Dr. Jordan's Statement," *Long Runner,* Aug. 1942, 2, MS 756 15:1.

47. Mimeographed History of Koinonia Farm, 2-11-57, MS 756 19:1.

48. "Dr. Jordan's Statement," *Long Runner,* Aug. 1942, 2, MS 756 15:1; Clarence Jordan to Buddy Jordan, 7-1-42, MS 756 2:2.

49. Martin England to Mack Goss, 7-15-42, in MS 2340, Clarence Jordan/Koinonia Farm Papers, box 1, folder 1942, Hargrett Rare Book and Manuscript Library of the University of Georgia Libraries, Athens.

50. Ibid.; Clarence Jordan to Fred Brownlee, 7-27-42, MS 756 2:2; Martin England to Dr. Howard, 5-17-42, MS 756 2:1.

51. For more on southern liberals, see Sosna, *In Search of The Silent South;* Krueger, *And Promises to Keep;* Newberry, "Without Urgency or Ardor"; and for a critique, Chappell, *Inside Agitators.*

52. On rural rehabilitation cooperatives and communities, see Royer, "A Comparative Study"; Dunbar, *Against the Grain;* Couto, *Aint's Gonna Let Nobody Turn Me Round.*

53. Royer, "A Comparative Study," 47.

54. Clarence, Florence, Martin, and Mabel to Friends, 9-23-42, MS 2340 1:1942; Clarence Jordan to Dr. D. J. Meador, 8-7-42, MS 756 2:3; Lee, *Cotton,* 33.

55. Paul W. Chapman, "Report on Agriculture," 1937, in box 24, file 5, "Agriculture, November 1937," Josephine Wilkins Papers, Emory University Library, Atlanta; pt. 2 of Report on Agriculture, "Human Aspects," Wilkins 24:6; "Religious, Civic, and Social Forces in Georgia," Aug. 1938, Wilkins 25:9.

56. Sumter County Farm Statistics, MS 756 26:5.

57. Interview with Ludrell Pope, 9-17-91; with Doris Pope, 9-16-91.

58. Clarence Jordan to Walnut Street Women's Missionary Society, 1-10-39, Mary Nelle Lyne to Clarence Jordan, 1-23-39, Clarence Jordan to V. V. Cooke, 11-26-40, MS 756 1:11.

59. Marjorie Moore to Clarence Jordan, 5-16-42, 5-21-42, MS 756 2:2.

60. Lee, *Cotton,* 31–34.

3. Incarnation

1. Interview with Harry Atkinson, 6-5-92; with Willie Pugh Ballard, 6-2-92; Lee, *Cotton*, 35, 41.

2. Lee, *Cotton*, 36–42; "Clarence Jordan letters to Florence Jordan, 2-21-43" [read by Lenny Jordan], KP tape collection, no. CJ57C.

3. Interview with Willie Pugh Ballard, 10-20-90.

4. T. Howard Johnson Jr. to Clarence Jordan, 8-11-42, MS 756 2:3.

5. Lee, *Cotton*, 45–46; interview with Howard Johnson, 11-24-90; with Harry Atkinson, 6-5-92; with Willie Pugh Ballard, 10-20-90.

6. Interview with Howard Johnson, 11-24-90, 7-20-92. The incident Johnson recalls is told in Kelley, *Hammer and Hoe*, 49–52.

7. Interview with Howard Johnson, 11-24-90.

8. Interview with Willie Pugh Ballard, 10-20-90.

9. Interview with Harry Atkinson, 6-5-92. Pugh, Johnson, and Atkinson were just three of the men and women who joined Koinonia in the 1940s. They were among the first and stayed longer than many others, thus forming a core for the early years of the community. I have chosen to present their brief biographies as representative of others who came to Koinonia at the same time.

10. Fellowship of Intentional Communities newsletter, 2(1) (October 1952), MS 756 22:4; interview with Howard Johnson, 7-20-92; "Koinonia Farm: Second Anniversary" brochure, 1944, in the Koinonia Partners Archives at Koinonia Partners, Sumter County, Georgia.

11. Interview with Con Browne, 11-17-90; with Howard Johnson, 11-24-90.

12. Interview with Howard Johnson, 7-20-92.

13. Interview with Foy Valentine, 10-8-90; with Carranza Morgan, 3-1-91.

14. Interview with Harry Atkinson, 6-5-92.

15. Interview with Con Browne, 11-17-90; with Chester Jackson, 11-4-90.

16. Deatrick, "Koinonia"; 12.

17. Interview with Harry Atkinson, 6-5-92, and Clarence Jordan Diary, 3-9-43, 3-10-43, MS 756 18:3.

18. Clarence Jordan Diary, 3-13-43, 4-21-43, 4-22-43, MS 756 18:3; Robert J. Messuer of Shank Electric Hatchery to Clarence Jordan, 3-20-43, MS 756 2:4, S. R. Winters, "Parson—Poultryman," *Progressive Farmer*, Jan. 1951, 100–101, MS 756 29:12A; interview with Con Browne, 11-17-90; "Clarence Jordan Tells the Koinonia Story," n.d., KP tape collection, no. CJ55A.

19. Jordan, "Christian Community in the South"; interview with Alma Jackson, 7-9-90; "Program of Outreach," n.d., MS 756 19:2.

20. Interview with Con Browne, 11-17-90.

21. Martin, "The Fellowship of Southern Churchmen."

22. Notes on Christian Service Foundation, SRC 17:587; "Reflections and Notes on the Big Ridge Retreat of the FSC," 8-25 to 9-1-42, box 1, file 3, Fellowship of Southern Churchman Papers at the Southern Historical Collection at Wilson Library, University of North Carolina, Chapel Hill; Report of the Activities of Howard Kester, secretary of the FSC for August 1941 to February 1942, FSC 1:2.

23. Eugéne Smathers, "I Work in the Cumberlands," *Prophetic Religion* 3(4) (Nov. 1939): 5–10.

24. Report of the State Director, 4-19-48, SRC 64:1989; Annual Meeting, 1940 notes, box 15, file 746, Howard Odum Papers, MS 3167 in the Southern Historical Collection at Wilson Library at the University of North Carolina, Chapel Hill; see also notes on various conferences, including the Tuskegee Rural Life Conference, the Emory Seminary Town and Country School, and the Home Missions Council of the National Council of the Churches of Christ in the USA Church and Family Farm institutes, SRC 23:796; Recommendations of the Rural Reconstruction Commission, January–February 1945, FSC 1:7.

25. Membership list for January 1945 (note next to Jordan's name indicates his membership dated from 1942), FSC 1:7; Nelle Morton to Martin Harvey, 9-18-45, FSC 2:12.

26. Gil Butler to Howard Johnson, 8-27-48, MS 756 2:11.

27. Clarence Jordan to Henlee Barnette, 11-1-44, HB correspondence; interview with Willie Pugh Ballard, 6-2-92.

28. Minutes, 1-11-49, MS 2341 4:16; interview with Chester Jackson, 11-4-90.

29. Norman Long to Clarence Jordan, 9-20-49, MS 756 2:12.

30. Interview with Willie Pugh Ballard, 6-2-92, 10-20-90; Fellowship of Intentional Communities newsletter, 2(1) (October 1952), MS 756 22:4; Minutes 6-13-56, MS 756 19:1, "Program of Outreach," n.d., MS 756 19:2.

31. Interview with Willie Pugh Ballard 6-2-92; letter to author from Con Browne, 4-24-91.

32. Interview with Chester Jackson, 11-4-90.

33. Clarence Jordan to Arthur Steilberg, December 1942 [?], MS 2340 1:1942; Clarence Jordan to Henlee Barnette, 11-1-44, HB correspondence; Margaret Wittkamper interview, 6-12-89, KP tape collection, no. CJ58E.

34. Fellowship of Intentional Communities newsletter, November 1954, MS 756 22:4; Margaret Wittkamper interview, 6-12-89, KP tape collection, no. CJ58E; Claud Nelson to Hans Hermann Arnold, 2-2-55, MS 2340 1:1955; "Program of Outreach," n.d., MS 756 19:2; Claud to Clarence and Will, 12-25-54, MS 756 3:1.

35. Rutledge, *Mission to America*, 137, 140, and chaps. 8 and 9; see also Sorrill, "Southern Baptist Laywomen."

36. Interview with Marion and Howard Johnson, 11-24-90.

37. Interview with Alma Jackson, 7-9-90.

38. Julius Belser, "Notes on the Meeting at Koinonia Farm, February 10–12, 1962," MS 756 19:1; interview with Harry Atkinson, 6-5-92.

39. Florence Jordan, "The Witness Was What Counted," interview by Pat Coy, *Round Table,* Summer 1984, 2–7, MS 2341 4:5.

40. Interview with Willie Pugh Ballard, 6-2-92; with Harry Atkinson, 6-5-92; with Gene Singletary, 10-25-90.

41. Interview with Con and Ora Browne, 9-7-89, KP tape collection, no. CJ58F.

42. Interview with Willie Pugh Ballard, 6-2-92; "Florence Jordan on Koinonia," n.d., KP tape collection, no. CJ58A.

43. Interview with Willie Pugh Ballard, 6-2-92.

44. "Letter from Koinonia Farm," Dec. 1942, MS 756 2:3; Clarence Jordan Diary, Jan. 1943, MS 756 18:3.

45. Clarence Jordan to Mack Goss, 2-14-43, MS 2340 1:1943.

46. Interview with Harry and Allene Atkinson, 6-5-92; Deatrick, "Koinonia," 16.

47. Interview with Harry Atkinson, 6-5-92.

48. Clarence Jordan to Henlee Barnette, 11-1-44, HB correspondence.

49. Interview with Foy Valentine, 10-8-90; Clarence Jordan Diary, 1943, especially 1-16, 1-17, 1-31, 2-8, and 4-25, MS 756 18:3.

50. Lawrence P. Fitzgerald to Clarence Jordan, 11-4-46, 1-21-49, MS 756 2:9, 12.

51. Lee, *Cotton,* 38.

52. "The Story of Koinonia Farms," January 1957, MS 756 19:1.

53. Interview with Chester Jackson, 11-4-90; with Alma Jackson, 7-9-90.

54. Interview with Carranza Morgan, 3-1-91.

55. Interview with Alma Jackson, 7-9-90.

56. Interview with Con Browne, 11-17-90.

57. Interview with Chester Jackson, 11-4-90.

58. Interview with Alma Jackson, 7-9-90.

59. Interview with Howard and Marion Johnson, 11-24-90; with Con and Ora Browne, 11-17-90; with Doris Pope, 9-16-91; Avis Crowe, "With Flair and Faithfulness: An Appreciation of Koinonia Partners," unpublished manuscript dated July 1986 in possession of Koinonia Partners.

60. Interview with Harry and Allene Atkinson, 5-21-90, 6-5-92; typed report on the Rehobeth incident, ca. 1950, MS 756 19:2.

61. Ira B. Faglier to Clarence Jordan, 8-9-50, MS 756 2:13.

62. Lee, *Cotton,* 77–78.

63. Interview with Chester Jackson, 11-4-90.

4: Christian Community

1. *Community* is a term which has been used in so many ways that its meaning has become ambiguous. Most simply put, a community is a place where people feel mutual responsibility and concern, believe that they in some sense belong together, and share many, but not necessarily all, aspects of their lives with one another. A community may be a specific geographic territory, as in a town or neighborhood. Recently sociologists have argued that it can also be the network of relationships formed in professional or social groups. The "community of scientists" or the "academic community" are examples. Finally, a community can be a place where people have gathered together in an "attempt to create a whole way of life molded by an idea," i.e., an "intentional community." Koinonia was a mid-twentieth-century example of an intentional community. *The Encyclopedia of American Religious Experience* (1988), s.v. "Communitarianism," by Charles H. Lippy; see also Bender, *Community and Social Change,* chaps. 1, 3, 4, and pp. 5–8, 108, 123.

2. See Gaston, *Women of Fairhope;* Fish, "The Christian Commonwealth Colony."

3. See Royer, "A Comparative Study"; Dunbar, *Against the Grain.*

4. For a study of Macedonia, see Orser, *Searching for a Viable Alternative;* on postwar religious awakening and community, see Bloesch, *Centers of Christian Renewal;* Wuthnow, *Restructuring of American Religion,* chap. 3, "A Vision of Promise and Peril."

5. Mildred Young to Clarence Jordan, 7-20-42, Aubrey J. Hudson to Clarence Jordan, 8-13-42, MS 756 2:2, 3.

6. Howard and Marion Johnson to author, July 1991; Con and Ora Browne to author, 7-15-91; interview with Harry Atkinson, 5-24-90; Harry Atkinson to author, 7-16-91; Willie Pugh Ballard to author, July 1991.

7. Interview with Con and Ora Browne, 9-7-89, KP tape collection, no. CJ58F.

8. Howard Johnson became a permanent resident in 1949, but because of his frequent visits, constant correspondence, and input into farm life beforehand, I have put him with the earlier core group.

9. Florence Jordan, "The Witness Was What Counted," interview by Pat Coy, *Round Table,* Summer 1984, 2–7, MS 2341 4:5.

10. Interview with Ora Browne, 11-17-90.

11. Interview with Con Browne, 11-17-90.

12. Minutes, 1-14-49, MS 2341 4:16.

13. Minutes, 1-18-49, 1-20-49, MS 2341 4:16.

14. Interview with Marion Johnson, 11-24-90; Minutes, 11-16-50, in folder marked "Minutes 1949–52" in possession of Koinonia Partners as office files. These are kept separate from the archives and this will be hereafter cited as KP Min or FM

Min according to the markings on the folders. Note that the dates on the labels do not always match the dates on the material.

15. For a history of the Brüderhof, see Zablocki, *Joyful Community.*

16. Interview with Howard Johnson, 11-24-90; Lee (of Primavera hof) to Friends, 2-19-49, Hermann Arnold to Clarence Jordan, 4-18-49, MS 756 2:12.

17. Con and Ora Browne to Clarence Jordan, 6-26-49, MS 756 2:12; interview with Con Browne, 11-17-90.

18. Minutes, 11-12-50, KP Min 49-52.

19. Deatrick, "Koinonia," 20; interview with Con Browne, 11-17-90.

20. Florence Jordan, "The Witness Was What Counted," interview by Pat Coy, *Round Table,* Summer 1984, 2–7, MS 2341 4:5.

21. Deatrick, "Koinonia," 29-32; Minutes, 2-3-49, MS 2341 4:16.

22. Minutes, 1-18-49, 1-20-49, MS 2341 4:16; interview with Howard Johnson, 7-20-92; with Willie Pugh Ballard, 10-20-90.

23. Minutes, 11-12-50, KP Min 49-52.

24. Minutes, 3-21-51, KP Min 49-52.

25. Interview with Willie Pugh Ballard, 6-2-92, 10-20-90. On the contrast between inner- and outer-directed communities, see Perkins, "Some Observations of My Sabbatical Experience"; Kanter, *Commitment and Community,* pt. 3.

26. Interview with Willie Pugh Ballard, 6-2-90, 10-20-90.

27. Koinonia Commitment, MS 2341 4:11.

28. The Atkinsons signed in 1954. The Ballards and Singletarys did not sign. Thereafter the designation "member" was reserved for people who signed the commitment. I use "Koinonians" to refer to anyone in the process, from novice to full member. Others at the farm are called visitors, volunteers, and workers.

29. Interview with Willie Pugh Ballard, 10-20-90; with Gene Singletary, 10-25-90.

30. Minutes, 7-8-51, 5-29-51, 8-14-51, 5-8-51, KP Min 49-52; Minutes, 6-7-53, 6-14-53, KP Min 53-55; Minutes, 9-5-54, KP Min 54-55.

31. Minutes, 12-13-54, KP Min 53-55; brochure for Koinonia Farm camp, 1955, KPA.

32. Claud Nelson to Dr. and Mrs. Paul E. Pfuetzer, 3-1-55, MS 756 3:3; letter to Summer 1955 Campers, 12-14-55, MS 2341 4:10; brochure for Koinonia Farm Camp, 1955, KPA; Con Browne to Ethel Miller, 7-21-55, MS 756 3:3.

33. Minutes, 9-5-54, KP Min 54-55.

34. Minutes, 11-17-54, KP Min 53-54.

35. On Engram, see Minutes, May, June, and July 1951; on the Jacksons, see Minutes 11-17-54, KP Min 53-54, and 1-13-56, KP Min 57; interview with Alma Jackson, 7-9-90; with Chester Jackson, 11-4-90, 4-26-92.

36. Interview with Sue Angry, 12-22-90.

37. Claud Nelson to Clarence Jordan, 10-20-54, MS 756 3:1; Minutes, 10-2-54, KP Min 53–55; Claud Nelson to Florence Jordan, 10-20-54, MS 756 3:1; Minutes, 11-4-56, KP Min 57.

38. Kramer, "Criteria," 50; Conkin, *Two Paths to Utopia,* 3–9.

39. Lee, *Cotton,* 98; interview with Con Browne, 11-17-90; Claud to Koinonia, 11-19-55, MS 2340 1:1955; Claud to Gilbert Butler, 2-1-56, MS 756 3:5.

40. Hermann Arnold to Koinonia, 7-14-49, MS 756 2:12; Duff to Paul Shiman, 1-10-[?], Shiman Papers on temporarily loan to author; John Maendel to Clarence Jordan, 2-28-55, MS 756 3:2; interview with Howard Johnson, 11-24-90; Claud and Billie to Gil, 8-19-55, MS 2340 1:1955; Minutes 12-11-56, KP Min 57.

41. Minutes, 5-29-51, KP Min 49–52; Florence Jordan, "The Witness Was What Counted," interview by Pat Coy, *Round Table,* Summer 1984, 2–7, MS 2341 4:5.

42. Interview with Howard Johnson, 11-24-90.

43. Harry to Heini, 2-14-56, MS 756 3:5; summary statement made by Norman Long, 2-8-56, MS 756 19:1.

44. Minutes, 2-4-55, KP Min 53–55.

45. Heini to Claud and Billie, 1-25-56, MS 756 3:5; Clarence Jordan to Carroll F. King, 12-3-57, MS 2340 1:1957C.

5. The Crucible

1. Lee, *Cotton,* 105.

2. For a succinct explanation of the rise of race and civil rights as an issue for northern liberals, see Kellogg, "Civil Rights Consciousness in the 1940s."

3. Myrdal et al., *American Dilemma;* Braden, "The Southern Freedom Movement in Perspective," 55–151; Patton, "Southern Liberals and the Emergence of the New South," chap. 7.

4. On the poll tax, see Durr, *Outside the Magic Circle,* chap. 9; on southern liberalism, see Sosna, *In Search of the Silent South,* chap. 8; Newberry, "Without Urgency or Ardor," chap. 1; Krueger, *And Promises to Keep,* chap. 7; Egerton, *Speak Now against the Day.* At the same time there was a rise in local-level African-American activism, in particular around returning veterans. For examples, see Dittmer, *Local People.*

5. Fellowship of Southern Churchmen newsletter, March 1954.

6. Bolster, "Civil Rights Movements," 143; for southern response to events before and after the *Brown* decision, see Bartley, *Rise of Massive Resistance;* for the liberals' reaction to *Brown,* see Newberry, "Without Urgency or Ardor," chaps. 5, 6.

7. "Editorial," 1-18-54, 2:1.

8. Interview with Howard Johnson, 7-20-92; with Harry Atkinson, 6-5-92. See also Bolster, "Civil Rights Movements," chap. 2, on Georgia's early NAACPs, including the one in Americus; interview with Lorena Barnum Sabbs, 3-3-91.

9. "Editorial," *ATR,* 5-18-54, 2:1.

10. "White Citizens Council Rally Attacks Justices Who Ordered Segregation," *ATR,* 6-23-55, 1:4; "Advertizement," *ATR,* 1-6-56, 2.

11. Interview with Lenny Jordan, 5-24-92.

12. Clarence to Nelsons and Johnsons, 4-1-56, MS 756 3:6; Deatrick, "Koinonia," 43–44; Koinonia Farm newsletter no. 3, 8-18-56.

13. KFN no. 1, 7-26-56; KFN no. 8, 11-23-56; KFN no. 10, 1-18-57.

14. Clarence Jordan to Fred, 12-29-56, MS 756 3:9; "Koinonia Farm under Siege," *Christian Century,* 2-20-57, p. 219; KFN no. 13, 4-24-57; KFN no. 11, 2-10-57.

15. KFN no. 10, 1-18-57; KFN no. 13, 4-24-57; statement of Zoltan Martenye and John Eustice, 3-21-57, MS 2341 4:14; Elizabeth Morgan at Koinonia Farm to Emory Via, 2-21-57, SRC 31:1037.

16. André Fontaine, "The Conflict of a Southern Town," *Redbook,* Oct. 1957, 48–51, 100, MS 756 29:12.

17. Lee, *Cotton,* 124; KFN no. 12, 3-9-57; interview with Margaret Wittkamper, 6-12-89, KP tape collection, no. CJ58F.

18. KFN no. 10, 1-18-57; Will D. Campbell to Fred Routh, 2-21-57, SRC 31:1037; "Koinonia Farm Undergoing Race Relations Difficulties," *Atlanta Constitution,* 2-16-57, typed copy in the vertical file, Koinonia Farm Folder (1), Hargrett Rare Book and Manuscript Room at the University of Georgia Library, Athens.

19. Lee, *Cotton,* 122; Clarence Jordan to Ray Brewster 2-11-57, MS 756 4:2; Osgood Williams to Guy Wells 2-13-57, SRC 31:1037.

20. Interview with Ora Browne, 11-17-90; report of John Gabor, 3-27-57, MS 2341 4:14.

21. Norman Long to Eugene Cook, 4-4-57, MS 756 4:4; interviews with Gene Singletary, 7-10-90, 10-25-90.

22. Sumter Co. vs. Koinonia Farm Inc., deposition in case of Board of Commissioners of Roads and Revenue of Sumter County, acting for and in behalf of the Sumter County Health Dept v. Koinonia Farms Inc. and Clarence L. Jordan, Deponent Clarence Jordan, MS 2340, box 32.

23. Injunction filed 6-25-56 by Finch et al., MS 756 20:3.

24. Interview with Con Browne, 11-17-90; KFN no. 6, 9-24-56.

25. Interview with Willie Pugh Ballard, 10-1-93.

26. "Koinonia Farm Inquiry by GBI Agents Revealed," *Macon Telegraph,* 2-27-57, vertical file, Koinonia Farm Folder (1); transcript of conversation between Emory Via and Norman Long, 2-28-57, SRC 31:1037.

27. Subpoena to Clarence Jordan, 3-26-57, MS 2341 4:15; Clarence Jordan to the Johnsons, 3-29-57, MS 756 4:5; Emory Via to Ben Segal, 4-2-57, SRC 31:1037.

28. See Durr, *Outside the Magic Circle;* Braden, *Wall Between;* see also the effect of anticommunism on the Southern Conference for Human Welfare in Krueger, *And Promises to Keep,* and on Highlander in Adams and Horton, *Unearthing Seeds of Fire.*

29. Interview with Alma Jackson, 7-9-90.

30. "Grand Jury Strongly Believes That Koinonia Is a Communist Front," *ATR,* 4-5-57, 1:1.

31. Press statement, 4-7-57, MS 2341 5:1.

32. Norman Long to Jack Ross, 4-20-57, MS 756 4:6.

33. Ibid.

34. Interview with Con and Ora Browne, 9-7-89, KP tape collection, no. CJ58F.

35. KFN no. 8, 11-23-56.

36. Conversation with Willis Shiver, 1-22-57 [summary by Clarence Jordan], MS 756 19:1.

37. Clarence Jordan to Mr. and Mrs. Longstreth, 7-17-57, MS 2340 1:1957C.

38. "A Shocking Episode" and "Mysterious Blast Breaks Three Store Fronts Here, *ATR,* 5-20-57, 1:2.

39. Lee, *Cotton,* 150; conversation between local citizens and members of Koinonia, MS 2340, tape no. 50/2.

40. Conversation between local citizens and members of Koinonia, MS 2340, tape no. 50/2.

41. KFN no. 16, 10-9-57.

42. KFN no. 22, 11-1-59; form letter from Koinonia to several businessmen in Americus, 12-3-59, MS 756 5:7.

43. Interview with Con and Ora Browne, 11-17-90.

44. Interview with Harry Atkinson, 5-24-90.

45. Report by Bill and Nita Hinley, 4-10-57, MS 756 19:1.

46. Charles Crisp quoted in W. A. Emerson and J. B. Cumming, "Everyman's Land or No Man's Land?: Koinonia Farm," *Newsweek,* 2-25-57, p. 37.

47. Jim Laxson, "Americus Biracial Farm: A Cancer on Community?" *Macon Telegraph,* 2-17-[?], 1:1, vertical file, Koinonia Farm Folder (1).

48. Report of Bill and Nita Hinley, 4-10-57, MS 756 19:1.

49. Interview with Carranza Morgan, 3-1-91; with Doc Champion, 10-26-90.

50. Clarence Jordan to Hallock Hoffman, 11-27-57, MS 2340 1:1957C.

51. Interview with Alma Jackson, 7-9-90; Minutes, 6-19-57, KP Min 57.

52. Interview with Con Browne, 11-17-90; sermon by Rev. Paul Ritch, 1-20-57, MS 2340 32:Miscellaneous; report of Bill and Nita Hinley, 4-10-57, MS 756 19:1.

53. Anne Braden to Clarence Jordan, 10-21-58, MS 756 5:2.

6. Fellowship of Believers

1. Bender, *Community and Social Change,* 1–9, 108–10, 123–36, 147.

2. I leave out of this list the growing number of African Americans who were agitating for change. I do so because, with the exception of the members of Vernon John's church in Montgomery, Koinonia's contact with black activists outside of Americus or Albany was relatively minor until the early 1960s.

3. On postwar activism, see Wittner, *Rebels against War;* Meier and Rudwick, *CORE;* Sosna, *In Search of the Silent South;* Newberry, "Without Urgency or Ardor"; Boyle, *Desegregated Heart;* Crook and Coggins, *Seven Who Fought;* Martin, "The Fellowship of Southern Churchmen"; Egerton, *Speak Now Against the Day.*

4. "The Other Cheek Is Turned in Georgia Bombing," *Christian Century,* 8-22-56, p. 965; "Embattled Fellowship Farm," *Time,* 9-17-56, p. 79; "Editorial," *Nation,* 9-22-56, p. 229; William A. Emerson Jr. and Joseph B. Cummings Jr., "Every Man's Land—Or a No Man's Land?" *Newsweek,* 2-25-57, p. 37.

5. Ben Willeford Jr. to Clarence Jordan, 11-1-43, MS 756 2:6; Alice N. Spearman to Clarence Jordan, 6-16-55, MS 756 3:3.

6. George Haynes to Koinonia, 2-3-57, MS 756 4:2; Lawrence P. Fitzgerald, to Koinonia, 10-17-56, MS 756 3:8; Mrs. Elliot E. Collison to Koinonia Farm, 4-9-57, MS 756 4:6; Joe T. Howard to Clarence Jordan, 2-5-57, MS 756 4:2; Seymour Eichel to Clarence Jordan, 11-16-56, MS 756 3:8.

7. Carol Hunt to Koinonia, 3-3-57, MS 756 4:4; James Maley to Koinonia, 4-12-58, MS 756 5:2; Rev. T. M. Howze to Koinonia, 1-22-57, MS 756 4:1.

8. Actions of the Presbytery of Athens, 1-29-57, MS 756 19:1; press release from Rev. Edward A. Driscoll, 4-29-57, MS 756 19:1.

9. An Open Letter to Christian Ministers in Georgia, 4-7-57, MS 756 4:6; KFN no. 10, 1-18-57.

10. Horace Hunt to Clarence Jordan, 12-14-56, MS 756 3:9; interview with Lorraine Williams Monroe, 1-27-91.

11. Valida Diehl to Eisenhower, 3-5-57, MS 756 4:4; Emory Via to President Eisenhower, 3-27-57, copy of letter from Clarence Jordan to President Eisenhower, 1-22-57, Herbert Brownell to Clarence Jordan, 2-28-57, SRC 31:1037; Mrs. George T. Johannesen to President Eisenhower, 4-26-57, MS 756 4:6.

12. Bill Hinley to Koinonia, 2-15-57, to Rev. Carruth, 2-26-57, MS 756 4:2, 3; "Report of the Relationship of Bill and Nita Hinley to Koinonia Farm, the Middle of February 1957 to April 10, 1957," MS 756 19:1.

13. Ernest Bromley to Lawrence Scott et al., 4-2-57, file 187, Morris R. Mitchell Papers in the Southern Historical Collection of the University of North Carolina, Chapel Hill.

14. All quotes are from "Report of the Relationship of Bill and Nita Hinley," MS

756 19:1; see also André Fontaine, "Conflict of a Southern Town," *Redbook,* Oct. 1957, 48–51, 100, MS 756 29:12.

15. Deatrick, "Koinonia," 96.

16. Helen Corson to Clarence Jordan, 1-24-57, MS 756 4:1.

17. Floyd M. Irwin to Koinonia Farm, 12-6-56, William M. Brooks to Clarence Jordan, n.d. ["probably 1957"], Charles R. Bell to Koinonia Farm, 12-5-56, Floyd M. Irwin to Harold Still, 12-5-56, MS 756 3:9; Bob Childers to Clarence Jordan, 1-17-59, MS 2340 2:1959A.

18. Swisshelm to Swift and Co., 2-3-61, Koinonia to Paul, 2-22-61, Paul M. Koger to Mrs. F. D. Roosevelt, 3-3-61, Carl A. Carson to Mrs. Roosevelt, 3-31-61, MS 756 6:3.

19. Con and Ora Browne to author, 4-10-91; Jack and Sharon to Koinonia, 8-4-56, MS 756 3:7; KFN no. 6, 9-24-56; McNeil, *God Wills Us Free,* 155–56.

20. Clarence Jordan to Morris R. Mitchell, 2-2-57, MRM file 184.

21. Open letter from Koinonia Community, 3-25-57, SRC 31:1037; Norman Long to Wendall Bull, 4-4-57, MS 756 4:6, Clarence to Rev. Alfred Schmalz, 8-1-57, MS 2340 1:1957; KFN no. 14, 5-29-57.

22. "Florence Jordan on Koinonia," KP tape collection, no. CJ58A, pt. 2; Clarence to Mr. and Mrs. Longstreth, 7-18-57, open letter to Friends of Koinonia, D.C., 8-15-57, MS 2340 1:1957.

23. Clarence Jordan to John Thomas, 12-8-56, MS 756 3:9; Koinonia Farm to Bob, 5-22-57, MS 756 4:7.

24. Memo to Friends of Koinonia—Groups and Individuals, June 1957, and memo from Wallace Nelson and Maurice McCracken, MS 756 19:1, 2.

25. "Support Koinonia," *CORE-lator,* Spring–Summer 1957, 4, MS 756 24:9; Thomas F. Gossett to Dr. Guy Wells, 4-6-57, SRC 31:1037.

26. Emory Via to Clarence Jordan, 4-2-57, to Norman Long, 4-2-57, to George Doss Jr., 4-2-57, Norman Long to Emory Via, 3-4-57, SRC 31:1037.

27. Septima Clark to Con Browne, 3-2-58, MS 756 4:1; Koinonia to Ralph Helstein, 3-27-57, MS 756 5:1.

28. James R. Robinson to James T. McCain, 9-9-57, ser. 5, folder 258, Papers of the Congress of Racial Equality, 1941–67, microfilm.

29. E. R. Diamond to Clarence Jordan, 6-14-60, MS 756 6:2.

30. Mrs. T. C. Steinhire to Clarence Jordan, 10-8-57, MS 2340 1:1957B.

31. Ed Gaylord to Koinonia, 8-2-59, MS 756 5:7.

32. Miller, *Harsh and Dreadful Love,* 283–86; Meier and Rudwick, *CORE,* 74–76.

33. Beth L. Irwin to Koinonia Farm, 1-10-56, MS 756 3:5; Bill and Helen Hammon to Koinonia Farm, 1-9-57, MS 756 4:1; Willa Christianson to Koinonia, 12-9-56, Horace Hunt to Clarence Jordan, 12-14-56, MS 756 3:9.

34. Iola Eustice to Rev. and Mrs. Graetz, 4-28-57, MS 756 4:6; Ralph D. Abernathy to Clarence Jordan, 1-28-58, Martin Luther King Jr. to Clarence Jordan, 2-6-58, MS 2340 1:1958A.

35. Paul Turner to Clarence Jordan, 8-18-59, MS 756 5:7; Clarence Jordan to "Friends," June 1959, MS 756 5:6; Anne Braden to Clarence, 3-24-61, 8-8-61, MS 756 6:2, 4; "Patty" [Sarah Patton Boyle] to Clarence Jordan, 8-23-58, MS 756 5:2.

36. Interview with Jim Jordan, 6-15-92.

37. Raymond J. Magee to Clarence Jordan, 11-18-57, MS 2340 1:1957C.

38. Con Browne to Jack Burdin, 9-5-57, MS 756 4:10.

39. Harry to Chris, 3-7-58, Harry and Allene to Con and All, 3-27-58, MS 756 5:1; Iola Eustice to Raymond J. Magee, 11-22-57, MS 2340 1:1957C.

7. To Bear Witness

1. Interview with Sue Angry, 12-22-90.

2. Allene to Koinonia Farm, 2-14-57, MS 756 4:2; Report on Hidden Springs by Harry and Allene, 2-27-57, MS 756 22:7; Atkinsons and Angrys to Koinonia, 4-4-57, MS 756 4:6.

3. Harry and Allene to Koinonia, 4-5-57, MS 756 4:6, KFN no. 14, 5-29-57; Koinonia Farm to the Atkinsons and Angrys, 2-19-57, MS 756 4:3.

4. John Gabor to Koinonia, 6-10-57, MS 756 4:8.

5. "Biracial Farm Unit Buying Jersey Sites," *New York Times,* 4-4-57, 34:4; Allene to Koinonia, 2-14-57, MS 756 4:2.

6. Interview with Sue Angry, 12-22-90; Allene to Clarence and Others, 8-22-57, MS 2340 29:Clarence.

7. Allene to Clarence, 7-11-57, MS 2340 1:1957; Atkinsons to Koinonia, 12-19-57, MS 756 4:14; Allene to Clarence and others, 8-22-57, MS 2340 29:Clarence.

8. Allene to Clarence, 7-17-57, MS 2340 29:Clarence; KFN no. 16, 10-9-57; Harry to Clarence, 12-26-57, MS 2340 29:Clarence.

9. Atkinsons to Koinonia, 12-19-57, MS 756 4:14.

10. Clarence for Koinonia to Joe Vise, 11-26-57, MS 2340 1:1957C; Atkinsons to Koinonia, 12-19-57, MS 756 4:14.

11. Atkinsons to Koinonia, 12-19-57, MS 756 4:14.

12. Gross Alexander to Koinonia, 10-22-57, MS 2340 1:1957B.

13. Minutes, 6-16-57, 6-30-57, FM Min 57.

14. Minutes, 11-5-57, FM Min 57; Iola Eustice to Sarah Patton Boyle, 10-10-58, in the Sarah Patton Boyle Papers, box 8003a, folder 31, marked "1958–1963 Materials re: Koinonia Farm," University of Virginia Library, Charlottesville; "Hidden Springs Conference," MS 2340 tape no. 54.

15. Harry to Chris, 3-7-58, MS 756 5:1.

16. Harry and Allene to Koinonia, 2-7-58, Harry and Allene to Con and all, 3-27-58, MS 756 5:1.

17. John Gabor to Koinonia, 6-10-57, MS 756 4:8.

18. Heini Arnold to Koinonia Farm, 2-11-57, Gross Alexander to Clarence Jordan, 6-22-57, Mary Gates to Koinonia Farm, 6-13-57, MS 756 4:2, 8; Gross Alexander to Con Browne, 2-7-58, MS 756 5:1.

19. John Thomas quoted in Atkinsons to Koinonia, 12-19-57, MS 756 4:14; Gross Alexander to Con Browne, 2-7-58, MS 756 5:1.

20. Halleck Hoffman statement on Koinonia for the Board of the Fund for the Republic, 8-21-57, MS 2340 1:1957.

21. Minutes, 1-31-57, 4-5-57, FM Min 57.

22. Con Browne to Brother Gross, 2-1-58, MS 756 5:1.

23. Clarence Jordan to Maurice McCrackin, 7-23-57, MS 2340 1:1957; Clarence Jordan to Rev. Gross W. Alexander, 6-19-57, MS 756 4:8; Connie to All in New Jersey, 1-29-58, MS 756 5:1.

24. Interview with Margaret Wittkamper, 10-25-90; "Hidden Springs Conference," MS 2340 tape no. 54; interview with Jim Jordan, 6-15-92; Ross Anderson to Rufus, Sue and all, 1-31-58, MS 756 5:1; Lee, *Cotton,* 178.

25. Con Browne quoted in Don Mosely, "Koinonia: Nonviolence in Action," *Fellowship,* August 1984, 10–12, MS 2341 4:9.

26. Ross Anderson to Rufus, Sue, and all, 1-31-58, MS 756 5:1; Clarence Jordan to Halleck Hoffman, 8-12-57, MS 2340 1:1957.

27. Ross Anderson to Rufus, Sue, and all, 1-31-58, Con Browne to Brother Gross, 2-1-58, MS 756 5:1.

28. Ross Anderson to Rufus, Sue, and all, 1-31-58, MS 756 5:1.

29. "Florence Jordan on Koinonia," n.d., KP tape collection, no. CJ58A.

30. During the crisis the Eustices, Butlers, and Norman Long also left. Chris and Jeanette Drescher returned to Koinonia Farm in Georgia. The next year Chris moved to another community while Jeanette remained. See Minutes, 4-1-58, FM Min 57–58.

31. Con and Ora to Harry, Allene, Rufus, and Sue, 3-20-58, MS 756 5:1.

8. *Wandering in the Desert*

1. KFN no. 23, 9-20-60; KFN no. 22, 11-1-59; KFN no. 21, Oct. 1959; KFN no. 25, Oct. 1961; John Veldhuizen to his family, 6-9-60, photocopy in possession of author; interview with Jan Jordan, 5-1-91.

2. Kirby, *Rural Worlds Lost,* chap. 8; Williford, *Americus through the Years,* chap. 16; *Eighteenth Census of the United Stated, 1960: Population* 12:352; *Nineteenth Census of the United States, 1970: Population* 12:561.

3. Julius Belser, "Notes on the Meeting at Koinonia Farm, February 10–12, 1962," MS 756 19:1.

4. Edgar Stoesz to Clarence Jordan, 6-21-62, MS 2341 1:1.

5. Ora to Dick Baker, 5-29-58, MS 756 5:1.

6. KFN no. 20, 12-21-58.

7. Clarence Jordan to Mrs. Carl R. Christiansen, 12-9-58, MS 2340 1:1958C.

8. KFN no. 22, 11-1-59.

9. "Ministers under Pressure," transcript of a speech by a member of Koinonia Farm, n.d., MS 2340 6:23; interview with Willa Mae Champion, 10-26-90.

10. Durward V. Cason Sr. to Clarence Jordan, 2-9-59, MS 2340 2:1959A; KFN no. 26, 4-1-62; Con Browne to author, 4-24-91; C. C. Browne to Leslie Dunbar, 2-15-63, SRC 31:1037.

11. See, for example, the programs of the Community Church in Honolulu, 3-16–18-60, Raleigh Intercollegiate Conference, 2-25–26-61, Commencement Exercises for the Class of '61 of the Mather School, Beaufort, S.C., 5-28-61, and Religious Emphasis Week at the North Carolina College at Durham, 3-26–30-61, MS 756 9:7.

12. KFN no. 21, 5-1-59.

13. "Florence Jordan on Koinonia," n.d., KP tape collection, no. CJ58A; Clarence Jordan to Don McKee, 10-21-63, MS 756 6:8.

14. Interview with Lora Browne, 3-9-91.

15. Interview with Con Browne, 11-17-90; Jeanette and Don Devault to Koinonia, 7-11-59, MS 756 5:6; Dorothy Swisshelm to the Chief of Social Service, 1-5-60, MS 756 6:1.

16. Interview with Don and Jeanette Devault, 10-22-90; Jeanette Devault to Koinonia, 3-26-58, Jeanette and Don Devault to Con Browne and Koinonia, 7-6-58, Con Browne to Jeanette and Don, 8-8-58, MS 756 5:1, 2.

17. Joan and John Veldhuizen to the Jordans, 7-28-59, MS 756 5:6; John Veldhuizen Diary, n.d., photocopy in possession of author; interview with Joan and John Veldhuizen, 5-4-91; KFN no. 23, 9-20-60.

18. Interview with Dorothy Swisshelm, 2-3-91; Dorothy Swisshelm to Representative Jimmy Carter, 8-23-63, CORE 1:1; Lee, *Cotton*, 178; KFN no. 19, 9-15-58.

19. Minutes, 1-1-61, 4-29-62, FM Min 60–63.

20. Interview with Lenny Jordan, 5-24-92; Lora Browne Diary, 6-4-59[60?], photocopy in possession of author; Joan Veldhuizen to her family, 2-14-60, 3-28-60, photocopies in possession of author; interview with Jan Jordan, 5-1-91.

21. Dorothy to Brothers and Sisters in Christ, 3-13-61, MS 756 6:3.

22. Interview with Carol King, 2-28-91; interview with Jan Jordan, 5-1-91; with Dorothy Swisshelm, 2-3-91; Koinonia to Reba Place and Forest River, 1-13-60, MS 756 6:1.

23. Ross to Fellowship of Intentional Communities, June 1960, MS 756 6:2; Minutes, 9-29-60, FM Min 60; Minutes, 12-20-60, FM Min 60–63.

24. Koinonia to Mr. and Mrs. John Beecher, 8-1-58, MS 756 5:2; Clarence Jordan to Bob Lee, 10-16-59, MS 2340 2:1959B.

25. Minutes, 9-29-60, 2-7-60, FM Min 1960.

26. Interview with John Veldhuizen, 5-4-91.

27. Jefferson Poland to Koinonia, 5-20-61, MS 756 6:3.

28. Interview with Joan Veldhuizen, 5-4-91; numerous letters and cards from Ross Anderson to Koinonia, Jan.–May 1961, MS 756 6:3.

29. Minutes, 2-10-60, FM Min 1960.

30. Minutes, 1-22-61, FM Min 60–63.

31. Koinonia to Mr. and Mrs. Gerald Dorrell, 4-3-61, MS 756 6:3.

32. Lee, *Cotton,* 175–76; "Handwritten Notes on June 10–12, 1960, Meeting" and "Summary of Meeting of June 10–12, 1960," MS 756 22:3.

33. "Handwritten Notes on June 10–12, 1960, Meeting," MS 756 22:3; Koinonia to John Miller and John Lehman, 4-3-63, MS 756 6:7; interview with Con Browne, 11-17-90.

34. Al to Koinonia, 3-12-63, MS 756 6:7.

35. Edgar Stoesz to Clarence Jordan, 6-21-62, MS 2341; Koinonia to Reba Place, Peoria St., Forest River, and Staughton Lynd, 2-1-62, MS 756 6:6.

36. Minutes, 1-22-62, 1-25-62, FM Min 60–63.

37. Minutes, 1-25-62, 2-1-62, 2-4-62, FM Min 60–63.

38. Ibid.

39. Minutes, 2-15-62, FM Min 60–63.

40. Minutes 1-7-63, 1-22-62, FM Min 60–63.

41. "Some Matters Discussed," 10-9–10-63, MS 756 19:1.

42. Interview with Con Browne, 11-17-90; with Lora Browne, 3-9-91; "Material for the Mennonite Central Committee," 7-8-63, MS 756 19:1.

43. "Material for the Mennonite Central Committee," 7-8-63, MS 756 19:1.

44. Clarence Jordan to Rev. Seido Ogawa, 12-18-63, MS 756 6:8.

9. Koinonia and the Movement

1. Incarnational evangelism was a phrase used by Jordan. It essentially meant acting out in life your beliefs and by demonstration teach them to others. See Jordan, "Incarnational Evangelism," *Substance of Faith.*

2. "Southern Regional Council Midsummer Report of Program Activities, 1958," Emory Via Papers, box 1278, file 13, Southern Labor Archives, Georgia State University, Atlanta; SCEF Field Secretary's Report, 1958, Wilkins 4:16.

3. Interview with Con Browne, 11-17-90; Koinonia to Nelsons and Johnsons,

3-30-56, MS 756 3:6; Conference on Christian Faith and Human Relations, book of press releases, April 1957, MS 756 24:7; "Letter from Mary Kolb," *Racial Equality Bulletin,* June 1957, 2, MS 756 24:4.

4. Interview with Lorena Barnum Sabbs and Thelma Barnum, 3-3-91; with Carol King, 2-28-91.

5. Carson, *In Struggle,* 56–57.

6. Smith and Zepp, *Search for the Beloved Community,* chap. 6; interview with Charles Sherrod, 3-1-91; Vincent G. Harding, "Community as a Liberating Theme in Civil Rights History," in Robinson and Sullivan, *New Directions in Civil Rights Studies,* 17–29.

7. Typed notes on discussion about integration, n.d., in KPA folder marked "Community: Notes on '62–'63."

8. Jordan, "Distinct Identity: The Mind of Christ in the Racial Conflict," *Substance of Faith,* 105.

9. Carson, *In Struggle,* 56.

10. Bolster, "Civil Rights Movements," 283–84.

11. Clarence Jordan, "Negro America Is Talking About," *Between the Lines,* n.d., MS 756 25:2.

12. Carson, *In Struggle,* 56; Branch, *Parting the Waters,* 527; interview with Carol King, 2-28-91; "Negro Students Demonstrate in Albany Incident," *ATR,* 11-28-61, 1:8; "Police Arrest 150 Negroes at Albany Hearing," *ATR,* 12-12-61, 1:3; "Negroes Attempt to Integrate Albany Library," *ATR,* 1-11-62, 4:6; "Albany Abandons Buses after Negro Boycott," *ATR,* 2-1-62, 1:1.

13. Interview with Dorothy Swisshelm, 2-3-91.

14. Lora Browne Diary, June 1962, photocopy in possession of author.

15. Koinonia to Reba Place, 12-18-61, MS 756 6:5.

16. Lora Browne Diary, June 1962, photocopy in possession of author.

17. Koinonia to Friends, Dec. 1962, MS 756 6:6; interview with Carol King, 2-28-91.

18. Hiley H. Ward, "Minister Sees Hope in South," *Detroit Free Press,* 9-10-62, 3:1, MS 756 28:23; KFN no. 27, 9-1-62; interview with Carol King, 2-28-91.

19. Interview no. 2 with Frances Pauley by Cliff Kuhn, 5-3-88, Georgia Government Documentation Project in the Georgia State University Special Collections.

20. Interview with Charles Sherrod, 3-1-91; guest lists, MS 756 20:4; interview with Con Browne, 11-17-90; Minutes, 1-11-63, FM Min 60–63; interview with Dorothy Swisshelm, 2-3-91; KFN no. 27, 9-1-62; Con Browne to SNCC, 11-12-62, Papers of the Student Nonviolent Coordinating Committee, microfilm reel 7, file 206.

21. "The Southwest Georgia Project: Report and Proposals," 12-27-63, p. 7,

SNCC 37:63; Clarence to Betts Huntley, 2-13-63, MS 2340 2:1963; interview with Rev. J. R. Campbell, 12-12-90.

22. Zev to Jim, Marcia, et al., 4-20-64, CORE 3:122; Don Harris, "Memo re SNCC Southwest Georgia Project," 7-12-64, SNCC 19:103; Zev to Nooker, Marcia, Marv, et al., 7-26-64, CORE 5:31.

23. Fact sheet, Americus, Ga., 1963, SNCC 37:37; *Upside Down Justice: The Albany Cases,* pamphlet circulated by the National Committee for the Albany Defendants, p. 7, MS 756 24:9; "Police Brutality in Georgia," n.d., CORE 3:175; Dorothy Swisshelm to Rev. Benjamin Hartley, 8-22-63, CORE 1:1; several ministers to Honorable T. O. Marshall, 9-16-63, SNCC 6:8; Claud Sitton, "Strict Law Enforcement Stifles Negroes' Drive in Americus, Ga," *New York Times,* 9-29-63, clipping, MS 756 28:24.

24. "Negro Enters JP Race Here," *ATR,* 7-9-65, 1:6; interview with Rev. J. R. Campbell, 12-12-90.

25. Interview with Rev. J. R. Campbell, 12-12-90; "Community Relations Committee Named Here," *ATR,* 7-26-65, 1:7; "Negroes Continue Marches in Protest of Jailing," *ATR,* 7-27-65, 1:7.

26. KFN no. 28, Sept. 1963; Robert Mants Jr., "Report on Americus, Georgia," 9-30–10-5-63, SNCC 17:20.

27. Zev Aelony to Jim, Marcia, et al., 8-11-63, CORE 3:122; interview with Greg Wittkamper, 11-18-90; statement of an anonymous citizen, taken by Zev Aelony and witnessed by Greg Wittkamper, 8-11-63, and Zev to Nooker, Marcia, Marv, et al., 7-26-64, CORE 5:31.

28. Interview with Jan Jordan, 5-1-91; with Dorothy Swisshelm, 2-3-91; Zev to Nooker, Marcia, Marv, et al., 7-26-64, CORE 5:31; Zev to Jim, Marcia, et al., 4-20-64, CORE 3:122; Dorothy Swisshelm to Rev. Benjamin Hartley, 8-22-63, CORE 1:1.

29. Dorothy Swisshelm to Representative Jimmy Carter, 8-23-63, CORE 1:1; More from Zev Aelony to Friends, 9-14-63, CORE 3:122.

30. "Americus Bitter," clipping [presumably from *Atlanta Journal,* 9-29-63], SNCC 19:104.

31. "Americus, Place of Courage," *Southern Patriot* 23(9) (Nov. 1965): 2, MS 756 24:10.

32. Interview with Lenny Jordan, 5-24-92.

33. Interview with Lenny Jordan, 5-24-92; with Millard Fuller, 12-13-90.

34. Interview with Jan Jordan, 5-1-91.

35. Interview with Con and Ora Browne, 11-17-90; with Margaret Wittkamper, 10-25-90; Minutes, 4-12-62, FM Min 60-63.

36. Interview with Ora Browne, 11-17-90.

37. Interview with Con and Ora Browne, 11-17-90; with Millard Fuller, 12-13-90.

38. Clarence Jordan, "A Parable of No Violence, Some Violence, and Great Violence," KFN no. 30, April 1965.

39. Clarence Jordan to Glenn H. Asquith, June 1963, MS 756 6:7.

40. Jordan, "God Movement: The Lesson on the Mount—II," *Substance of Faith,* 72, 74.

41. Interview with Charles Sherrod, 3-1-91.

42. Minutes, 6-24-63, FM Min 60–63.

43. C. Browne to William Porter, April 1964 [?], MS 756 6:7; Mrs. Jordan to Don [Harris], 7-6-64, MS 756 6:10; interview with Con and Ora Browne, 11-17-90.

44. Zev to Jim McCain, 12-15-64, CORE 3:122.

45. KFN no. 30, April 1965; Clarence to Marjorie Moore Armstrong, 4-23-66, MS 756 7:1; Clarence Jordan to "Friend," April 1965, Martin Luther King Jr. Papers, box 14, folder 18, Martin Luther King Center, Atlanta.

46. KFN no. 31, Sept. 1965; Clarence Jordan to "Friend," April 1965, MLK 14:18; Maurice McCrackin newsletter, Summer 1968, MS 756 24:2; form letter from Koinonia Farm, 1966, John Ramsay Papers, box 1588, file 359, Southern Labor Archives, Georgia State University, Atlanta; KFN no. 30, April 1965; KFN no. 31, Sept. 1965.

47. A. E. Cox to Harold Fleming, 7-9-59, Harold Fleming to A. E. Cox, 7-10-59, SRC 23:795; Programs for Farmers' Cooperative and Job Training Conference, Sept. 1963 and A Better Life for Mississippi's Farm Families, 2-29–3-1-64, SRC 46:1598; Michael Miles, "Black Cooperatives," *New Republic,* 9-21-68, p. 21; for recent work on cooperatives and the civil rights movement, see Mills, *This Little Light of Mine;* Dittmer, *Local People.*

48. Bolster, "Civil Rights Movements," 346–47; interview with Charles Sherrod, 3-1-91.

49. Zev Aelony to John Due et al., 6-11-63, to Marcia, Jim, et al., 7-28-63, 8-11-63, CORE 3:122; Zev to Nooker, Marcia, Marv, et al. 7-26-64, CORE 5:31.

50. Zev to Jim McCain, 12-15-64, CORE 3:12.

51. "Bar-B-Que Picnic for Maid's Union and Quilt Cooperative Sunday," *Voice of Americus,* July 1963, 1: Zev to Nooker, Marcia, Marv, et al., 7-26-54, CORE 5:31.

52. KFN no. 33, April 1966.

53. Clarence to F. Robert Otto, 5-22-63, MS 2340 2:1963; KFN no. 30, April 1965.

54. Clarence Jordan to Lyle Tatum, 2-16-65, MS 756 6:10.

55. "The Committee of Southern Churchmen," June 4, 1963, and proposal for a conference on "The Integration of a Desegregated Society," 1-5-62, SRC 43:1502.

56. James Solheim, "We Need a God Movement: An Interview with Clarence Jordan," *Greater Works,* June 1968, 16–21, MS 2341 3:5.

57. Clarence Jordan to Sam Emerick, 5-17-68, MS 756 7:15.

10. Partners

1. Lee, *Cotton,* 178–79; Koinonia to Reba Place, Peoria Street, Forest River, and Staughton Lynd, 2-1-62, MS 756 6:6.

2. Quoted in Esther Ho, unnamed article in the *Messenger,* 2-8-66, MS 756 7:1; Clarence Jordan to Will Powers Jr., 4-19-67, MS 756 7:3.

3. Clarence to Henry W. Friesen, 3-14-64, MS 756 6:9; Clarence Jordan to Will R. Getz, 1-6-67, MS 2340 3:1966; Clarence Jordan to Lyall W. Scott, 4-21-67, MS 756 7:3.

4. KFN no. 33, April 1966; Frances Pauley to Al Henry, 1-9-67, to Clarence Jordan, 1-9-67, Frances Pauley Papers, 1919–92, box 9, file 11, Special Collections Department, Robert W. Woodruff Library, Emory University, Atlanta; Clarence Jordan to Kit Havice, 4-19-67, MS 756 7:3.

5. "Florence Jordan on Koinonia," n.d., KP tape collection, no. CJ58A.

6. Marilyn Meininger to Clarence Jordan, 2-3-65, MS 756 6:11; Tom Todd to Koinonia, 7-13-64, MS 756 6:10; Farns Lobenstine to Koinonia, 2-13-64, Gene McCormack to Florence, 8-26-64, MS 756 6:9.

7. Tal D. Fowler to Clarence Jordan, 2-5-66, Deborah Keelin and Rick Margolis to Koinonia, 6-3-67, MS 756 7:1, 3; Donald F. Clausen to Clarence Jordan, 1-29-66, MS 756 7:1; on the "hippy" communes, see Kanter, *Commitment and Community,* chap. 1; Fairfield, *Utopia, U.S.A.;* Hedgepeth, *Alternative;* and a series of articles in *Alternatives! Newsmagazine* in the early 1970s, especially "Directory of Intentional Communities" in volume 1 (1971).

8. Florence Jordan to Farns Lobenstine, 2-17-64, MS 756 6:9.

9. Clarence Jordan to Lyall W. Scott, 4-21-67, MS 756 7:3.

10. "Draft Aged and Rich: D. C. Forum Speaker Urges Annihilation Alternatives," *Defiance Crescent News,* 10-25-66, 14:1, MS 756 19:3; Clarence Jordan, "Love Your Enemies," *PostAmerican* 2(1973): 4–5; "Little Thots" [by Clarence Jordan], MS 756 25:7.

11. Clarence Jordan to Jim Jordan, 2-27-66, MS 756 7:1.

12. Ibid.; interview with Margaret Wittkamper, 10-25-90; Ann Morris to Clarence Jordan, 2-2-68, Marge Chapman to Clarence Jordan, 3-5-68, Michel to Clarence Jordan, n.d., Clarence Jordan to Everett Mischler, 5-14-68, MS 756 7:5; Sam Emerick to Clarence Jordan, 4-11-68, MS 756 7:15.

13. Interview with Margaret Wittkamper, 10-25-90; with Greg Wittkamper, 11-18-90; with Lenny Jordan, 5-24-92.

14. Clarence Jordan to Ann Morris, 4-26-68, to Sam Emerick, 5-17-68, MS 756 7:5, 15.

15. Biographical material on Millard Fuller from Fuller and Scott, *Love in the Mortar Joints,* chap. 4.

16. "A Personal Letter from Clarence Jordan," KFN, 10-21-68; Fuller and Scott, *Love in the Mortar Joints,* chap. 5.

17. Millard and Linda to Clarence, 5-27-66, MS 756 7:1.

18. Fuller and Scott, *Love in the Mortar Joints,* 64; Millard to Clarence Jordan, 5-4-68, MS 756 7:5; "A Personal Letter from Clarence Jordan," KFN, 10-21-68.

19. "A Personal Letter from Clarence Jordan," KFN, 10-21-68.

20. Fuller and Scott, *Love in the Mortar Joints,* 67–68; Millard to Clarence, 6-26-68, MS 756 7:6; interview with Millard Fuller, 12-13-90; Lee, *Cotton,* 205–6. Four of the men were African Americans; the rest were whites. Women were conspicuously absent from the list. No one commented on this omission at the time, however. Fuller spoke of his wife as an equal partner in his decisions and said that while she may have been absent from the meeting, her wishes were on his mind. Both Jordan and Fuller also consulted at length with their wives before the discussions. Will Wittkamper participated in the meeting but did not take an active role.

21. Lee, *Cotton,* 207.

22. "Koinonia Partners Conference," Aug. 1968, KP tape collection, no. 54.

23. Ibid.

24. Interview with Millard Fuller, 12-13-90.

25. "A Personal Letter from Clarence Jordan," KFN, 10-21-68.

26. Lee, *Cotton,* 209–11; Chancey, "Restructuring Southern Society," 94–95; "A Personal Letter from Clarence Jordan," KFN, 10-21-68; "Koinonia Partners Conference," Aug. 1968, KP tape collection, no. 54.

27. "A Personal Letter from Clarence Jordan," KFN, 10-21-68.

28. KFN no. 37, Feb. 1968.

29. Interview with Millard Fuller, 12-13-90; KFN no. 37, Feb. 1968.

30. Howard Thorkelson to Jean Fairfax, 7-14-66, Frances Pauley to Howard Thorkelson, 8-3-66, FP 9:10; Quarterly Report to the SRC, Jan.–March 1967, FP 10:3; Notes on Cooperative League, 2-28-67, SRC 19:669; Quarterly Report, April to June 1967, July to September 1967, and Annual Report, 1967, FP 10:3, 5.

31. KFN, Summer 1969.

32. Clarence Jordan to Mrs. Perry A. Howard, 1-28-69[?], and open letter from Clarence Jordan, 2-21-69, MS 756 8:1.

33. "Discipleship School," 6-6–9-69[?], MS 756 19:1.

34. Clarence Jordan to Kathleen A. Turitto, 4-15-69, MS 756 8:1.

35. Interview with Millard Fuller, 12-13-90.

36. Millard Fuller to Leon Capsuano, 9-5-69, MS 756 19:1.

37. Janice Meredith to Clarence Jordan, 8-27-68, MS 756 7:6; "Personal Letter from Clarence Jordan," KFN, 10-21-68; Fuller and Scott, *Love in the Mortar Joints,* 72; "Lori's Letters," May 1969, MS 756 8:1; KFN, Summer 1969.

38. Lee, *Cotton,* 229–32; Fuller, *Bokotola,* 22.

39. Lee, *Cotton*, 233; Fuller, *Bokotola*, 22–23.

40. "Lori's Letters," May 1969, MS 756 8:1; Lee, *Cotton*, 238.

41. "Lori's Letters," May 1969, MS 756 8:1.

42. Chancey, "Restructuring Southern Society," 100.

43. National Public Radio Koinonia Farm segment, 9-7-71, MS 2340 tape no. 58.

44. Interview with Jim Jordan, 6-15-92.

45. Phrase is borrowed from the title of chapter 8 in Fuller and Scott, *Love in the Mortar Joints*.

Epilogue

1. The story of Habitat for Humanity is told in Fuller and Scott, *Love in the Mortar Joints*.

2. Employees' Petition to the Board of Directors, 1989[?], in possession of Koinonia Partners.

3. "A Proposal for Racial Reconciliation for Koinonia Farm," 1989, in possession of Koinonia Partners.

4. Koinonia Employees' Mission Statement, 1992, "What Is Koinonia??" in possession of Koinonia Partners.

5. Koinonia Partners Mission Statement, 1992, in possession of Koinonia Partners.

6. These impression and others about the restructuring of the mid-1990s are drawn from a series of interviews conducted in 1992, 1993, and 1995. Because of the sensitive nature of the discussions and continued tensions and uncertainty at the community, interviewees were promised anonymity. Furthermore, I promised not to quote directly from the interviews of 1995.

Bibliography

Manuscript Collections

Clark Atlanta University Center, Robert W. Woodruff Library, Atlanta
  Southern Regional Council Papers, 1944–68 (available on microfilm)
Hargrett Rare Book and Manuscript Library, University of Georgia Libraries, Athens
  Clarence Jordan Papers, MSS no. 756, 2340, 2341
  Vertical file
Koinonia Partners, Americus, Ga.
  Koinonia Partners Archives
  Koinonia Partners Tape Collection
Library of Congress, Washington, D.C.
  Congress of Racial Equality Papers, 1941–67, and Addendum, 1944–68 (Available on microfilm)
Martin Luther King Center Archives, Atlanta
  Martin Luther King, Jr., Papers
  Student Nonviolent Coordinating Committee Papers, 1959–72 (available on microfilm)
Southern Historical Collection, University of North Carolina Library, Chapel Hill
  Fellowship of Southern Churchmen Papers
  Morris R. Mitchell Papers
  Howard Odum Papers
Southern Labor Archives, Georgia State University, Atlanta
  John Ramsay Papers
  Emory Via Papers
Special Collections Department, Robert W. Woodruff Library, Emory University, Atlanta
  Frances Pauley Papers
  Josephine Wilkins Papers
Special Collections Department, University of Virginia Library, Charlottesville
  Sarah Patton Boyle Papers

Miscellaneous

Barnette, Henlee. "Clarence Jordan: A Prophet in Blue Jeans." A lecture presented at the Southern Baptist Theological Seminary, April 1983. Transcription and correspondence on microfilm in possession of author.

Browne, Lora. Diary. Photocopy in possession of author.

Interview no. 2 with Frances Pauley by Cliff Kuhn, 5-3-88, in the Georgia Government Documentation Project in the Georgia State University Special Collections, Atlanta.

Letters to author from Con and Ora Browne, dated 4-10, 4-24, and 7-15-91.

Private papers of John and Joan Veldhuizen, photocopies in possession of author.

Interviews

Sue Angry, 12-22-90, 7-17-92

Harry and Allene Atkinson, 5-21-90, 6-5-92

Willie Mae Pugh Ballard, 10-20-90, 6-2-92

Claude Broach, 4-6-91

Con and Ora Browne, 11-17-90

Lora Browne, 3-9-91

G. McLeod Bryan, 5-31-92

Mathew Burton, 9-17-91

J. R. Campbell, 12-12-90

Peggy Campbell, 4-26-92

Doc and Willa Mae Champion, 10-26-90

Don and Roberta Devault, 10-22-90

William Wallace Finlator, 4-30-91

Warren Fortson, 9-19-91

Robert Freeman, 10-25-90

Millard Fuller, 12-13-90

Alma Jackson, 7-9-90

Annabel Jackson, 9-18-91

Chester Jackson, 11-4-90, 4-26-92

Bo Johnson, 9-18-91

Howard Johnson, 7-20-92

Howard and Marion Johnson, 11-24-90

Jan Jordan, 5-1-91

Jim Jordan, 6-15-92

Lenny Jordan, 5-24-92

Carol King, 2-28-91

Lorraine Williams Monroe, 1-27-91
Carranza Morgan, 3-1-91
Lee Morgan, n.d.
Doris Pope, 9-16-91
Ludrell Pope, 9-17-91
Lorena Barnum Sabbs with Thelma Barnum, 3-3-91
Charles Sherrod, 3-1-91
Gene Singletary, 7-10-90, 10-25-90
Dorothy Swisshelm, 2-3-91
Annie Thornton, 9-18-91
John and Joan Veldhuizen, 5-4-91
Greg Wittkamper, 11-18-90
Margaret Wittkamper, 10-25-90

Magazines and Periodicals

Americus Times-Recorder
Atlanta Constitution
Baptist Student
Between the Lines
Christian Century
Liberation
New York Times
Motive
Peacemaker
Student Voice

Books, Articles, Dissertations, and Theses

Adams, Frank, with Myles Horton. *Unearthing Seeds of Fire: The Idea of Highlander.* Winston-Salem, N.C., 1975.
Ammerman, Nancy Tatum. *Baptist Battles: Social Change and Religious Conflict in the Southern Baptist Convention.* New Brunswick, N.J., 1990.
Ashmore, Harry S. *Hearts and Minds: The Anatomy of Racism from Roosevelt to Reagan.* New York, 1982.
Bailey, Kenneth K. *Southern White Protestantism in the Twentieth Century.* New York, 1964.
Barkun, Michael. "Communal Societies as Cyclical Phenomena." *Communal Societies* 4 (Fall 1984): 35–48.

Bartley, Numan. *The Creation of Modern Georgia.* Athens, Ga., 1990.

————. *The Rise of Massive Resistance: Race and Politics in the South during the 1950s.* Baton Rouge, La., 1969.

Bender, Thomas. *Community and Social Change in America.* New Brunswick, N.J., 1978.

Bloesch, Donald G. *Centers of Christian Renewal.* Philadelphia, 1964.

Bolster, Paul Douglas. "Civil Rights Movements in Twentieth Century Georgia." Ph.D. diss., University of Georgia, 1972.

Boyle, Sarah Patton. *The Desegregated Heart: A Virginian's Stand in Time of Transition.* New York, 1962.

Braden, Anne. "The Southern Freedom Movement in Perspective," in David Garrow, ed., *We Shall Overcome: The Civil Rights Movement in the United States in the 1950s and 1960s.* New York, 1969, p. 55–151.

————. *The Wall Between.* New York, 1958.

Branch, Taylor. *Parting the Waters: America in the King Years, 1954–1963.* New York, 1988.

Brewer, Pat Bryan. "Lillian Smith: Thorn in the Flesh of Crackerdom." Ph.D. diss., University of Georgia, 1982.

Broach, Claude Upshaw. *Before It Slips my Mind.* Charlotte, N.C., 1975.

Carson, Clayborne. *In Struggle: SNCC and the Black Awakening of the 1960s.* Cambridge, Mass., 1981.

Chancey, Andrew S. "A Demonstration Plot for the Kingdom of God: The Establishment and Early Years of Koinonia Farm," *Georgia Historical Quarterly* 75(2) (1991): 321–53.

————. "Restructuring Southern Society: The Radical Vision of Koinonia Farm." M.A. thesis, University of Georgia, 1990.

Chappell, David L. *Inside Agitators: White Southerners in the Civil Rights Movement.* Baltimore, 1994.

Conkin, Paul Keith. *Two Paths to Utopia: The Hutterites and the Llano Colony.* Lincoln, Nebr., 1964.

Connelly, Thomas L. *Will Campbell and the Soul of the South.* New York, 1982.

Couto, Richard. *Ain't Gonna Let Nobody Turn Me Around: The Pursuit of Racial Justice in the Rural South.* Philadelphia, 1991.

Crawford, Vicki, et al., eds., *Women in the Civil Rights Movement: Trailblazers and Torchbearers, 1941–1965.* Brooklyn, N.Y., 1990.

Crook, William H., and Ross Coggins. *Seven Who Fought.* Waco, Tex., 1971.

Crowe, Avis. "With Flair and Faithfulness: An Appreciation of Koinonia Partners," 1986. MS in the possession of Koinonia Partners.

Deatrick, Juanita. "Koinonia: A Twentieth Century Experiment in Communal Living." M.A. thesis, University of Georgia, 1968.

Dittmer, John. *Local People: The Struggle for Civil Rights in Mississippi.* Urbana, Ill., 1994.

Dunbar, Anthony. *Against the Grain: Southern Radicals and Prophets, 1929–1941.* Charlottesville, Va., 1981.

Durr, Virginia. *Outside the Magic Circle: The Autobiography of Virginia Foster Durr.* Ed. Hollinger F. Barnard. New York, 1985.

Egerton, John. *Speak Now against the Day: The Generation before the Civil Rights Movement in the South.* New York, 1994.

Eighmy, John Lee. *Churches in Cultural Captivity: A History of Social Attitudes of Southern Baptists.* Knoxville, Tenn., 1972.

———. "Religious Liberalism in the South during the Progressive Era." *Church History* 38(3): 359–72.

Ellis, Ann. "The Commission on Interracial Cooperation, 1919–1944: Its Activities and Results." Ph.D. diss., Georgia State University, 1975.

Encyclopedia of American Religions. 1978 ed. s.v. "The Communal Family." By J. Gordon Melton.

Encyclopedia of American Religious Experience. 1988 ed. s.v. "Communitarianism." By Charles H. Lippy.

Evans, Sara Margaret. *Personal Politics: The Roots of Women's Liberation in the Civil Rights Movement and New Left.* New York, 1979.

Fairfield, Dick. *Utopia, U.S.A.* San Francisco, 1972.

Fish, John O. "The Christian Commonwealth Colony: A Georgia Experiment, 1896–1900." *Georgia Historical Quarterly* 57(1973): 213–26.

Fuller, Millard. *Bokotola.* Piscataway, N.J., 1977.

Fuller, Millard, and Scott, Diane. *Love in the Mortar Joints: The Story of Habitat for Humanity.* Piscataway, N.J., 1977.

Gaston, Paul. *Women of Fairhope.* Athens, Ga., 1984.

Giddings, Paula. *When and Where I Enter: The Impact of Black Women on Race and Sex in America.* New York, 1984.

Glen, John M. *Highlander: No Ordinary School, 1932–1962.* Lexington, Ky., 1988.

Goldfield, David. *Black, White, and Southern: Race Relations and Southern Culture, 1940 to Present.* Baton Rouge, La., 1990.

Hall, Jacquelyn Dowd. *Revolt against Chivalry: Jessie Daniel Ames and the Women's Campaign against Lynching.* New York, 1979.

Hedgepeth, William, with Dennis Stock. *Alternative: Communal Life in the New America.* London, 1970.

Hill, Samuel S., Jr. *Religion in the Solid South.* Nashville, 1972.

———. *Southern Churches in Crisis.* New York, 1966.

Hinson, E. Glenn. "Southern Baptists and the Liberal Tradition in Biblical Interpretation, 1845–1945." *Baptist History and Heritage* 19(3) (1984): 16–20.

Hollyday, Joyce. "The Legacy of Clarence Jordan." *Sojourners,* Dec. 1979, 1–5.

Jacklin, Thomas M. "Mission to the Sharecroppers: Neo-Orthodox Radicalism and the Delta Farm Venture, 1936–1940." *South Atlantic Quarterly* 78(1979): 302–16.

Jordan, Clarence. "Christian Community in the South." *Journal of Religious Thought* 14(1956–57): 27–36.

———. *The Cotton Patch Version of Matthew and John.* New York, 1970.

———. "Impractical Christianity." *Young People's Quarterly,* 1948, 2.

———. "Is It an Impossible Job?" *Young People,* Aug. 12, 1956, 9–10.

———. "Is Nonviolence Enough?" *Baptist Leader,* Feb. 1964, 12–13.

———. "Love Your Enemies." *PostAmerican* 2(1973): 4–5.

———. *The Substance of Faith and Other Cotton Patch Sermons.* Ed. Dallas Lee. New York, 1972.

———. "Thy Kingdom Come—Now." *High Call,* Summer 1950, 33–34.

———. "Thy Kingdom Come—On Earth." *High Call,* Summer 1950, 31–32.

———. "What Is the Kingdom of God?" *High Call,* Summer 1950, 29–30.

Jordan, Clarence, and Bill Lane Doulos. *Cotton Patch Parables of Liberation.* Scottdale, Pa., 1976.

Kanter, Rosabeth Moss. *Commitment and Community Communes and Utopias in Sociological Perspective.* Cambridge, Mass., 1972.

Kelley, Robin D. G. *Hammer and Hoe: Alabama Communists during the Great Depression.* Chapel Hill, N.C., 1990.

Kellogg, Peter J. "Civil Rights Consciousness in the 1940s." *Historian* 42 (Nov. 1979): 18–41.

Kelsey, George D. *Social Ethics among Southern Baptists, 1917–1969.* Metuchen, N.J., 1973.

Kirby, Jack Temple. *Rural Worlds Lost.* Baton Rouge, La., 1987.

Knott, Alice G. "'Bound by the Spirit, Found on the Journey': The Methodist Women's Campaign for Southern Civil Rights, 1940–1968." Ph.D. diss., Ilift School of Theology, 1989.

Kramer, Wendell Barlow. "Criteria for the Intentional Community: A Study of the Factors Affecting Success and Failure in the Planned, Purposeful, Cooperative Community." Ph.D. diss., New York University, 1955.

Krueger, Thomas A. *And Promises to Keep: The Southern Conference for Human Welfare, 1938–1948.* Nashville, 1967.

Lee, Dallas. *The Cotton Patch Evidence.* New York, 1971.

Leonard, Bill J. "Southern Baptists and Southern Culture." *American Baptist Quarterly* 4(June 1985): 200–213.

Luker, Ralph E. *The Social Gospel in Black and White: American Racial Reform, 1885–1912.* Chapel Hill, N.C., 1991.

Lynn, Susan. *Progressive Women in Conservative Times: Racial Justice, Peace, and Feminism, 1945 to the 1960s.* New Brunswick, N.J., 1992.

McAdam, Douglas. *Freedom Summer.* New York, 1988.

McClellan, Albert. "The Shaping of the Southern Baptist Mind." *Baptist History and Heritage* 13(3) (1978): 2–11.

McClendon, James William, Jr. *Biography as Theology: How Life Stories Can Remake Today's Theology.* Nashville, 1974.

McDowell, John Patrick. *The Social Gospel in the South: The Women's Home Mission Movement in the Methodist Episcopal Church, South, 1886–1939.* Baton Rouge, La., 1982.

McNeil, Robert. *God Wills Us Free: The Ordeal of a Southern Minister.* New York, 1965.

Martin, Robert Francis. "The Fellowship of Southern Churchmen." M.A. thesis, University of North Carolina at Chapel Hill, 1970.

———. *Howard Kester and the Struggle for Social Justice in the South, 1904–77.* Charlottesville, Va., 1991.

Maston, Thomas Bufford. *"Of One": A Study of Christian Principles and Race Relations.* Atlanta, 1946.

Mathews, Donald G. *Religion in the Old South.* Chicago, 1977.

Meier, August, and Elliott Rudwick. *CORE: A Study in the Civil Rights Movement, 1942–1968.* Chicago, 1975.

Miles, Michael. "Black Cooperatives." *New Republic,* Sept. 21, 1968, 21.

Miller, Timothy. *American Commune, 1860–1960: A Bibliography.* New York, 1990.

Miller, William D. *A Harsh and Dreadful Love: Dorothy Day and the Catholic Worker Movement.* New York, 1973.

Mills, Kay. *This Little Light of Mine: The Life of Fannie Lou Hamer.* New York, 1993.

Mow, Merrill. *Torches Rekindled: The Bruderhof's Struggle for Renewal.* Ulster Park, N.Y., 1990.

Myrdal, Gunnar, with Richard Sterner and Arnold Rose. *An American Dilemma: The Negro Problem and Modern Democracy.* New York, 1941.

Newberry, Anthony Lake. "Without Urgency or Ardor: The South's Middle of the Road Liberals and Civil Rights, 1945–1960." Ph.D. diss., Ohio University, 1982.

Orser, W. Edward. *Searching for a Viable Alternative: The Macedonia Cooperative Community, 1937–1958.* New York, 1981.

Oved, Yaacov. *Two Hundred Years of American Communes.* New Brunswick, N.J., 1988.

Patton, Randall Lee. "Southern Liberals and the Emergence of the New South, 1938–1950." Ph.D. diss., University of Georgia, 1990.

Perkins, Richard. "Some Observations of My Sabbatical Experience." Paper delivered at the Communal Studies Association meeting, Oct. 15–17, 1992.

Queen, Edward L., II. *In the South the Baptists Are the Center of Gravity: Southern Baptists and Social Change, 1930–1980.* New York, 1991.

Reed, Linda. *Simple Decency and Common Sense: The Southern Conference Movement, 1938–1963.* Bloomington, Ind., 1991.

Robinson, Armstead L., and Patricia Sullivan. *New Directions in Civil Rights Studies.* Charlottesville, Va., 1991.

Rosenberg, Ellen M. *The Southern Baptists: A Subculture in Transition.* Knoxville, Tenn., 1989.

Royer, Donald M. "A Comparative Study of Three Experiments in Rural 'Community' Reconstruction in the Southeast." M.A. thesis, University of North Carolina at Chapel Hill, 1943.

Rutledge, Arthur B. *Mission to America: A Century and a Quarter of Southern Baptist Home Missions.* Nashville, 1969.

Salmond, John A. "The Fellowship of Southern Churchmen and Interracial Change in the South." *North Carolina Historical Review* 69(2) (1992): 179–99.

Shenker, Barry. *Intentional Communities: Ideology and Alienation in Communal Societies.* London, 1986.

Smathers, Euguene. "I Work in the Cumberlands." *Prophetic Religion* 3(4) (1939): 5–10.

Smith, Kenneth L., and Ira G. Zepp, Jr. *Search for the Beloved Community: The Thinking of Martin Luther King, Jr.* New York, 1986.

Snider, P. Joel. *The "Cotton Patch" Gospel: The Proclamation of Clarence Jordan.* New York, 1985.

Sorrill, Bobbie. "Southern Baptist Laywomen in Missions." *Baptist History and Heritage* 22(3) (1987): 21–28.

Sosna, Morton. *In Search of the Silent South: Southern Liberals and the Race Issue.* New York, 1977.

Sullivan, Patricia Ann. "Gideon's Southern Soldiers: New Deal Politics and Civil Rights Reform, 1933–1948." Ph.D. diss., Emory University, 1983.

Taylor, Frances Sanders. "'On the Edge of Tomorrow': Southern Women, the Student YWCA, and Race, 1920–1944." Ph.D. diss., Stanford University, 1984.

United States Department of Commerce. Bureau of the Census. *Eighteenth Census of the United States, 1960: Population* 12:352.

———. *Nineteenth Census of the United States, 1970: Population* 12:561.

Valentine, Foy D. *A Historical Study of Southern Baptist and Race Relations, 1917–1947* Ph.D. diss., 1949; published New York, 1980.

Vickers, Gregory. "Southern Baptist Women and Social Concerns." *Baptist History and Heritage* 23(4) (1988): 3–13.

Warnock, Henry Young. "Moderate Racial Thought and Attitudes of Southern Baptists and Southern Methodists, 1900–1921." Ph.D. diss., Northwestern University, 1963.

Whisenhunt, Donald W. "Utopias, Communalism, and the Great Depression." *Communal Societies* 3 (Fall 1983): 101–10.

White, Ronald C., Jr. *Liberty and Justice for All: Racial Reform and the Social Gospel, 1877–1925.* San Francisco, 1990.

Williamson, Joel. *The Crucible of Race: Black-White Relations in the American South since Emancipation.* New York, 1984.

Williford, William Bailey. *Americus through the Years.* Atlanta, 1975.

Wittner, Lawrence S. *Rebels against War: The American Peace Movement, 1941–1960.* New York, 1969.

Wuthnow, Robert. *Meaning and Moral Order: Explorations in Cultural Analysis.* Berkeley, Calif., 1987.

———. *The Restructuring of American Religion: Society and Faith since World War II.* Princeton, N.J., 1988.

Yance, Norman A. *Religion Southern Style: Southern Baptists and Society in Historical Perspective.* Perspectives in Religious Studies Special Series no. 4. Danville, Va., 1978.

Zablocki, David Benjamin. *The Joyful Community: An Account of the Bruderhof, a Communal Movement Now in Its Third Generation.* Baltimore, 1971.

Index